Constitutional Sunsets and Experimental Legislation

ELGAR MONOGRAPHS IN CONSTITUTIONAL AND ADMINISTRATIVE LAW

Series Editors: Rosalind Dixon, *University of New South Wales, Australia,* Susan Rose-Ackerman, *Yale University and* Mark Tushnet, *Harvard University, USA*

Constitutions are a country's most important legal document, laying the foundation not just for politics, but for all other areas of law. They allocate power among different levels and branches of government, record and promote a society's shared values, and protect the rights of citizens. Countries around the world are adopting written constitutions, though what defines a constitution is evolving to include a variety of sources beyond canonical texts, such as political conventions, statutes, judicial decisions and administrative law norms.

This cosmopolitan monograph series provides a forum for the best and most original scholarship in constitutional and administrative law, with each book offering an international, comparative, or multi-jurisdictional approach to this complex and fascinating field of research.

Titles in the series include:

Political Technology and the Erosion of the Rule of Law
Normalizing the State of Exception
Günter Frankenberg

Constitutional Sunsets and Experimental Legislation
A Comparative Perspective
Sofia Ranchordás

Constitutional Sunsets and Experimental Legislation

A Comparative Perspective

Sofia Ranchordás

Assistant Professor, Tilburg University, the Netherlands

ELGAR MONOGRAPHS IN CONSTITUTIONAL AND ADMINISTRATIVE LAW

Edward Elgar

Cheltenham, UK • Northampton, MA, USA

Published by
Edward Elgar Publishing Limited
The Lypiatts
15 Lansdown Road
Cheltenham
Glos GL50 2JA
UK

Edward Elgar Publishing, Inc.
William Pratt House
9 Dewey Court
Northampton
Massachusetts 01060
USA

A catalogue record for this book
is available from the British Library

Library of Congress Control Number: 2014947042

This book is available electronically in the ElgarOnline.com Law Subject Collection, E-ISBN 978 1 78347 895 8

FSC
www.fsc.org
MIX
Paper from
responsible sources
FSC® C013056

ISBN 978 1 78347 894 1

Typeset by Columns Design XML Ltd, Reading
Printed and bound in Great Britain by T.J. International Ltd, Padstow

For my mother

and in memory of my grandparents

Wenn du nicht irrst, kommst du nicht zu Verstand.
Willst du enstehn, entsteh auf eigne Hand.

J.W. Goethe, *Faust* (1832)

Contents

Acknowledgements

The genesis for this book lies in my unpublished PhD dissertation entitled 'Sunset Clauses and Experimental Legislation: Blessing or Curse for Innovation?', the themes from which are extrapolated and further developed in this book. I would like to start by thanking Professors Rob van Gestel and Patricia Popelier for their time, friendship, and insights. Thank you for treating me like the senior researcher you always saw in me. I am on my way thanks to your advice.

I would also like to thank a number of scholars with whom I had the opportunity to discuss some aspects of my work. I am particularly grateful to Professors Martin Eifert, Christoph Engel, William Eskridge, W. Hoffmann-Riem, Ernst Hirsch Ballin, Bernd Holznagel, Günter Krings, Pierre Larouche, Anne Meuwese, Edward Rubin, Charles Sabel, Gert-Jan Veerman, Wim Voermans, Felix Uhlmann and Pauline Westerman.

I would like to express my particular gratitude toward my colleagues at the University of Antwerp for their friendship and support. My sincere appreciation is also extended to the Portuguese Catholic University (Porto) where I 'learned to crawl', to Vieira de Almeida e associados, law firm (Lisbon) where I 'learned to walk', and Tilburg University where I 'learned to run'.

Last but not least, I owe my deepest gratitude to my mother and my sister. Words cannot describe how grateful I am to my Mom for having given me wings to fly, for believing in me and particularly, for the unconditional love that has nourished and will continue to nourish and inspire my work.

PART I

Introducing sunset clauses and experimental legislation

1. Lawmaking in a time of change

> 'He's very sad', Ursula answered, 'because he thinks that you're going to die'. 'Tell him', the colonel said smiling, 'that a person doesn't die when he *should* but when he *can*'.
>
> Gabriel García Márquez, *One Hundred Years of Solitude* (1967)

1.1 INTRODUCTION

In the ideal world, laws 'mirror society': they are based on perfect information, regulate social behaviour in its multiple forms and rapid mutations, and reflect the social, economic and political conditions of their time.[1] These 'perfect laws' are born of an informed, deliberative and efficient process, in other words, key legislative decisions are only made when sufficient and relevant information has been gathered, 'a full interchange of views and arguments among those making the decisions' has taken place and 'legislative proposals [have been] disposed of in the time available'.[2] In addition, in the ideal world, laws are the result of a fair decision-making process impermeable to political hurdles and lobbying,[3] lead a life of effective and efficient implementation, and expire when they are no longer necessary. Unfortunately in the real world, laws do not expire when they *should*, but when they *can*. Moreover, reflecting the current society has become increasingly challenging due to the rapid 'social and technological acceleration of society'.[4] This acceleration of reality does not interact well with slow-going legislators, resistance to

[1] Charles Montesquieu, *The Spirit of Laws* (first published 1748, Cosimo Classics, 2011); for a modern conception of the 'mirror theory', see Brian Z. Tamanaha, *A General Jurisprudence of Law and Society* (Oxford University Press, 2001).

[2] Henry M. Hart, Jr and Albert M. Sacks, *The Legal Process: Basic Problems in the Making and Application of Law* (Foundation Press, 1994) 695.

[3] For an analysis of the 'real' rules governing the legislative process, see Ittai Bar-Siman Tov, 'Lawmakers as Lawbreakers' (2010) 52 *William and Mary Law Review* 805.

[4] William E. Scheuerman, *Liberal Democracy and the Social Acceleration of Time* (Johns Hopkins University Press, 2004).

legal change, obsolete laws, excessive administrative burdens and a perception of the rule of law as 'a law of [permanent] rules'.

Most jurisdictions have been struggling for the past decades with legislative and regulatory challenges. On the one hand, legislators and regulators are required to be 'smarter', enact 'simpler' rules, minimize bad laws and regulations, regulate without stifling innovation, and reduce unnecessary costs or burdens on the private sector.[5] However, these challenges are particularly difficult to surmount due to the abundance of unnecessary and obsolete statutes and regulations, their poor quality and contradictory character, and the risk-aversion and scarce information of legislators and regulators. These challenges do not mean that in a time of frequent and complex changes, law should stop aiming to 'mirror society'. Rather, a greater awareness of the interaction between the evolution of society and the adoption and implementation of laws should be developed.[6] Briefly, in a time of change, dynamic legislative instruments must be sought, not cosmetic mirrors. A quest for such instruments implies, first of all, an understanding of the main informational challenges posed by the modern society and its evolution, and then an introductory analysis of two valuable legislative instruments that can offer an adequate response to these circumstances: experimental legislation and sunset clauses. These legislative instruments will be the leading actors in this book.

1.1.1 The Ignorance Society

Knowledge – understood as clear and valid operative schemes of the observation of the world and not as assemblages of information – is a key element to understand modern society[7] and, consequently, to regulate it. However, as originally claimed by Ulrich Beck[8] and later by Hoffmann-Riem, the '*Wissensgesellschaft*' (knowledge society) can be merely regarded as a euphemism. In a risk-society we are often impeded from perceiving what really matters due, on the one hand, to the abundance of

---

[5] Wendy L. Gramm and Gerald D. Gay, 'Leading a Regulatory Agency: Lessons from the CFTC' (1994) 17(4) *Regulation* 1.

[6] Wolfgang Hoffman-Riem, 'Législation expérimentale en Allemagne' in Charles Morand (ed.), *Évaluation législative et lois expérimentales* (Presses Universitaires d'Aix-Marseille, 1992) 177.

[7] Alfons Bora, 'Innovationsregulierung als Wissensregulierung' in Wolfgang Hoffmann-Riem and Martin Eifert (eds), *Innovationsfördernde Regulierung: Innovation und Recht II* (Duncker & Humblot, 2009) 24.

[8] Ulrich Beck, *Risk Society: Towards a New Modernity* (Sage, 1992).

information, and, on the other, to the lack of concrete details as to the potential risks of new products and their regulation. There is too much of the same, and too little of what we really need: insight on the effects of new laws and regulations. We thus live in a '*Nichtwissensgesellschaft*': an ignorance society.[9] Resembling what Kuhnian 'normal science' does, law can only pretend to know 'what the world is like'.[10]

According to the German literature, in the context of innovative fields, the mentioned lack of knowledge is enhanced by the rapid changes of society and technology, converting lawmaking into a greater challenge. Here, lawmaking implies regulating knowledge (*Wissen*), its evolution or even the lack of it.[11] To wit, legislators are required to consider different forms of knowledge: *Prognosewissen* as the attempt to predict the expected innovations and make a prognostic of their potential regulation; *Risikoentscheidungs-Wissen* referring to the knowledge or the conscious acceptance of the unknown risks and opportunities involved; and finally *regulierungstechnisches Wissen*, comprising the complete sum of empirical and theoretical political and legal research on the regulation.[12]

Like scientists, legislators are, amongst others, 'problem-solvers',[13] who seek to understand the problem they are asked to solve and try to find the most effective and efficient solution within the boundaries of law. When dealing with novel and complex situations, these problem-solvers do not know everything, but they are asked to acquire the above-mentioned forms of knowledge. While scientists search for evidence through 'trial and error', lawmakers often try to justify their Bills by *ipse dixit* or on the grounds of mysterious opinions, without relying

---

9 Wolfgang Hoffmann-Riem, *Die Governance-Perspektive in der rechtswissenschaftlichen Innovationsforschung* (Nomos, 2011) 23.

10 Thomas S. Kuhn, *The Structure of Scientific Revolutions* (3rd edn, University of Chicago Press, 1996).

11 Bora, 'Innovationsregulierung als Wissensregulierung', n. 7 above, 24, 31.

12 *Ibid.* 24, 31–4.

13 Gert-Jan Veerman, *Het meesterschap van de wetgevingsjurist* (SdU, 2011) 9–10. Legislation does not always aim at solving a problem; it can also, for example, have a symbolic function. See Bart M.J. van Klink, *De wet als symbool: over wettelijke communicatie en de Wet gelijke behandeling van mannen en vrouwen bij de arbeid* (Tjeenk Willink, 1998). For an analysis of the multiple functions of legislation, see Gert-Jan Veerman and Robin Mulder, *Wetgeving met beleid* (Boom Juridische uitgevers, 2010) 39; Ph. Eijlander, *De verbindende wetgever. Over de verhouding tussen staat, markt en samenleving*, Inaugural lecture (KUB, 2000).

on the facts and on the criterion of 'reason informed by experience'.[14] Nowadays, a consultation with the Oracle of Delphi will not be a sufficiently strong ground to justify legislation. The world is far too complex and the Oracle of Delphi has ceased to keep up with reality. New problem-solving methodologies and information-gathering instruments are required. Legislators must admit their 'ignorance', engage in a pursuit of facts and evidence in order to make prognostics as to the effects of new laws.

Making prognostics (*Prognosewissen*) is decisive for the enactment of legislation and implies predicting the most effective approach and rules to a societal problem. Recalling Hart and Sacks' criteria of 'legislative quality', these predictions often constitute the most 'relevant information' that should be gathered before making the key decisions as to new Bills.[15]

Gathering information is, however, not enough: periodic oversight and monitoring are essential to ensure that lawmakers and drafters learn from the implementation of new laws. More than two decades ago, Robert Seidman tried to put us on 'the right track', arguing that 'every social intervention, including all legislation, necessarily generates new data; each constitutes an experiment. ... All legislation should contain provisions so as to make periodic assessment of its performance likely'.[16] The inclusion of sunset clauses was one of the suggested instruments. *Ex ante* evaluations and impact assessments could potentially provide a part of the information required. Nonetheless, they would not submit new rules to a true 'reality test', allying prognostics with real-world evidence. Sunset clauses and, particularly, experimental legislation do. Experimenting with new rules with a small sample may enable lawmakers to make predictions for the current or future periods.[17] The information gathered through experimental provisions can be then used to assist lawmakers in the process of learning about the effects of a new legal regime or innovation-oriented policy. This justifies why this legislative instrument is valuable in a time of fast social and technological changes.

---

[14] Robert B. Seidman, 'Justifying Legislation: A Pragmatic, Institutionalist Approach to the Memorandum of Law, Legislative Theory, and Practical Reason' (1992) 29 *Harvard Journal on Legislation* 1.

[15] Henry M. Hart, Jr and Albert M. Sacks, *The Legal Process: Basic Problems in the Making and Application of Law* (Foundation Press, 1994) 695.

[16] Seidman, 'Justifying Legislation', n. 14 above, 75.

[17] Yair Listokin, 'Learning through Policy Variation' (2008) 118 *Yale Law Journal* 480.

1.1.2 An Experiment Named Lawmaking

Although the safety of innovative products has often been previously tested in a laboratory, the information resulting from these tests may not provide sufficient information or insight as to their effective regulation. In the case of social innovations, the legislator will have even less knowledge as to the most effective instruments to regulate them. The concept of experimental legislation is a broad term which comprises statutes but, in most cases, new temporary regulations (secondary legislation) with a circumscribed scope that, derogating from existing law or waiving the observance of a number of rules or standards, are designed to try out novel legal approaches or to regulate new products or services so as to gather more information about them. Experimental regulations imply close monitoring and are submitted to a periodic or final evaluation.[18] Once evaluated, an experimental legislative instrument denoting positive outcomes can be adapted in conformity with the results observed and transformed into a permanent act.[19] The terms 'experimental legislation', experimental rules or clauses are the most common in the literature, these 'experiments' are usually executed through the enactment of

---

[18] For a historical perspective on the origins of experimental legislation, see J. Williams, 'Experiment in Legislation' (1888) 14 *Law Magazine and Review* 299. According to this author, the roots of this type of legislation can be traced back to Ancient Greece. There are limited sources explaining the evolution of experimental legislation between Ancient times and the emergence of experimental laws in England in the last few centuries and how they spread to other countries. Older examples of these legislative instruments can be found in the former British colonies. This is the case of the seventeenth century experimental legislation on land tenure enacted in the American colonies (see Henry W. Farnam and C. Day, *Chapters in the History of Social Legislation in the U.S. to 1860* (Lawbook Exchange Ltd, 2000) 25). Another illustration of early experimental laws is the Pánjab Municipal Act of 1850 regarding the taxation of the inhabitants of that state without previous consultation. The government justified the experimental character of the measure with the 'need to take the opportunity of judging of its operation' while adapting the tax to the local specificities. See Council of Governor-General of India, *Laws and Regulations* (Authority of the Governor-General, 1869) vol. VII. As will become clear, the United Kingdom is not included in this study; however, reference to this country is made for historical and contextual purposes. The United States is one of the jurisdictions under analysis and appears to have inherited this legislative instrument from the former British Empire.

[19] See also Gabriel Doménech Pascual, 'Los experimentos jurídicos' (2004) 164 *Revista de Administración Publica* 149.

regulations. For example, in the Netherlands, Parliament typically delegates the competence to experiment with a number of dispositions in an Act of Parliament to the executive, agencies or other public bodies with regulatory powers.

Experimental legislation implies submitting new rules to a 'reality check', but allows legislators to gather more information, progressively extend the new rules to other parts of the jurisdiction in question, and adapt and improve existing laws based on evidence of what works and what does not.

The idea of converting the lawmaking process into an experimental and learning process is far from being recent. In 1953, Jahrreiss, in Germany, stated that 'legislating is [always] an experiment with human destinies'.[20] To wit, it is impossible to predict beforehand whether a certain law will achieve its objectives, generate undesirable side-effects, or respond adequately to the social imperatives for which it was enacted. In addition, this uncertainty increases in the case of rapidly evolving sectors where the reality under regulation today might be drastically another one tomorrow.

Nevertheless, when the legislator's priority resides in guaranteeing a continuous legislative oversight so as to avoid laws becoming ineffective or even obsolete, legislators can opt for sunset clauses.

1.1.3 Setting the Sun on Legislation

Both sunset clauses and experimental legislation are temporary legislative instruments that provide legislators with the required flexibility to determine the destiny of legislative provisions according to the evolution of society, economy and technology. While experimental regulations aim to be a first step towards lasting legislation, sunset clauses are usually 'born' to fulfil a mission and then 'die' after a fixed period.

Sunset clauses (or provisions) are dispositions that determine the expiration of a law or regulation within a period determined beforehand. A sunset clause submits a legislative act to a final evaluation, on the grounds of which renewal based on exceptional circumstances can occur.[21] Since a sunset clause is designed to be terminated at a certain point in time, its renewal implies an inversion of the burden of proof:

---

[20] Hermann Jahrreiss, *Größe und Not der Gesetzgebung* (Schünemann, 1953) 32: 'Gesetzgeben ist ein Experimentieren mit Menschenschicksalen'.

[21] Anthony Davis, 'Review Procedures and Public Accountability in Sunset Legislation: An Analysis and Proposal for Reform' (1981) 33 *Administrative Law Review* 393.

contrarily to permanent legislation, parties claiming that a sunset clause should be reauthorized must prove that this reauthorization is necessary. Sunset clauses allow for the adjustment of regulation to changing social or technological circumstances and determine the expiration of unnecessary acts, avoiding in this way 'overregulating' the sector and placing more burdens on the industry. In addition, the introduction of temporary laws may be useful to assess the underlying risks of a novel policy. In this context, sunset clauses can be used as a 'precautionary instrument' to assess new policies and verify whether relevant risks for the environment or public health may emerge from technological novelties.[22]

1.2 STRANGE SILENCES AND GUIDING VOICES

Despite the above-mentioned virtues of sunset clauses and experimental legislation, these legislative instruments do not proliferate in most legal orders. In practice, sunset clauses and experimental laws are almost unknown instruments to legal practitioners and represent a minority of the annual production of legislation in the three jurisdictions under analysis: the United States, the Netherlands and Germany.[23] In the three mentioned jurisdictions, diverse examples of these legislative instruments can be found, but it is clear that sunset clauses and experimental legislation are not systematically used. According to a thorough study conducted by Zachary Gubler, federal agencies in the United States have rarely employed experimental rules in the last decades (*c.* 1 per cent of total enacted regulations).[24] Up until now, little research has been conducted on the reasons underlying the scarce enactment of sunset

---

[22] Ph. Eijlander and R.A.J. van Gestel, *Horizonwetgeving: effectief middel in de strijd tegen toenemende regeldruk?: een onderzoek naar de functie van werkingsbeperkingen in wetgeving ter vermindering van regeldruk* (Ministerie van Justitie, 2006) 23.

[23] As to the Netherlands, see Frans Jan Douglas and Tessa van den Berg (ZENC, study commissioned by ACTAL), *Horizonwetgeving Dichterbij: onderzoek naar horizonwetgeving en regeldrukvermindering voor bedrijven* (ZENC, 2010): the authors concluded that sunset clauses still constitute an almost known term to most civil servants and policy-makers; Simon Bulut and Gert-Jan Veerman, *Over horizon- en experimenteerbepalingen* (Ministerie van Justitie, 2010) 36: according to the authors, between 1985 and 2009, only 85 Bills contained a sunset clause.

[24] Zachary Gubler, 'Experimental Rules' (2014) 55 *Boston College Law Review* 129.

clauses and experimental legislation.[25] This strange silence is broken in this book by the following question: in a time of fast and complex changes, why have sunset clauses and experimental legislation been so scarcely used?

The reluctance towards a broader enactment of sunset clauses and experimental legislation can be partially explained, both in different European countries and in the United States, by legal and non-legal reasons. There is first a notorious concern that these instruments may endanger a number of fundamental values and principles of law. Lawyers, legal academics and other actors such as environmental NGOs view experimental dispositions with suspicion, fearing that an experimental approach to legislation may open the door to unpredictable rules, unprincipled legislative compromise and pose a threat to the fundamental precepts of the rule of law.[26] On the one hand, legislators in Europe and in the United States are explicitly or implicitly constrained not only by the rule of law but also by a number of principles that derive from it. Laws are expected to be long-standing, predictable, reasonable and non-discriminatory. However, sunset clauses and experimental laws and regulations expire within a period determined beforehand and one could argue that it is not always possible to predict whether these dispositions will be renewed or terminated after their evaluation.

From a traditional legal perspective, temporary legislation has been conceived as a 'contradictio in adjecto':[27] if legislation is normally perceived as a synonym of continuity and a source of stability and predictability, the enactment of temporary rules, outside emergency scenarios, appears to defy a common perception of legislation as a lasting phenomenon. Citizens should be able to understand clearly what laws require and entitle them to do so as to be able to exercise their autonomy and effectively manage their affairs.[28] Achieving this stability has implied ensuring the continuity of laws, restricting the number of amendments to

---

[25] A recent law and economics study on the enactment of temporary legislation worth mentioning is Frank Fagan, *Law and Limits of Government: Temporary versus Permanent Legislation* (Edward Elgar, 2013).

[26] Bradley C. Karkkainen, 'Adaptive Ecosystem Management and Regulatory Penalty Defaults: Toward a Bounded Pragmatism' (2003) 87 *Minnesota Law Review* 943–4.

[27] Antonis Chanos, *Möglichkeiten und Grenzen der Befristung parlamentarischer Gesetzgebung* (Duncker & Humblot, 1999) 12.

[28] Maimon Schwarzschild, 'Keeping it Private' (2007) 44 *San Diego Law Review* 677, 681; William N. Eskridge, Jr and Philip P. Frickey (eds), *Hart and Sack's, The Legal Process: Problems in the Making and Application of Law* (Foundation Press, 1994) 686.

them, which meant that lawmakers often had to act as if they were already aware of all relevant circumstances at the time of the legislative drafting.[29] The preservation of stability has been highly valued over time since, as Fuller explains, legislative inconstancy could be one route to the failure of any legal system.[30] This does not mean that laws cannot be amended. Instead, this scholar's criticism targets mainly frequent and capricious changes in law. Fuller compares the problems of sudden changes in law to the evils of retrospective law; however, the scholar, citing the US Supreme Court in *Ochoa* v. *Hernandez y Morales*, acknowledges the possibility of amending law 'while the time is still running, and so that a reasonable time still remains for the commencement of an action'.[31] This type of amendment could allow legislators to incorporate new information in a preliminary period so as to adapt new laws not only to changing realities but also to the progressive acquisition of information.

Moreover, experimental regulations will only deserve this designation if a differentiation occurs, that is, not all citizens will be equal before the law since only experimental rules are only applicable to a part of the population. The other questions that should break the vast and strange silences on the present topic are: is the rule of law threatened by a law of 'sunset and experimental rules'?[32] What are constitutional sunsets and experimental regulations?

1.3 APPROACH AND METHOD

1.3.1 Approach

This is not a technical book on sunset clauses and experimental legislation. Instead, this is a comparative law study that reflects on the framework, potentialities and constitutional limits of these legislative instruments. These legislative instruments are nowadays enacted in

---

[29] For a brief historical insight on the perception of 'legal certainty', see Patricia Popelier, 'Five Paradoxes on Legal Certainty and the Lawmaker' (2008) II *Legisprudence* 51.

[30] Lon Fuller, *The Morality of Law* (Yale University Press, 1969) 39.

[31] *Ibid.* 80–81. See *Ochoa* v. *Hernandez y Morales*, 230 U.S. 139, 161–2 (1913).

[32] The expression is inspired by the article by Justice Scalia: Antonin Scalia, 'The Rule of Law as a Law of Rules' (1989) 56 *University of Chicago Law Review* 1175.

diverse Western jurisdictions, notably Germany, the Netherlands, the United States, Spain, the United Kingdom, France and Switzerland, and even at the EU level.[33] For the purposes of this study, the United States, the Netherlands and Germany have been selected. These jurisdictions were selected since, on the one hand, in all of them experimental legislation and sunset clauses have been enacted in the last decades – though under different designations. On the other, these jurisdictions have different experiences with their implementation. In none of these jurisdictions is there a clear framework for the enactment and implementation of sunset clauses and experimental legislation. There is thus room for learning in the three countries. An introductory overview of these jurisdictions is provided here.

(a) United States

In the United States, sunset clauses were mainly used at state level to tackle the overwhelming power of agencies in the 1970s,[34] but they have also been more recently adopted by Congress in the fight against terrorism (USA Patriot Act).[35] In addition, a substantial number of programmes aiming to stimulate investments in research and development (R&D) have included sunset clauses.[36] Since the United States has a long experience with the implementation of sunset clauses, valuable lessons can be drawn from the rise and failure of state sunsets.

Experimental legislation has a relatively old tradition in the United States, and some examples date back to child labour laws at the very

---

33 For France, see Florence Crouzatier Durand, 'Refléxions sur le concept d'expérimentation legislative (à propos de la loi constitutionnelle du 28 mars 2003 relative ä l'organisation décentralisée de la République)' (2003) 56 *Revue Francaise de Droit Constitutionnel* 675; for Spain, see for example, Gabriel Doménech Pascual, 'Los Experimentos Juridicos' (2004) 164 *Revista de Administración Publica* 145. For Switzerland, see Luzius Mader, 'Evaluating the Effects: A Contribution to the Quality of Legislation' (2001) 22(2) *Statute Law Review* 119. For a historical perspective in the United Kingdom, see James Williams, 'Experiment in Legislation' (1888) 14 *Law Magazine and Review* 299.

34 Dan R. Price, 'Sunset Legislation in the United States' (1978) 30(3) *Baylor Law Review* 401.

35 John E. Finn, 'Sunset Clauses and Democratic Deliberation: Assessing the Significance of Sunset Provisions in Antiterrorism Legislation' (2010) 48 *Columbia Journal of Transnational Law* 442.

36 Wendy H. Schacht, *Cooperative R&D: Federal Efforts to Promote Industrial Competitiveness*, Report for Congress, Order Code RL33526 (Congressional Research Service, 2008).

beginning of the twentieth century.[37] Moreover, policy and legislative experimentation has been regarded here as a motor of innovation and an instrument to further federalism. In 1932, Justice Brandeis, dissenting in *New State Ice Co.* v. *Liebmann*, pled for 'power in the States and the Nation to remold, through experimentation, our economic practices and institutions to meet changing social and economic needs'.[38] Brandeis stated that 'it [was] one of the happy incidents of the federal system that a single courageous State may, if its citizens choose, serve as a laboratory; and try novel social and economic experiments without risk to the rest of the country'.[39] Most experiments with laws are still performed at state level through the use of waivers: states may apply for an exemption of the observance of a number of federal dispositions, experimenting with policy and legislative solutions that fit their socio-economic conditions. As it will be explained later in this book (see Chapter 2), experimental regulations are also conceivable at the federal level and federal agencies could benefit from this instrument when regulating complex problems.

(b) Germany

In Germany, experimental legislation is not a recent phenomenon,[40] but it has been traditionally implemented in the context of municipal law.[41] In addition, it has constituted an important tool in the last decade in the process of modernizing the public administration.[42] In the last two decades, experimental laws have been placed in the context of the regulation of innovative fields in order to guarantee legislative updates.

---

37 'New Labor Law works well: experimental statute in Capital reduces number of children employed', *New York Times*, 24 August 1909: experimental law introduced in the District of Columbia in 1908 imposed work permits and limited child labour to an eight-hour day.

38 Justice Brandeis, dissenting, in *New State Ice Co.* v. *Liebmann,* 285 U.S. 265, 303; 52 S. Ct. 371; 76 L.Ed. 747 (1932).

39 *Ibid.* 311.

40 See Julius Ofner, 'Das Experiment im Recht, Vortrag gehalten in der Juristischen Gesellschaft in Wien 28 Dezember 1881' in *Beiträge zur exacte Rechtswissenschaft* (1883).

41 Georg Strätker, 'Experimentierklauseln im Kommunalrecht' in Maximilian Wallerath (ed.), *Verwaltungserneuerung* (Nomos, 2001).

42 Volker Maβ, *Experimentierklauseln für die Verwaltung und ihre verfassungsrechtlichen Grenzen* (Duncker & Humblot, 2001) 19.

However, in the 1990s experimental legislation and other types of temporary legislation raised doubts as to their constitutionality.[43]

The debate regarding the introduction of experimental acts and sunset clauses has re-emerged in the past decades and occurred, for example, in the postal and telecommunications sectors in the context of the process of deregulation. Sunset clauses have also been suggested in Germany as a tool to combat excessive bureaucracy and regulatory pressure.[44]

(c) The Netherlands

The Netherlands does not have a long experience with either experimental legislation or sunset clauses. However, this jurisdiction has revealed a growing curiosity as to these instruments, which has been accompanied by a vast silence in the literature and the Dutch Council of State's frequent critical remarks.[45] This may explain why sunset clauses and experimental legislation have been regarded here as an *ultimum remedium*. A number of constitutional objections have been raised against experimental legislation and sunset clauses, namely, the potential violation of the principles of legal certainty, equal treatment, proportionality and legality.

1.3.2 Method

The research underlying this book was mainly based on qualitative research into the nature of sunset clauses and experimental legislation and the literature on the regulation of innovation. Empirical data was only indirectly used in the process of exploring the outcomes of the implementation of sunset clauses and experimental laws.[46] For this purpose, evaluation reports elaborated by sunset commissions, ministries and national or local committees, and other documents containing

---

[43] Hans-Detlef Horn, *Experimentelle Gesetzgebung unter dem Grundgesetz* (Duncker & Humblot, 1989).

[44] In 2005, the introduction of a sunset clause was suggested in every new regulation in order to tackle overregulation, see for example, the proposal submitted to the Bundestag, on the enactment of sunset clauses in the context of the combat of terrorism, available at www.bundestag.de/blickpunkt/101_Themen/0507/0507044_3.htmlhttp://www.bundestag.de/dokumente/analysen/2007/Terrorismusbekaempfung_kor.pdf.

[45] The opinions of the Dutch Council of State regarding the legality of experimental legislation in the light of the basic principles of law will be analyzed in Chapter 3.

[46] For an empirical study of the enactment of temporary legislation, see Frank Fagan, *Law and Limits of Government: Temporary versus Permanent Legislation* (Edward Elgar, 2013).

empirical data about the execution of pilot projects, have been selected. Since most lawyers are not familiar with sunset clauses and experimental legislation, a number of examples of these instruments from different jurisdictions will be provided throughout the book.

1.4 ROADMAP TO CONSTITUTIONAL SUNSETS AND EXPERIMENTAL REGULATIONS

This is not a book just about sunset clauses and experimental legislation. It is also a book that aims to unveil important debates on legislative studies. First, the study of these legislative instruments implies rethinking our perception of lawmaking: from opinion-based to evidence-based, from a tendentially static approach to a dynamic one (particularly in Europe). Secondly, by analyzing the relationship between sunset clauses and experimental legislation and fundamental constitutional principles, the urge to adopt a dynamic perspective of lawmaking and a living interpretation of the mentioned principles will be also demonstrated. Thirdly, non-legal elements underlying the legislative process are also analyzed in this book, reminding us that the lawmaking process cannot be isolated from political, social and economic considerations.

This book is divided into four parts. The first part is dedicated to an overview, definitions, historical background, functions and legal framework of sunset clauses and experimental legislation (Chapters 1, 2 and 3). The terms 'experimental legislation' and 'experimental regulations' are used interchangeably, however, the first term is broader and includes in this context both experimental statutes and regulations (secondary legislation). There will in principle be less experimental statutes than regulations since the details concerning the implementation of experiments do not fit the primordial tasks of Congress (or its equivalent in other countries). The legislature often remains the 'master of the experiment' but its execution must be delegated to the executive. This is why, in Chapter 3, the principles of separation of powers and legality are analyzed. Chapter 3 reflects upon a 'legality framework' for sunset clauses and experimental legislation: according to what legal conditions can sunset clauses and experimental legislation be implemented? Another important question discussed in this chapter refers to the situations and fields where sunset clauses and experimental legislation should be implemented: is there a 'promised land' for these instruments? And is there a 'forbidden fruit'?

In the second part of this book, the 'constitutionality' of sunset clauses and experimental legislation is scrutinized in light of the literature and case law of the jurisdictions under analysis. This analysis is focused on a number of fundamental principles that could be potentially endangered by sunset clauses and experimental legislation. Chapter 4 departs from the rule of law as a source of predictability. This chapter tries to combine the American and European perspectives on the principle of legal certainty as an imperative guarding the stability and predictability of legislation. Chapter 5 devotes more attention to experimental legislation and its relationship with the principle of equal treatment. Chapter 6 inquires when and how sunset clauses and experimental legislation should be regarded as proportionate legislative responses to social or economic problems. In order to understand whether sunset clauses and experimental legislation are at odds with these principles, their meaning will be analyzed not only in light of their traditional meanings, but also considering their current significance in a fast-changing world. In a time of rapid and complex changes, fundamental principles of law can only remain meaningful if they reflect and accompany the most significant changes in society, economy and technology. Thus, besides examining the constraining function of these principles on the enactment of sunset clauses and experimental legislation, I also explore whether these legislative instruments can further the concrete application of fundamental principles of law in a time and world of changes (see Chapters 3 to 6).

Nonetheless, legal objections do not exhaust the repertoire of arguments against sunset clauses and experimental legislation. Lawmakers are not only influenced by legal arguments but are equally under pressure from interest groups, politics and economic limitations. This is the tension between law and politics that plays an inevitable role in the choice and implementation of the legislative instruments under analysis. Although this tension cannot easily be resolved, it deserves considerable attention: experimental legislation and sunset clauses can be, depending on the subject in question, an appealing or a repulsive instrument to realize certain political goals. This is the topic of the third part of the book (Chapter 7). Here I also investigate whether unsuccessful experiences may explain why lawmakers may be reluctant to enact these instruments in other contexts. Chapter 7 analyzes the intellectual, practical, and political reasons underlying the limited enactment of sunset clauses and experimental legislation.

In the fourth and last part of this book, the conclusions and 'instructions for use' are presented. Chapter 8 provides an overview of the legal framework to be taken into account by legislators when drafting sunset clauses and experimental legislation.

2. The past and present of sunset clauses and experimental legislation

Oh, do not ask, 'What is it?'
Let us go and make our visit.
T.S. Eliot, *The Love-Song of J. Alfred Prufrock* (1915)

2.1 INTRODUCTION

Temporary legislation is a broad term used to refer to different forms of temporary legislation and regulations, such as temporary effects legislation, emergency legislation, sunset clauses and experimental legislation. The terms 'temporary legislation' '*Gesetzgebung auf Zeit*' (in Germany)[1] or '*tijdelijke wetgeving*' (in the Netherlands) stand for laws and regulations that terminate at the end of a period established beforehand, except if the legislator decides otherwise.[2] As introduced in Chapter 1, temporary laws are not enacted on a systematic basis in Germany, the Netherlands and the United States, but they are no rarity.[3] In these three jurisdictions, temporary laws appear to serve specific purposes.

[1] The German literature employs different terms to refer to temporary laws, other possibilities are '*Gesetze mit Verfallsdatum*' and '*Zeitgesetze*'.

[2] Jacob E. Gersen, 'Temporary Legislation' (2007) 74 *University of Chicago Law Review* 247.

[3] For the Netherlands, see P.O. de Jong and M. Herweijer, *Alle regels tellen – de ontwikkeling van het aantal wetten, AMvB's en ministeriële regelingen in Nederland* (WODC/Boom, 2004) 45–6: the scarcity of sunset clauses and experimental legislation can be indirectly concluded from the data on the average duration of laws (40 years) and regulations (21 years). The laws and regulations with duration of less than five years were a substantial minority. For Germany, see Ingo von München, 'Die Zeit im Recht' (2000) I *Neue Juristische Wochenschrift* 4. Until the reunification, experimental legislation was enacted mostly in the former Federal Republic of Germany, see Wolfgang Hoffman-Riem, 'Législation expérimentale en Allemagne' in Charles Morand (ed.), *Evaluation législative et lois expérimentales* (Presses Universitaires d'Aix-Marseille, 1992) 179. For the United States, see Gersen, 'Temporary Legislation', n. 2 above.

Temporary legislation is often regarded as an extraordinary tool or even a 'necessary evil' for problems that permanent legislation would not be able to solve. To illustrate, a rapid legislative response to calamities or to political instability requires extraordinary but temporary measures (for example, curfew laws) and cannot afford to wait for the end of the bureaucratic legislative process. Temporary laws can, however, be employed for a number of other less common reasons, including the production of information, resolution of uncertainties or search for political consensus. In this chapter, two types of temporary legislation and their functions are 'demystified': sunset clauses and experimental legislation. Both legislative instruments are characterized by their temporary character and can be used to perform a number of functions.

This chapter aims to understand where sunset clauses and experimental legislation come from (2.2); what their nature is and how they can be distinguished from apparently similar instruments (2.3); and what functions they perform (2.4). Finally, attention will be devoted to fields or circumstances where sunset clauses and experimental legislation could and should play an important role, in place of permanent legislation (2.4).

2.2 HISTORICAL BACKGROUND

In this subsection, the roots of sunset clauses and experimental legislation are analyzed. The overview of the history of these legislative instruments does not aim to be extensive and it refers to their 'broader roots', including different approaches over the years to subjects such as legal change, legislative obsolescence and experimentalism. The discussion of these topics in the literature and case law prepared the ground for the later emergence of sunset clauses and experimental legislation.

2.2.1 Sunset Clauses

The concern that legislation should mirror the evolution of society mentioned in Chapter 1 is far from being a recent one. Instead, in 1789, in a letter to James Madison, Thomas Jefferson argued that 'no society can make a perpetual constitution, or even a perpetual law. The earth belongs always to the living generation. [Therefore] every constitution … and every law naturally expires at the end of thirty-four years'.[4] Less than

---

[4] Thomas Jefferson, *Letter to James Madison*, 6 September 1789, *The Federalist Papers*, available at www.thefederalistpapers.org/founders/jefferson/thomas-jefferson-september-6-1789: this letter referred to the possibility 'of the

a decade later, Jefferson's plea for termination of laws appeared to be heard when the Sedition Act of 1798 was enacted.[5] This Act included a sunset clause determining its expiry in 1801. The charter establishing the first national bank in the United States in 1791 also included a sunset provision with the duration of twenty-one years.[6] According to Jacob Gersen, temporary legislation played a significant role not only in colonial legislatures but also in the early years of the US Congress.[7]

This idea of terminating legislation was later revived by Robert Luce, who, without referring to the Founding Father, questioned in 1930 the validity of lasting laws and the extent to which they represented the values of that generation.[8] Luce refers in this context to Blackstone who asserted 'the right of each generation to think for itself' and Francis Lieber, who argued that 'all that is in a code which is not conformable to the spirit of society must fall to the ground'.[9] According to Luce, it was important for the legislator to embrace the new challenges of society and try to 'escape the prison of custom and old law'.[10] Obsolescence of legislation could be the price to pay for holding on to rules that last longer than the phenomena they originally aimed to regulate.

The described awareness that constitutions and laws should not last forever does not mean that they should necessarily terminate after a fixed period as claimed by Jefferson. On the one hand, while some laws naturally lag behind the evolution of society and technology, others survive different generations or can be updated through statutory interpretation. To wit, while the regulation of telecommunications devices must be frequently reviewed so as to reflect the evolution of this sector, rules on marriage or family relationships tend to evolve at a different pace and may survive several decades without becoming obsolete. On the other, termination is not the only means to guarantee that constitutions and laws remain updated. In the case of constitutions, a living perception

---

representatives of a nation validly engag[ing] debts beyond what they may pay in their own time, that is to say, within thirty-four years of the date of the engagement'.

5 Sedition Act, s. 4, 1 Stat. 596, 597 (14 July 1798).

6 See Frank H. Easterbrook, William N. Eskridge, Jr, Philip K. Howard, Thomas W. Merrill and Jeffrey S. Sutton, 'Showcase Panel IV: A Federal Sunset Law, The Federalist Society 2011 National Lawyers Convention' (2011) 16 *Texas Review of Law and Politics* 339.

7 Gersen, 'Temporary Legislation', n. 2 above, 248.

8 Robert Luce, *Legislative Principles: The History and Theory of Lawmaking* (Lawbook Exchange, 1971, first published in 1930).

9 *Ibid.* 14, 16.

10 *Ibid.* 13.

of the constitution and an effort to guarantee that constitutions remain open to the future, may be the route to a long constitutional life and avoid their periodic termination, as advocated by Jefferson. While it is true that 'the past cannot fully control the future', as Jack Balkin explains, 'there are not enough rules in the world adequate to navigate centuries of change and crisis.[11] A constitutional project is developed over time and there are inevitably course corrections', rather than terminations. Moreover, according to Balkin, 'the legitimacy of a constitution can be enhanced by the fact that people in the past, in the present and in the future can and will disagree about the future'.[12] While the mentioned 'course corrections' imply openness to the future and the capacity of a constitution to be adapted to the evolution of relevant socio-economic, political and even technological circumstances, nothing is mentioned about the need to terminate constitutional dispositions.

As far as statutes are concerned, the goal of maintaining them up-to-date can be equally achieved by promoting, for example, evaluations and periodic reviews. However, sunset clauses provide additional benefits in comparison to these instruments. In the second half of the twentieth century, sunset clauses re-emerged as instruments that combine the idea of termination of unnecessary rules with the need to evaluate legislation.

The idea of combining enhanced legislative oversight with temporary legislative instruments emerged later in the second half of the twentieth century. In 1969, Theodore Lowi proposed a 'Tenure of Statutes Act' with a sunset of five to ten years on the duration of agencies and their regulatory programmes in order to ensure their reassessment after this period of time.[13] However, the idea of terminating agencies and regulatory programmes had earlier been suggested in 1937 by Justice William O. Douglas.[14]

In the 1970s, the United States experienced a 'sunset clause boom' at the state level: the state of Colorado, influenced by the lobby group Common Cause, took the lead in passing sunset clauses that determined

---

[11] Jack Balkin, *Constitutional Redemption: Political Faith in an Unjust World* (Harvard University Press, 2011) 9.

[12] *Ibid.* 9.

[13] See Theodore J. Lowi, *The End of Liberalism: The Second Republic of the United States* (W.W. Norton, 1979).

[14] Michael D. Crain, 'Time for the Sun to Rise on Federal Sunset Legislation' (2000) 8 *Public Law* 10.

the extinction of agencies and unnecessary programmes.[15] Sunset provisions emerged as a reaction to the general discontentment with uncontrolled governmental growth, excessive bureaucracy and public spending. Between 1976 and 1982, 36 state legislators enacted laws containing sunset clauses.[16] States also established sunset advisory commissions which were created to periodically evaluate and review existing sunset clauses; hold hearings on this subject; and decide upon their extinction or renewal. The extant Texas Sunset Advisory Commission is one of the most well-known examples.

The first attempt to enact a federal sunset law was discussed in 1978. Nonetheless, it remained at the 'attempt level' since the Bill did not obtain the support of the House of Representatives.[17]

During the 1980s, sunset clauses were adopted in order to control and limit the powers of agencies, solve the 'ills' of the executive,[18] control public spending[19] and increase political accountability.[20] In the mid-1980s, the disappointment with sunset clauses was clear: the underlying goals of these instruments were often not achieved, the inertia of politicians and legislators often resulted in the automatic renewal of sunset clauses, and the reauthorization of sunset clauses occurred with disregard for the evaluation reports.[21]

Despite the disenchantment with sunset clauses, the urge to combat the obsolescence of law – in other words, statutes that 'no longer fit the legal topography' and 'lack current legislative support' – had not diminished.[22] In 1982, Guido Calabresi criticized the growing disconnection between law and reality due to the obsolescence of legislation and case law.[23] In *A Common Law for the Age of Statutes*, Calabresi argued that updating law

---

[15] The first sunset law was enacted in 1976 in Colorado, see Mark B. Bickle, 'The National Sunset Movement' (1985) 9 *Seton Hall Legislative Journal* 209.

[16] Landon Curry, 'Politics of Sunset Review in Texas' (1990) 50 *Public Administration Review* 58.

[17] Easterbrook *et al.*, 'Showcase Panel IV', n. 6 above, 339, 342.

[18] Rebecca M. Kysar, 'The Sun Also Rises: The Political Economy of Sunset Provisions in the Tax Code' (2006) 40 *Georgia Law Review* 335.

[19] Bickle, 'The National Sunset Movement', n. 15 above.

[20] Lewis Anthony Davis, 'Review Procedures and Public Accountability in Sunset Legislation: An Analysis and Proposal for Reform' (1981) 33 *Administrative Law Review* 393.

[21] Bickle, 'The National Sunset Movement', n. 15 above.

[22] Guido Calabresi, *A Common Law for the Age of Statutes* (Harvard University Press, 1982) 2, 51.

[23] *Ibid.*

implies enforcing consistency within the legal system since the latter is necessarily 'contextual, interactive and dynamic'. This scholar rejected, conversely, the use of sunset clauses in this battle against the obsolescence of legislation, arguing that these dispositions were too 'mechanical' and could easily be converted into a mere formality. Instead, judges were advised to update legislation or, in some cases, invalidate legislation that no longer fits the 'legal topography'.

More than one decade later, in *Quill* v. *Vacco*, Calabresi suggested that obsolete statutes whose 'bases have been deeply eroded over the last hundred and fifty years ... [and no longer] remain in place today ... inevitably raise doubts about the current support for these laws'.[24] Laws whose 'original reason have ceased to exist or whose fit with the rest of the system is dubious' and threaten fundamental interests, should be declared unconstitutional, except if the court can demonstrate why these laws are still defensible in the contemporary setting.[25] Calabresi regarded legislation as the result of a rational and deliberative process where there is no room for obsolete rules that no longer fit the legal landscape they were originally designed to inhabit.[26] Calabresi insisted, however, that judges and legislators should therefore engage in a frank dialogue to update legislation.[27] Calabresi is one of several different American scholars pleading for a dynamic interpretation of statutes.[28] In the last decades, William N. Eskridge has also pointed out that 'as time passes,

---

[24] Calabresi, Circuit Judge, concurring in *Quill* v. *Vacco*, 80 F.3d 716 (2d Circ. 1996), see also *Vacco* v. *Quill*, 521 U.S. 793 (1997): in this case the validity of two New York statutes criminalizing assisted suicide was discussed. The court was requested to strike down these statutes in so far as they apply to 'terminally ill, mentally competent patients, who would self-administer drugs' since they were allegedly violative of the Equal Protection Clause of the Fourteenth Amendment.

[25] Calabresi, Circuit Judge, concurring in *Quill* v. *Vacco*, 80 F.3d 716 (2d Circ. 1996).

[26] William D. Popkin, *Materials on Legislation: Political Language and the Political Process* (5th edn., Foundation Press, 2009) 1130.

[27] Ursula A. Petrozzi, 'The Forgotten Lesson in *Quill v. Vacco*: A Perspective on the Modern Judicial Role as the Calabresian Remedy to the Statutory Obsolescence' (1998) 44 *Wayne Law Review* 343.

[28] This perspective was already visible in Henry M. Hart, Jr and Albert M. Sacks, *The Legal Process: Basic Problems in the Making and Application of Law* (Foundation Press, 1994).

the legal constitutional context may change', compelling the interpreter to perform a dynamic interpretation of the statute.[29]

Although the use of sunset clauses has been heavily criticized in the last decades in the United States,[30] its impact in Europe is undeniable. In Germany and in the Netherlands, sunset clauses have not mainly been employed to periodically review or terminate agencies. In Europe, agencies' powers cannot be compared to the American 'fourth branch of government'. Instead, these legislative instruments have been used to limit the duration of laws and regulations in general and submit them to an *ex post* evaluation, upon which their renewal or termination is dependent (see 2.3).[31] Nonetheless, the mentioned sunset boom in the United States produced an undeniable influence in Europe.

In the Netherlands, the first timid signs of the impact of this sunset movement started to be visible in the literature in the 1970s.[32] In the 1980s, a group of Dutch researchers saw in sunset clauses (*horizon-bepalingen*) a legislative translation of the need to reflect policy dynamics and terminate policies when the objective for which they were enacted had been achieved, or when the policy at stake proved to be ineffective to attain it.[33] This study appeared along with the ideas of Roel in't Veld who advocated that since problems shift in the course of time – often even before they are solved – so should policies, in order to avoid obsolescence.[34]

---

29 William N. Eskridge, Jr, 'Dynamic Statutory Interpretation' (1987) 135 *University of Pennsylvania Law Review* 1479.

30 See Kysar, 'The Sun Also Rises', n. 18 above.

31 Bertelsmann Stiftung, *Sunset Legislation and Better Regulation: Empirical Evidence from Four Countries* (2010), available at www.bertelsmann-stiftung.de/cps/rde/xbcr/SID-E8B3D0D1-5443791C/bst_engl/xcms_bst_dms_35739__2.pdf.

32 See J.I.R. Kindt, 'Horizonwetten' (1979) 64 *Economische-Statistische berichten: algemeen weekblad voor handel, nijverheid, financiën en verkeer* 130, 130–33.

33 Th. Camps, W.J.M. Kickert and A.F.A. Korsten, 'Horizonwet, een nieuwe coloradokever' (1982) 2 *Bestuur* 10, 10–11.

34 The most relevant works in this field in the Netherlands appear either to have been conducted or directed by Roel in't Veld, see Roel in't Veld, *Verandering en bestuur: een pleidooi voor een bescheiden bestuurskunde-*afscheidscollege (Nijmegen, 1982); Roel in't Veld, *De verguisde staat* (VUGA, 1989).

Sunset clauses have been progressively implemented in more fields since the 1980s and an even broader implementation of sunset clauses in the Netherlands has been studied and discussed.[35]

In Germany, it was particularly in the last decade that sunset clauses (*Gesetze mit Verfallsdatum* or, more specifically, *Auslaufklauseln*) began to enter the political debate and the first references in the literature were made.[36] In 2004, it was advocated in the German literature that the enactment of sunset clauses in rapidly changing regulated markets like telecommunications would avoid endangering their 'free and innovative development' since they could encompass 'soft' deregulatory reforms and reduce the risk of overregulation.[37] A broader use of sunset clauses was suggested here as a way to ensure that unnecessary regulatory burdens would be extinguished, thereby creating favourable regulatory conditions for investment and innovation. Fewer regulatory burdens could signify more resources to invest in research and development.[38] Nonetheless, the connection between the enactment of sunset clauses, the reduction of regulatory pressure, and the consequent stimulation of innovation has only been argued but never sufficiently demonstrated. No attempt to prove the causal relationship between the enactment of sunset clauses and the reduction of regulatory pressure is attempted here either.

---

[35] For the political debate, see for example, the VVD electoral programme for the 1986 elections for Parliament (Tweede-Kamer) where the introduction of sunset clauses is suggested at 14, available at http://dnpp.eldoc.ub.rug.nl/FILES/root/programmas/Verkiezingsprogramma/1986/vvd86.pdf. In the context of the reduction of administrative burdens on companies, a broader use of sunset clauses was also advocated by the Commissie Wientjes, see Commissie Regeldruk Bedrijven, report available at www.rijksoverheid.nl/documenten-en-publicaties/brieven/2011/04/22/advies-toezicht-20-van-de-commissie-regeldruk-bedrijven.html. For an early study of sunset clauses in the Netherlands, see A.F.A. Korsten, *Horizonwetgeving en wetsevaluatie: Ervaringen in de Verenigde Staten en in Nederland* (Ministerie van Binnenlandse Zaken, 1984).

[36] See Jörg Steinhaus, *Gesetze mit Verfallsdatum* (Books on Demand, 2008).

[37] A. Freytag and K. Winkler, *The Economics of Self-Regulation in Telecommunications under Sunset Legislation*, Friedrich-Schiller-Universität Jena Working Paper No. 17/2004 (2004).

[38] Opinion of the Council of Economic Advisors (Advies van de Raad van Economisch Adviseurs), 19 May 2005, *De wetten en regels die droom en daad verstoren; Bureaucratisering en overregulering,* Tweede Kamer, 2004–2005, 30 123, no. 2. See also ZENC, *Horizonwetgeving Dichterbij: onderzoek naar horizonwetgeving en regeldrukvermindering voor bedrijven*, study commissioned by ACTAL (ZENC, 2010), available at www.actal.nl/upload/Eindrapport_Onderzoek_Horizonwetgeving.pdf.

Since the enactment of sunset clauses in the Netherlands and Germany is fairly recent, illustrations of the latter will be analyzed below (2.3).

2.2.2 Experimental Legislation

Like sunset clauses, experimental legislation is far from being an invention of our times; instead it has a long tradition in Europe.[39] The first signs of experimental legislation in France date back to the kingdom of Louis XVI and appear to have been motivated by 'the wish to improve the effectiveness of the administration [of the country]'.[40]

'Experimental legislation is the very method of social growth', affirmed W.S. Jevons in 1880.[41] This scholar argued that the employment of the experimental method, already successfully used in natural sciences, was applicable to law: legislators should undertake small steps in the enactment of any new law, submit it to the test of reality, adapt it to local specificities and assess its effects both empirically and statistically.[42] More than one century later, experimental legislation is still far from being a commonly used instrument in most jurisdictions. Nonetheless, the idea of experimenting with laws has drawn more interest in the twentieth and twenty-first centuries.

John Dewey was one of the twentieth century scholars who advocated the use of an experimentalist approach to policy and lawmaking. Dewey supported a pragmatic and 'experimentalist' problem-solving method to remedy various equal protection problems.[43] Dewey considered that legal precepts, like every social policy should be subject to 'a more experimental and flexible logic' in which rules and principles should be treated as 'working hypotheses' that should be constantly tested.[44] Dewey was 'a

---

[39] James Williams, 'Experiment in Legislation' (1888) 14 *Law Magazine and Review* 299.

[40] In France, experimental legislation is still implemented. The French Constitution explicitly recognizes that 'statutes and regulations may contain provisions enacted on an experimental basis for limited purposes and duration' (art. 37-1) and that territorial communities may 'derogate on an experimental basis for limited purposes and duration from provisions laid down by statute or regulation governing the exercise of their powers' (see art. 72).

[41] William S. Jevons, 'Experimental Legislation and the Drink Traffic' (1880) XXXVII *Contemporary Review* 177.

[42] *Ibid.*

[43] John Dewey, *The Public and its Problems: An Essay in Political Inquiry* (Holt Publishers, 1927).

[44] John Dewey, *The Quest for Certainty: A Study of the Relation of Knowledge and Action* (Gilford Lectures, 1929) 277.

man ahead of his time' who did not have in mind the concrete case of experimental legislation or the characteristics of experimental designs. Instead, as Bradley Karkkainen explains, Dewey simply advocated 'a dynamic, experimental, iterative, and adaptive problem-solving approach'.[45] Dewey's experimentalism has been described as a 'day-to-day process of self-government, which he equated with public problem-solving uncovering social needs and troubles and best judging how the trouble is to be remedied'.

Dewey's experimentalism cannot be confused with a plea for laboratory experiments. Instead, the philosopher insisted on the need to 'keep premises and conclusions open and subject to constant testing and revision'.[46] Dewey conceived state and regulation as dynamic realities that must evolve as the underlying social conditions do; and such evolution can be executed by constant experimentation.[47] Dewey had in mind a continuous process of learning by doing, accompanied by a cyclical system of planning, implementation, evaluation, and planning of alternative policies. One can almost see in Dewey's pragmatism a translation of the theory of evolution to the lawmaking process.[48] Policies and laws are assumed to be fallible and should therefore be systematically tested and corrected.

The re-emergence of an experimental approach to lawmaking in the twentieth century has equally much to owe to Justice Brandeis and his 'states-as-laboratories' metaphor. In Chapter 1, Brandeis' dissenting opinion in *New State Ice Co.* v. *Liebmann* has already been mentioned, but its multiple interpretations were not explored. Brandeis stated:

> It [was] one of the happy accidents of the federal system that a single courageous state may, if its citizens choose, serve as a laboratory, and try novel social and economic experiments without risk to the rest of the country.[49]

---

[45] Bradley C. Karkkainen, 'Toward a Smarter NEPA: Monitoring and Managing Environmental Performance' (2002) 102 *Columbia Law Review* 903; Bradley C. Karkkainen, 'Adaptive Ecosystem Management and Regulatory Penalty Defaults: Toward a Bounded Pragmatism' (2003) 87 *Minnesota Law Review* 943.

[46] B.L. Garrett and J.S. Liebman, 'Experimentalist Equal Protection' (2004) 22 *Yale Law and Policy Review* 261, 287–8.

[47] *Ibid.* 288–9.

[48] Bradley C. Karkkainen, 'Adaptive Ecosystem Management and Regulatory Penalty Defaults: Toward a Bounded Pragmatism' (2003) 87 *Minnesota Law Review* 943.

[49] *New State Ice Co.* v. *Liebmann*, 285 U.S. 262, 311 (1932).

Justice Brandeis firmly believed that legislation should be supported by social facts, experience and statistics.[50] In this states-as-laboratories metaphor, Brandeis praises state experimentation as a method of enhancing the 'triumphs of invention' in social and economic fields while safeguarding the legal order against the harms of failure. Should the experiment fail, then the damage would be limited to the 'courageous state' that decided to experiment.[51] Brandeis' dissenting opinion can first be interpreted as a plea for the use of experiments as instruments of innovation: states should have the right to enact experimental legislation and innovate beyond federal policies. This idea of states as laboratories of democracy was earlier present in the work of James Bryce who observed that federalism enabled 'a people to try experiments in legislation and administration which could not safely be tried in a large centralized country. A comparatively small commonwealth like an American state easily makes and unmakes its laws; mistakes are not serious, for they are soon corrected'.[52]

On the one hand, Bryce' and Brandeis' perceptions of 'states-as-laboratories' and experimentation can be interpreted as methods of converting the lawmaking process into a learning process. New laws are first tried on a small-scale basis, shaped by the facts, allowing 'other States [to] profit by the experience of a law or a method which has worked well or ill in the State that has tried it'.[53] On the other hand, a second interpretation of this metaphor could be associated with a plea for federalism. The 'states-as-laboratories' assertion can be read in the context of a Madisonian defense of diffusion of power to states and communities. This is a secondary interpretation, which is not developed in this study.[54]

In the 1950s, F.K. Beutel conceived the idea of a 'Science-State' guided by strict rationality where policies would be enacted according to

---

[50] David M. Speak, *Living Law: The Transformation of American Jurisprudence in the Early 20th Century* (Garland Publishing, 1987) 35.

[51] G. Alan Tarr, *Laboratories of Democracy*, available at http://camlaw.rutgers.edu/statecon/publications/lab.pdf.

[52] James Bryce, *The American Commonwealth* (3rd edn, Macmillan, 1893) 353.

[53] *Ibid.* 353.

[54] James A. Gardner, 'The 'States-as-Laboratories' Metaphor in State Constitutional Law' (1995) 30 *Valparaiso University Law Review* 475; Daniel O. Conkle, 'Free Exercise, Federalism, and the States as Laboratories' (1999) 21 *Cardozo Law Review* 493; Thomas K. McGraw, *Prophets of Regulation: Charles Francis Adams, Louis D. Brandeis, James M. Landis, Alfred E. Kahn* (Belknap Press, 1984).

the scientific method, tested and improved in conformity with the results observed.[55] Legal experiments would be particularly appropriate for fields characterized by frequent technical and social changes, such as road traffic and educational policies.[56] Experiments in law were 'the way' to implement innovative social reforms. Beutel did not conceive experimental legislation in its modern form as a temporary derogation of rules. Rather, his theory of the 'Science-State' referred to a more global approach to both experimental policy and lawmaking as a concretization of a learning approach.

Although it is unclear whether Brandeis' words produced any type of direct influence in Europe, experimental legislation emerged some decades later in the Netherlands and in Germany.

Experimental legislation emerged in Germany at a time of 'legislative crisis'. In the 1960s, trust in the virtues of law and legislation was severely eroded. The progressive widening of legal subjects, lack of clarity and intelligibility of rules, and excessive workload of the ministerial departments in charge of legislating and overseeing the legislative process contributed to a true crisis in legislation.[57] This awareness that the legislative process was 'getting out of hand' explains the enhanced attention for the field of Legislative Studies (*Gesetzgebungslehre*) in the 1960s.[58]

Peter Noll became a prominent character in the German debate regarding the development of a theory of legislation, arguing that the latter should be supported by scientific work.[59] This distrust in legislation and its implementation were at the root of the claims regarding the need to rationalize the lawmaking process, namely, by incorporating multidisciplinary and empirically-driven methodologies. Experimental lawmaking was then conceived as a process that would ensure that the regulation of society was based on facts and figures. This would be an alternative to the assumption that new laws purely based on theoretical

---

55 Frederick K. Beutel, *Some Potentialities of Experimental Jurisprudence as a New Branch of Social Science* (University of Nebraska Press, 1957).

56 Frederick K. Beutel, *Experimental Jurisprudence and the Science State* (Gieseking Verlag, 1975).

57 Hans-Detlef Horn, *Experimentelle Gesetzgebung unter dem Grundgesetz* (Duncker and Humblot, 1989) 17.

58 Hermann Jahrreiss, *Größe und Not der Gesetzgebung* (Schünemann, 1953).

59 Horn, *Experimentelle Gesetzgebung unter dem Grundgesetz*, n. 57 above, 20.

knowledge would be effective.[60] The main idea behind experimental legislation in Germany at the time was to submit laws to a reality check, gather information as to their effects, renew and optimize legislation through the incorporation of new elements.[61]

Experimental laws fit Peter Noll's discourse that 'all new laws are experiments'.[62] Every time the legislator implements a new law, it will inevitably draw valuable lessons from it. However, in practice, this was not always possible in the first examples of experimental laws in Germany. The experimental provisions on the qualifications of lawyers in the former Federal Republic of Germany in the 1970s illustrate this initial difficulty to 'learn' from experimental lawmaking (see example 2.1).

EXAMPLE 2.1 EXPERIMENTAL LEGISLATION ON LEGAL EDUCATION IN GERMANY

The first examples of experimental legislation in Germany date back to the 1970s, namely, to the experiment with the 'one-step' qualification of lawyers implemented in 1971. This experiment emerged in a period of student contestation and greater demand for a more dynamic regime for lawyers.[63] A political compromise was then achieved allowing the Länder to experiment for five years with a different curriculum and approach to the qualification and training of lawyers.[64] The 'experimental character' of these laws was not as explicit as it has been in more recent

[60] Segun Reinhold Zippelius, *Die experimentierende Methode im Recht* (Akademieabhandlung Mainz, 1991) 7. More recently, for the general use of evidence-based and other scientific evidence to support legislation, see the recent article by Werner Schroeder and Eva-Maria Kostenzer, 'Wissenschaftsbasierte Regulierung im EU-Produktrecht' (2013) 48 *Europarecht* 389.

[61] Wolfgang Beck and Claudia Schürmeier, 'Die kommmunalrechtliche Experimentierklausel als Reforminstrument' (2004) *Landes- und Kommunalverwaltung* 488; Rupert Stettner, 'Verfassungsbindungen des experimentierenden Gesetzgebers' (1989) *Neue Zeitschrift für Verwaltungsrecht* 806.

[62] See Peter Noll, *Gesetzgebungslehre* (Rowolt Taschenbuch Verlag, 1973).

[63] Wolfgang Hoffmann-Riem, 'Législation expérimentale en Allemagne' in Charles-Albert Morand (ed.), *Évaluation législative et lois expérimentales* (Presses universitaires d'Aix-Marseille, 1993) 177, 189.

[64] See Thomas Freund, *Kommunale Standardöffnungs- und Experimentierklauseln im Lichte der Verfassung* (WVB, 2003) 21–2; Ernst E. Hirsch, 'Experimentierklausel' (1971) 26 *Juristenzeitung* 286.

examples of experimental laws, but it clearly resulted from its context. Although this experiment was not a success and most of its participants abandoned it before the end of its duration period and evaluation,[65] this was the first of many experiments at the state level.

The field of education was one the first fields to welcome experiments, not only in Germany but also in the Netherlands. In this country, the first experimental rules emerged in the 1960s as a means to enhance the quality of education by experimenting with new methods (see example 2.2).

EXAMPLE 2.2 EXPERIMENTAL LAWS ON EDUCATION IN THE NETHERLANDS

Among the first Dutch examples of legislative acts containing experimental dispositions is the Statute of 14 February 1963. This statute granted, on an experimental basis, a greater leeway to secondary schools to decide upon educational programmes. The Experimental Statute on Education (Experimentenwet Onderwijs) of 9 July 1970 opened the door to a number of experiments. This statute conferred competence on the responsible Minister, after having consulted the Education Council, to promote experiments with other forms of secondary school programmes diverging from ordinary forms of education.[66] The statute did not specify exactly what type of alternative educational programmes could be experimented with. The initiative to promote an experiment could, however, be taken by numerous institutions as long as it was submitted for the approval of the Ministry of Education and Science and, as stated in article 2(2),

---

[65] Freund, *Kommunale Standardöffnungs- und Experimentierklauseln im Lichte der Verfassung*, n. 64 above, 21–2.

[66] Experimentenwet Onderwijs, Statute of 9 July 1970, Stb. 370 (modified by the statutes of 6 May 1971 (stb. 356) and 16 November 1972.

the duration of the experiment did not exceed the period of ten years (which could be prolonged for a five-year period).[67]

In the last decades, the interest in experimental legislation has increased in the Netherlands and Germany and examples of experiments can be found in multiple fields, including social and unemployment policies,[68] deregulation of telecommunications and road traffic.[69] These more recent examples, as well as the respective functions performed by sunset clauses and experimental legislation, are further examined in 2.4.

This brief overview of the historical background of sunset clauses and experimental legislation aimed to provide a glimpse of the context in which these instruments emerged. Although these legislative instruments still partially reflect this historical background, they have evolved and developed specific characteristics which allow us to identify them in legal texts and distinguish them from apparently similar instruments.

2.3 DEFINITION AND CHARACTERISTICS

What is the difference between a 'regular' temporary provision and a 'sunset clause'? Are 'experimental laws' and 'legislative experiments' synonyms? This subsection answers these and other questions regarding the nature of sunset clauses and experimental legislation, provides a terminological clarification of the concepts under analysis, and lists the essential characteristics of both legislative instruments.

---

67 Statute of 14 February 1963 (Stb. 74) (tot het verlenen van grotere vrijheid van inrichting van het onderwijs). The implementation of this law opened the doors for experiments involving different Dutch secondary school educational programmes (for example, the so-called HAVO). See Experimentenwet Onderwijs, Statute of 9 July 1970, Stb. 370 (modified by the statutes of 6 May 1971 (Stb. 356) and 16 November 1972).

68 In Germany, for example, s. 56 Abs. 3 a SGB III (Erprobung von Maßnahmen zur Beschäftigung von Arbeitslosenhilfebeziehern).

69 *Evaluatie praktijkvoeren Dynamische Maximumsnelheden (evaluatie rapport van Rijkswaterstaat, Ministerie van Verkeer en Waterstaat, Dynamische Maximumsnelheden)*, 15 July 2010, Bijvoegsel Kamerstukken II, 2010–2011, 32 646, no. 1, 9.

2.3.1 Sunset Clauses

'Sunset' can be defined as 'a statutory method of forcing legislators to make a periodic determination whether to allow a particular program or agency to continue'.[70] 'Sunsetting' implies the introduction of clauses regarding certain measures contained in a Bill, or establishing that an agency[71] or a programme will be extinguished after a certain period, except if the renewal of the clause is requested.[72] Although the Texas Sunset Advisory Commission still defines 'sunset clause' as 'the regular assessment of the continuing need for a state agency to exist', this term has been used in the literature to refer to a broader range of statutory or regulatory mechanisms entailing the termination of a statute after a period of time determined beforehand.[73]

Sunset clauses or provisions can be applied to entire statutes or determined provisions, regardless of the subject they regulate.[74] A specific *reason* to submit a law to a *time limit* should underlie the decision to enact a sunset clause. Sunset clauses are usually not the legislators' first choice, so it is important to understand why the legislator have opted in that particular case for a sunset clause. Legislative oversight could also be guaranteed by the adoption of a review or evaluation clause. In the case of sunset clauses, legislators should justify why a law should sunset. This is not, however, an essential element for the definition of sunset clauses. These legislative instruments can be normally identified by the presence of the following elements:

(i) temporary character: a sunset clause does not aim at continuity, rather it determines the expiration of a law after a fixed period, *unless* there are substantial reasons to believe that the former should be extended for a determined period;[75]

---

[70] Mark D. Young, 'A Test of Federal Sunset: Congressional Reauthorization of the Commodity Futures Trading Commission' (1978) 27 *Emory Law Journal* 853–4.

[71] See the glossary on the website of the Texas Sunset Advisory Commission, available at www.sunset.state.tx.us/guide.htm.

[72] Anthony Davis, 'Review Procedures and Public Accountability in Sunset Legislation: An Analysis and Proposal for Reform' (1981) 33 *Administrative Law Review* 393.

[73] John E. Finn, 'Sunset Clauses and Democratic Deliberation' (2009) 48 *Columbia Journal of Transnational Journal* 442.

[74] Easterbrook *et al.*, 'Showcase Panel IV', n. 6 above, 341.

[75] Philip Eijlander and Rob van Gestel, *Horizonwetgeving: effectief middel in de strijd tegen toenemende regeldruk? – een onderzoek naar de functie van*

(ii) *ex post* evaluation: the effects of the sunset disposition should be assessed in order to verify whether the objective for which it was enacted has been achieved. Depending on the evaluation report, it can be decided whether to let the provision sunset or renew it for another fixed period.

As far as the duration period of sunset clauses is concerned, this has varied in the countries under analysis depending on the subjects in question. In the Netherlands, for example, the duration of sunset clauses has oscillated between one year in the case of a temporary regulation designed to address the problem of the smuggling of drugs into the airport at Schiphol,[76] and six years, in the context of a statute on the integration of minorities in the labour market.[77] In the United States, the original average duration of sunset clauses appears to have been five years.[78] However, reauthorization has often occurred, so multiple acts were only terminated several years after the original sunset date. This was particularly visible during the sunset movement in the 1970s and 1980s, where successive reauthorization of sunset clauses occurred without any previous significant evaluation.

Renewal of sunset clauses is possible but it implies an inversion of the burden of proof: the institution interested in its reauthorization must demonstrate on what grounds this should occur.[79] The Dutch Council of State has underlined that continuation of sunsets should be justified on

---

werkingsbeperkingen in wetgeving ter vermindering van regeldruk (2006), available at www.portill.nl/articles/Eijlander/Horizonwetgeving.pdf.

[76] See Wet van 6 maart 2002 tot vaststelling van de tijdelijke wet voor de penitentiaire noodcapaciteit ten behoove van drugkoeriers (tijdelijke wet penitentiaire capaciteit drugkoeriers), Stb. 2002, 124.

[77] Voorstel van de leden Vos en Stuurman betreffende het wijzigen van de wet stimulering arbeidsdeelname minderheden, Advies van de Raad van State en reactie van de indieners, Kamerstukken II, 2003–2004, 29 275, no. 4, 1–2: this proposed amendment aimed to extend the duration period of a law on the integration of minorities in the labour market for six years (expiration in 2010). The proponents of this extension argued that the production of the desired positive effects was not fully achieved at the time, and it was, therefore, necessary to ensure the continuation of the law.

[78] See Bickle, 'The National Sunset Movement', n. 15 above.

[79] Bertelsmann Stiftung, 'Gutachten: Wirksamkeit von Sunset Legislation und Evaluationsklauseln' (2005) *Agenda Moderne Regulierung*, available at www.bertelsmann-stiftung.de/bst/de/media/xcms_bst_dms_16438__2.pdf.

imperative grounds to avoid laws being too easily renewed.[80] In any case, renewal should never occur before an evaluation has taken place.[81]

The requirement to conduct an evaluation does not need to be explicitly stated in the sunset clause; rather it should be understood as an inherent element of this legislative instrument. This evaluation might occur a few months before the expiration term. Periodic evaluations are also admissible and have been typically introduced in particularly dynamic settings, such as regulated sectors where it is important to assess the effects produced by the law submitted to the sunset.[82]

Having defined and identified the most important elements of sunset clauses, it is important to clarify that there is not only one type of 'sunset clause'. Instead, this legislative instrument has several different faces, which should not be confused with apparently similar instruments that do not fall within the qualification of 'sunset clause'.

(a) Different types of sunset clauses

Sunset clauses can be qualified as 'reflexive', when they are included in the rule or statute to expire; or 'irreflexive', if the clauses are placed outside it and the statute which they apply to.[83] Reflexive sunset clauses are the most common forms of sunset clauses and they are often contained in a specific section of the statute. Example 2.3 illustrates a reflexive sunset clause included in the US Federal Food, Drug Administration Safety and Innovation Act which is applicable to two specific provisions of the statute.

---

[80] Voorstel van de leden Vos en Stuurman betreffende het wijzigen van de wet stimulering arbeidsdeelname minderheden, Advies van de Raad van State en reactie van de indieners, Kamerstukken II, 2003–2004, 29 275, no. 4, 1–2.

[81] Tijdelijke verruiming artikel 668a van Boek 7 van het Burgerlijk Wetboek om arbeidsovereenkomsten voor bepaalde tijd aan te gaan in verband met het bevorderen van de arbeidsparticipatie van jongeren, Advies Raad van State en nader rapport, Kamerstukken II, 2008–2009, 32 058, no. 4, 3: the Dutch Council of State underlined here that the renewal of the law after the sunset period must depend on the results of the research and evaluation of its effectiveness.

[82] As discussed in Voorstel van wijziging van de Mededingingswet ter invoering van regels inzake ondernemingen die van overheidswege over een bijzondere positie beschikken en inzake ondernemingen die deel uitmaken van een publiekrechtelijke persoon of die hiermee zijn verbonden (Regels voor ondernemingen met een bijzondere taak, overheidsondernemingen en overheidsbedrijven), advies van Raad van State en nader rapport, Kamerstukken II, 2007–2008, 31 354, no. 4, 15.

[83] Finn, 'Sunset Clauses and Democratic Deliberation', n. 73 above.

EXAMPLE 2.3 SUNSET CLAUSE IN THE FEDERAL FOOD, DRUG ADMINISTRATION SAFETY AND INNOVATION ACT

207. SUNSET CLAUSE. IN GENERAL. – Sections 737 and 738 of the Federal Food, Drug, and Cosmetic Act (21 U.S.C. 739i; 739j) shall cease to be effective October 1, 2017. Section 738A (21 U.S.C. 739j–1) of the Federal Food, Drug, and Cosmetic Act (regarding reauthorization and reporting).[84]

Sunset clauses incorporated in specific legislative acts should not be confused with those that are applied to a wider group of laws or even the generality of regulations enacted by a particular lawmaker – the so-called general sunset clauses. To illustrate, in Germany, many Länder have employed sunset provisions imposing a general time limitation to their laws. This has been the case in North-Rhine Westphalia, Low-Saxony, Hessen and Bremen. According to an empirical research performed by the Bertelsmann Stiftung in 2010, the number of state regulations including sunset provisions varied between 6 per cent in Lower Saxony and more than 60 per cent in Hesse, North Rhine-Westphalia and Saarland.[85] The federation has only enacted sunset clauses on an ad hoc basis and for designated laws. The adoption of general sunset clauses was also suggested in the Netherlands in 2005 by the Council of Economic Advisors, but this proposal did not gather sufficient support.[86]

(b) True sunset clauses and 'the others'

Sunset clauses can be 'reflexive' or 'irreflexive', 'specific' or 'general', last five years or many more, but they are intrinsically characterized by the unavoidable event of termination. Pathologies are certainly visible in

---

[84] Food and Drug Administration Safety and Innovation Act 112th Congress, 2011–2013, S. 3187 (112th) text as of 27 June 2012 (Passed Congress/Enrolled Bill).

[85] Bertelsmann Stiftung, *Sunset Legislation and Better Regulation*, n. 31 above.

[86] Opinion of the Council of Economic Advisors (Advies van de Raad van Economisch Adviseurs) 19 May 2005, De wetten en regels die droom en daad verstoren; Bureaucratisering en overregulering, Tweede Kamer, 2004–2005, 30 123, no. 2.

the lawmaking world (see Part III), but sunset clauses distinguish themselves from the crowd of rules by: (i) their inherent temporary character; (ii) compulsory evaluation; and (iii) renewal on extraordinary grounds. Sunset clauses should not be confused with temporary laws enacted in scenarios of catastrophes and other emergencies. Emergency temporary rules depend on the duration of extraordinary circumstances and are only enacted to solve critical situations. Sunset clauses, on the contrary, have a broader scope of application since they are usually not adopted to respond to emergencies, but to tackle other temporary problems or to terminate rules that are not expected to remain effective or to be necessary after a fixed period.

Review clauses may appear similar to sunset clauses since they impose the evaluation of legislative dispositions; however, the former determine the continuation of dispositions, except if the legislator explicitly decides to terminate them,[87] while sunset clauses 'are born to die'.

'Sunset laws' have been described in the literature as the 'US equivalent' of European experimental legislation.[88] Nothing could be further away from the truth, for various reasons. First, as mentioned above, the idea of experimenting with law has a long history in the United States and this history is different from the reasons that underlie the emergence of sunset clauses. Secondly, although sunset clauses and experimental legislation share some characteristics such as their temporary character and evaluation clauses, they are distinct instruments. The basic distinction between sunset clauses and experimental legislation is the aspiration to permanence: the former does not have it; the latter is a preliminary step towards it. Notwithstanding the multifunctionality of sunset clauses (see below), sunset clauses are primarily instruments of policy termination,[89] while experimental legislation is the first attempt to introduce a good lasting regulation.

---

87 Mandelkern Group on Better Regulation, *Final Report* (13 November 2001) 17, available at http://ec.europa.eu/governance/better_regulation/documents/mandelkern_report.pdf.

88 Bertil Cottier, 'Les Sunset Laws: Des lois expérimentales à la mode américaine?' in Charles-Albert Morand (ed.), *Évaluation législative et lois expérimentales* (Presses Universitaires d'Aix-Marseille, 1993) 161.

89 Th. Camps, W.J.M. Kickert and A.F.A. Korsten, 'Horizonwet, een nieuwe coloradokever' (1982) 2 *Bestuur* 10.

2.3.2 Experimental Legislation

As the word 'experimental' indicates, experimental legislation suggests that new laws are tested.[90] Experimental legislation can be defined as laws or, in the majority of cases, regulations or dispositions that are enacted on an experimental basis in derogation of existing law for a fixed period. These 'experimental rules' are applicable to a limited group of citizens or a part of the jurisdiction which is selected on the grounds of objective criteria. The experiment is also subject to a periodic or final evaluation.

Like sunset clauses, experimental legislation is also characterized by a number of intrinsic elements. The first element of the definition of experimental legislation is its *temporary character*: an experimental law or regulation must have an *ab initio* limited duration. This essential element regarding the explicit duration of experimental dispositions does not appear to be contested in the Netherlands, Germany and in the United States. The duration and subsistence of a law beyond the original experimental period should be dependent on the attainment (or not) of the underlying objective of the experimental law.[91] If only mixed evidence has been gathered, it is reasonable to prolong the experiment for another period.

The second element is the *derogation* from existing law (rules or standards), which implies the observation of two requirements: first, there must be a statutory ground authorizing this derogation (principle of legality, see Chapter 3); and, secondly, it must be clear why this derogation through an experiment is necessary, meaning that the objective to be attained by the experiment must be clearly indicated.[92] Laws are often denominated 'experimental' because they introduce new rules in the legal order but no derogation occurs. In such cases, the essence of the idea of experimenting, which is to compare the results obtained in two groups – one submitted to the experimental regime and the other to the status quo – is to a great extent lost. Such laws can be qualified as

---

[90] Freund, *Kommunale Standardöffnungs- und Experimentierklauseln im Lichte der Verfassung*, n. 64 above, 16.

[91] Carl Böhret and Werner Hugger, *Test und Prüfung von Gesetzentwürfen: Anleitungen zur Vorabkontrolle und Verbesserung von Rechtsvorschriften* (Carl Heymanns Verlag, 1980) 51.

[92] Antonis Chanos, *Möglichkeiten und Grenzen der Befristung parlamentarischer Gesetzgebung* (Duncker and Humblot, 1999) 33–6.

ordinary temporary laws but they do not perform a serious experimental function, and the validity of the withdrawn lessons will necessarily be reduced.

The third element is the performance of an *evaluation*. The primary idea behind experimental legislation is to try out a new legal regime, see if it works, and learn from the positive and negative effects observed. The evaluation constitutes the opportunity to rethink the objective of the experiment. Legislators are then asked to decide whether the rules tried out can be extended to the rest of the population and consequently converted into general lasting rules.

A fourth and essential feature of experimental legislation is its *limited scope of application*. Experimental rules are only applicable to a part of the territory or to a group of citizens which are used as the 'sample group'. This group should be representative of the rest of the population and be selected for the implementation of the experimental legal regime on the grounds of objective criteria. Objective criteria for the selection of the sample group are, for example, demographic or wealth factors. The results obtained here will be compared with the ones observed in the 'control group', in other words, the rest of the population. The participation in an experiment can, therefore, be compulsory to those living in the area selected by the legislator, but it can also be voluntary. Contrarily to scientific experiments, the 'sample group' is not always objectively or randomly chosen but instead participation can be voluntary. As described in example 2.4, this last situation can be found in the Netherlands.

EXAMPLE 2.4 INNOVATIVE KINDERGARTENS IN THE NETHERLANDS

An illustration is the 2012 temporary governmental decree enacting 'an experiment in the context of innovative kindergartens' (*besluit experiment integraal dagarrangement*).[93] This involved an experiment regarding an innovative concept of kindergarten where children were offered a 'day arrangement' consisting of a combination between child day care and primary school subjects. The objective of the experiment was to gather information on the added value of this form of childcare and its

[93] Besluit van 14 september 2012, houdende tijdelijke regels voor een experiment in het kader van innovatieve kinderopvang (Besluit experiment integraal dagarrangement), Stb. 2012, 413.

repercussions on the school performance of these children, satisfaction of parents with this system and the quality of the kindergartens. Arising from the specific regulation under analysis, this experiment was based on cooperation agreements between primary schools and kindergartens authorized by the Ministry of Social Affairs and Employment. This meant that the children benefiting from this experimental programme would be the ones attending the schools or kindergartens which had applied for this 'day arrangement' and been granted the required ministerial authorization. Fifteen cooperation agreements were signed and the experiment is ongoing. This was a case of voluntary participation of schools and kindergartens, submitted to a ministerial authorization, but not randomly chosen.

Example 2.4 illustrates that it is not always possible to comply with the ideal requirements of an experimental law *stricto sensu*. However, when this is possible, it is important to underline that for the sake of the validity of the results of the experiment, these criteria should be respected. As will later be demonstrated, the lack of a framework guiding legislators on the enactment of experimental laws may explain the imperfect design of many experiments. In Chapter 8, a number of guidelines on methodological considerations for a better design of experimental legislation are put forward.

In addition to experimental legislation *stricto sensu*, there is a wide array of other forms of legislative experimentation: while some simply translate multiple variations of the category 'experimental legislation', others do not deserve this qualification. In addition, experimental legislation may also be implemented at different organizational levels for specific purposes and involve policy phenomena such as policy experimentation and policy variation.

(a) Different shades of experimental legislation

A glimpse into the German literature is enough to reveal that this legal order is populated by multiple terms referring to experiments with laws: *Standardöffnungsklausel, Testgesetz, Experimentierklausel, erprobende Gesetzgebung* and *Gesetzgebung zur Erprobung*.[94] In this list, there is no

[94] Volker Maaβ, *Experimentierklauseln für die Verwaltung und ihre verfassungrechtlichen Grenzen* (Duncker and Humblot, 2001) 30–31; Horn, *Experimentelle Gesetzgebung unter dem Gesetz*, n. 57 above, 21–8.

possible distinction between 'true experimental laws' and 'the others' (see above).

In some cases, experiments with laws can be very close to the 'legalization' of the scientific method, whereas in others, they will be mere derogations from existing rules. An example of the first was suggested in the reform of procedural laws in the United States. Laurens Walker suggested here the implementation of unrestricted or national experiments, implying the application of different rules to randomly assigned cases, or restricted field experiments to be conducted in a small number of US district courts.[95] True randomization as performed in scientific experiments may be neither feasible nor required in the case of experimental laws in order for meaningful results to be obtained. It is exactly the fact that this is an experimental law implemented in the real world and not in a laboratory under controlled conditions that imposes this need for flexibility.

Contrary to the concept of experimental legislation *stricto sensu* (see above), '*Standardöffnungklauseln*' do not necessarily introduce novel rules in the legal order or imply the use of randomly or objectively selected groups. Rather, these clauses can exempt federal states or local governments from applying existing standards or rules on an experimental basis. The legislative novelty and the learning opportunity often reside exactly in this exemption or derogation. Besides this type of provision, the German literature has also referred to the possibility to apply for a temporary '*Regulierungsfreistellung*'.[96] In the United States, a similar concept exists and is applied to facilitate state innovation: state 'waivers' enable states to accommodate federal statutes to their social or economic characteristics and, in doing so, facilitate the regulation of a particular social or technological innovation. These waivers should be categorized as experimental laws whenever they are enacted for a temporary period and with experimental purposes.

Experiments with law can vary between true experimental regulations that fulfil the criteria listed above and hybrid instruments that are enacted as apparent 'phased implementations' of new legislative acts. Experimental legislation appears here 'disguised' under the form of phased implementation with a clear learning component. This is the case of the

---

[95] Laurens Walker, 'Perfecting Federal Civil Rules: A Proposal for Restricted Field Experiments' (1988) 51 *Law and Contemporary Problems* 67, 75–6.

[96] Bernd Holznagel, 'Innovationsanreize durch Regulierungsfreistellung vom Umgang mit neuen Diensten und Märkten im Medien und TK-Recht' (2006) *MMR* 661.

EU Emissions Trading System (see example 2.5) which was launched in 2005 to combat climate change and the implementation of which was split into different trading periods, including a first 'learning phase'.[97]

EXAMPLE 2.5 EU EMISSIONS TRADING SCHEME

The EU Emissions Trading Scheme is an EU policy designed to combat climate change and reduce greenhouse emissions at the least cost to society.[98] The literature has qualified this system as the 'world's first large *experiment* with an emission trading system for carbon dioxide [which] is likely to be copied by others'.[99] Although the Directive enacting this system was not explicitly qualified as an 'experimental act', this results from the system itself. This system has been closely monitored by the Commission in the last few years and amendments resulting from the Commission's evaluation and the stakeholders' input have been proposed. The EU Emission Trading System entered its third phase in 2013 and this should run until 2020. Due to the evaluation performed in 2009, significant changes were introduced in the system for the third phase. Among these changes are the inclusion of additional sectors and gases; the establishment of a single, EU-wide cap on emissions replacing the previous system of national caps; and the institution of auctioning, not free allocation, as the default method for allocating allowances.[100]

---

[97] Directive 2009/29/EC of the European Parliament and of the Council of 23 April 2009 amending Directive 2003/87/EC so as to improve and extend the greenhouse gas emission allowance trading scheme of the Community [2009] OJ L140/63–87.

[98] See for example, Communication from the Commission to the European Parliament and the Council, Towards an Enhanced Market Oversight Framework for the EU Emissions Trading Scheme, COM/2010/0796 final.

[99] A. Denny Ellerman and Barbara K. Buchner, 'The European Union Emission Trading Schemes: Origins, Allocation, and Early Results' (2007) 1 *Review of Environmental Policy* 66, 66–87.

[100] For a short overview, see the European Commission webpage on climate change, http://ec.europa.eu/clima/policies/ets/index_en.htm.

In the following paragraphs, an overview of the distinction between experimental legislation *stricto sensu* and other forms of experimentation with law is presented.

(b) Other forms of legislative experimentation

Experimental laws and regulations *stricto sensu* coexist with 'legislative experiments'[101] or, adopting the terminology used in the German literature, '*Testmethoden*' that cannot be included in the broad category of 'experimental legislation' because they do not imply an alteration of rules in the real world.[102]

Legislative drafts can be submitted to tests beforehand. These trials are called legislative experiments and they can either be performed in a laboratory or in the context of field experiments. The German literature has used a varied terminology for these instruments, including *Gesetzgebungsexperiment, Modellversuch* and *Praxistest.* These empirical instruments used in the lawmaking process attempt to predict the results of the implementation of a new law.

Gesetzgebungexperimente, for example, are internal experiments executed in the drafting phase of a law and aim at carrying out an *ex ante* control of Bills. The main idea is to test the clarity of the legislative measures before the laws or regulations come into effect. These experiments are performed mainly by the Ministries involved in the drafting of legislation. Experimental legislation can be regarded as the external variant of these 'laboratory' legislative experiments: in the first case, the legislative disposition has already come into effect and is an 'experiment in the real world'. In the second, the experiment constitutes an *ex ante* instrument which may influence the content of the new legislative dispositions, but does not produce effects external to the legal order.

Field experiments involving law and legal policy are equally conceivable. These can be qualified as external legislative experiments. In the

---

[101] This distinction was originally suggested by Peter Fricke and Werner Hugger, *Test von Gesetzentwürfen,* vol. I, *Voraussetzungen einer testorientierten Rechtsetzungsmethodik*, Speyerer Forschungsberichte 11 (Speyer, 1979) 172; and later by Horn, *Experimentelle Gesetzgebung unter dem Grundgesetz*, n. 57 above, 24. A recent reference to 'legislative experiments' in a law and economics context but still in the sense adopted in this book as '*ex ante* experiments' with laws before they come into force, confirms the position adopted, see Christoph Engel, *Legislative Experiments: Mission Impossible?*, Erasmus Law Lectures 28 (Eleven International Publishing, 2013).

[102] Böhret and Hugger, *Test und Prüfung von Gesetzentwürfen*, n. 91 above, 49.

United States, experimental research using this instrument has revealed a positive effect on legal policy. This was the case of the 1984 Minneapolis Domestic Violence Experiment, which aimed to test which police action was more effective in deterring domestic violence.[103] A randomized test demonstrated that arrest (at the time less frequently used for minor cases of violence) produced less repeated violence than separating the abuser for eight hours from the victim or initiating advice and mediation procedures.

Besides the mentioned legislative experiments or *Testmethoden*, it is important to mention the Dutch *proeftuinen* and pilot projects. These instruments often resemble policy experiments and they have particular legal relevance, not only because they must be authorized by law but also because their results may influence the revision of legislation. *Proeftuinen* are centres or entities that conduct experiments. *Proeftuinen* are located between social experiments – in the sense that they test the effects of policy on human behaviour – and experimental legislation, since *proeftuinen* often require a legal ground. *Proeftuinen* are temporary small-scale experiments, publicly funded, targeting a specific goal, which may involve the collaboration of private entities. An evaluation should also occur at the end of the experimental period. In the Netherlands, important experiments with social and economic significance have been carried out under the form of a *proeftuin*. Examples include *proeftuinen* designed to improve the integration of immigrants and the development of social structures for better homecare; and the stimulation of innovation in the maritime sector by creating attractive investment conditions has been conducted under the form of a '*proeftuin*' (see example 2.6).

EXAMPLE 2.6 *PROEFTUINEN* IN THE NETHERLANDS

The *Proeftuin inburgering* aimed to improve the quality of the education provided to immigrants and consequently facilitate their integration into Dutch society, by analyzing the success factors and performance incentives.[104] This experiment was

[103] Lawrence W. Sherman and Ellen G. Cohn, 'The Impact of Research on Legal Policy: The Minneapolis Domestic Violence Experiment' (1989) 23 *Law and Society Review* 117.

[104] More information about this experiment can be found at www.proeftuininburgering.nl.

launched on 5 February 2010 and involved 27 *proeftuinen*. This experiment was performed in collaboration with different language institutes and municipalities. The final evaluation report revealed important conclusions as to the success factors of the learning process of these immigrants (notably learning the Dutch language).[105]

Another example of a *proeftuin* for the stimulation of innovation is the *Proeftuin Maritime Innovatie*.[106] This *proeftuin* was designed to create a network between institutions to promote regional investment in knowledge and investment in the maritime sector. While the first example is a national *proeftuin*, organized by the Ministry of Public Housing, Urbanism and Environment and involving the cooperation of public entities; the second is a local *proeftuin* structured by a group of municipalities in the neighbourhood of Dordrecht. In this case, (mostly) private entities were encouraged to participate in the *proeftuin*.

Proeftuinen can equally be used to assist the implementation of new statutes. This is the case of the 2005 *proeftuin* established to implement a statute on social support (Wet Maatschappelijke Ondersteuning) which involved 26 municipalities.[107] The idea was to discover what the structures established by this law would mean for the people in need of homecare and for the municipalities themselves. This experiment involved the creation of new social structures where different institutions would work together in order to assist people living in their area. The initiative for this *proeftuin* came from the Ministry of Health but involved the collaboration of the municipalities and several private entities.

It is important to summarize the differences between the instruments in question since they translate not only different forms and degrees of experimentation but also of underlying uncertainty, revealing the stage of the legislative process:

---

[105] Final evaluation report available at www.proeftuininburgering.nl/eindrapportage-297.html (in Dutch).

[106] For more information on Proeftuin Maritime Innovatie, see www.hme.nl.

[107] Proeftuin Wet Maatschappelijke Ondersteuning was launched on 20 June 2005 and the results were presented in 2007. For more information see www.invoeringwmo.nl/content/de-resultaten-van-twee-jaar-proeftuin-wmo.

(i) Legislative experiments are internal, *ex ante* experiments with new legislative dispositions which are conducted under controlled conditions.
(ii) *Proeftuinen* are social policy experiments that often involve a legal authorization and are publicly funded but do not necessarily imply a derogation from existing legislation. Results from them can influence the legislator to revise existing legislation.
(iii) Experimental legislation is in itself an experiment with laws: experimental provisions derogate from existing law so as to obtain more information about the legal regime being introduced in the legal order. These experimental provisions produce a clear impact on the rights and duties of citizens.
(iv) Pilot projects can be regarded as a preparation for a structural change, which has been sufficiently tested, whereas experimental legislation can be regarded (for example) as a method to 'observe (and learn from) the effects of the implementation of a policy of selection of students and differentiation of tuition fees'.[108] Pilot projects have been elected as alternatives to experimental provisions, revealing a rather imprecise use of the former.

In 2009, for example, the then Dutch Secretary of State for Labour Affairs stated that 'the general objective of pilots was to answer questions and eliminate any uncertainties' regarding the new legislative regime under analysis and gather enough information that would justify extending it to the whole jurisdiction.[109] This was notably done in the case of

[108] See the response of the Secretary of Education, Culture and Science, *Nader rapport (reactie op het advies)* van 5.10.200404, Opinion of the Dutch Council of State of 23August 2004, no. W05.04.0365/III, Voorstel van wet houdende tijdelijke regels betreffende experimenten in het hoger onderwijs op het gebied van vooropleidingseisen aan en selectie van aanstaande studenten en op het gebied van heffing van collegegeld (Experimentenwet vooropleidingseisen, selectie en collegegeldheffing), Kamerstukken II, 2004/2005, 29 819, no. 4.

[109] Tijdelijke regels voor een pilot ter bevordering van de participatie van personen met een arbeidsbeperking met behulp van loondispensatie (Tijdelijke wet pilot loondispensatie), advies van Raad van State en nader rapport. (See reaction of the Secretary of State for Social and Labour Affairs to the Opinion of the Council of State of 2 October 2009, no. W12.09.0349/III, Kamerstukken II, 2009–2010, 32165, no. 4, 2.

the 'temporary law on wage dispensation for disabled workers' (see example 2.7).[110]

> **EXAMPLE 2.7 PILOT PROJECT ON WAGE DISPENSATION FOR DISABLED WORKERS**
>
> Article 2 of the temporary statute in question (tijdelijke wet pilot loondispensatie) states that 'this pilot aims to reach a grounded decision on whether a wage dispensation could contribute to the integration of disabled workers, gain some insight on the effects of this instrument and assess the possible existing side-effects'.[111]

(c) Levels of enactment in federal states

Sunset clauses and experimental legislation can be used both in federal and unitary jurisdictions. As earlier mentioned, in the 1970s sunset clauses were a state phenomenon but there are nowadays examples of federal laws containing these provisions (see below). Since sunset clauses do not involve derogation from existing law and do not reveal particular affinity with the different levels of enactment and implementation, more attention will be paid here to experimental legislation.

Experimentation is common in federal states characterized by a greater diversity of races, cultural backgrounds, religions and political identities.[112] State and local unities will tend to experiment because 'different populations have different goals'.[113] Although most examples come from the United States and Germany, federalism is 'neither a necessary nor an

[110] Wet van 20 mei 2010 houdende tijdelijke regels voor een pilot ter bevordering van de participatie van personen met een arbeidsbeperking met behulp van loondispensatie (Tijdelijke wet pilot loondispensatie), Stb. 2010, 216.

[111] The Dutch Council of State also stated that the Bill lacks information regarding the implementation of the experiment, see Opinion of the Council of State of 2 October 2009, no. W12.09.0349/III, Kamerstukken II, 2009–2010, 32165, no. 4, 2–3.

[112] See Section 2.4 on the link between experimental legislation, innovation and the value of diversity.

[113] Yair Listokin, 'Learning through Policy Variation' (2008) 118 *Yale Law Journal* 480.

essential condition for policy [or legislative] experimentation'.[114] Rather, it has been claimed in the literature that experimentation is 'a happy incident of decentralization' which allows for variation of policy solutions: a wide variety of solutions gives a state the possibility of choosing the 'most desirable policies'.[115] Rubin and Feeley explain that experimentation can be useful for a decentralized state because the respective subunits usually share goals among each other and with the central level.[116] The same does not necessarily apply to a federalist system where state governments can define their own goals and are not limited to experimenting with new instruments to achieve common national goals. Experimentation in federal states may be particularly useful in the case of shared competences when the states have to implement federal legislation but have leeway to decide upon the means of implementation.

Distinguishing between the so-called 'policy variation', 'legal transplants' and experimental legislation in the sense of 'states as laboratories' is not a simple task. *Policy variation* signifies that states, within their competences, act independently in defining their own policies which, if proven successful, can eventually be transplanted to other states. This does not imply the enactment of temporary laws. Such transplantation can be regarded as a part of 'the grass is greener on the other side' effect of comparative law. Differently, in the case of experimental legislation, there is a derogation from existing law: in a scenario of shared competences, the federal level may authorize states to derogate from federal provisions on an experimental basis in order to find the best way to implement these rules in the state's circumstances.

Whereas federalism might particularly stimulate experimentation because 'multiple truth-seekers are more likely to uncover the truth than a single-seeker',[117] Rubin and Feeley stress that the key element lies in the existence of a multiplicity of distinct policy-makers.[118] A unitary but decentralized government can equally stimulate policy and legislative experimentation, namely, with the aim to develop policy innovation. According to the literature, smaller units such as municipalities should be given the competence to experiment with their own legislative solutions.

---

[114] Tarr, *Laboratories of Democracy?*, n. 51 above, 9.

[115] Malcom M. Feeley and Edward Rubin, *Federalism: Political Identity and Tragic Compromise* (University of Michigan Press, 2008) 26.

[116] *Ibid.* 26.

[117] Tarr, *Laboratories of Democracy?*, n. 51 above, 9.

[118] Edward Rubin and Malcolm Feeley, 'Federalism? Some Notes on a National Neurosis' (1994) 41 *University of California Los Angeles Review* 903, 924.

Should these experiments work, other units can try to borrow them.[119] According to a study on the diffusion of innovation, demographic factors and the availability of reduced financial resources were mentioned as correlates of this effect of policy innovation and policy diffusion: small decision-makers can 'afford' the luxury of experimenting because they can also afford the risk of failure (see Bryce' and Brandeis' positions above).[120] This is far more serious in the case of an entire nation, which may explain why nation-wide experiments are less common.

The majority of German experimental clauses have been implemented at the level of the Länder (states),[121] but the Kommunen (municipalities) are equally significant users of this instrument. There appears to be a preference for state or local experiments, since it is substantially more difficult to experiment at a national level due to the high costs involved and eventual lack of cooperation by all the relevant authorities.[122] As earlier demonstrated, in the Netherlands, experimental regulations and other forms of experiments with law are often implemented by municipalities.

The decision as to which level to choose for the implementation of experimental regulations depends notably on the objective and complexity of the experiment, competences and/or the field at stake.

2.4 FUNCTIONS OF SUNSET CLAUSES AND EXPERIMENTAL LEGISLATION

Both sunset clauses and experimental legislation are multifunctional legislative instruments that serve a number of purposes. Although these legislative instruments are often used to tackle temporary or uncertain problems, about which little is known, this subsection evidences that the versatility of sunset clauses and experimental legislation goes beyond the need to gather information about social or economic problems or their regulation.

---

[119] Tarr, *Laboratories of Democracy?*, n. 51 above, 9.

[120] Jack L. Walker, 'The Diffusion of Innovation among the American States' (1969) 63(3) *American Political Science Review* 880, 883.

[121] Freund, *Kommunale Standardöffnungs- und Experimentierklauseln im Lichte der Verfassung*, n. 64 above, 59.

[122] John Gerring and Rose McDermott, 'An Experimental Template for Case Study Research' (2007) 51(3) *American Journal of Political Science* 688, 693.

2.4.1 To Tackle Uncertainty, Lack of Information and Prognosis Problems

'Information is the lifeblood of regulatory policy' but lawmakers and regulators will often be unable to gather accurate information from private actors as to the risks and costs of their activities.[123] In the United States, in the area of environmental and occupational safety regulation, agencies have often encouraged firms to participate in pilot programmes so that information about their management practices is revealed.[124] However, this is not put in practice on a systematic basis through experimental rules.

Regulating without the necessary information can be risky since regulators and lawmakers should be able to understand the nature of the underlying problems in order to enact effective regulations. Lawmakers and regulators have often legislated and regulated with reduced information but concluding as to the success or failure of a regulation without scientific testing is, as Posner describes, a 'mere impression' with 'no verified knowledge'. Experimenting with alternatives, by proposing testable hypotheses, should be able to produce useful information and reflect the effectiveness of the rules being tested.[125]

In the case of innovative products and services, regulators will face not only the problem of information asymmetries caused by the reluctance of firms to disclose relevant information but also the absence of information regarding the best regulatory approaches to them. It is difficult to compel firms to produce information but the required information can be more easily provided over time through repeated interaction.[126] This 'repeated interaction' is notably enabled by sunset clauses and experimental legislation: due to the temporary character and periodic evaluations of these instruments, lawmakers can easily incorporate the information obtained either through observing the effects of the laws in question, by acknowledging the results of the participation of stakeholders or by taking into account the evaluation reports. Zachary Gubler claims that

---

[123] Cary Coglianese, Richard Zeckhauser and Edward Parson, 'Seeking Truth for Power: Informational Strategy and Regulatory Policymaking' (2004) 89 *Minnesota Law Review* 277, 279.

[124] *Ibid.* 312.

[125] Richard A. Posner, 'The Summary Jury Trial and Other Methods of Alternative Dispute Resolution: Some Cautionary Observations' (1986) 53 *University of Chicago Law Review* 366–7.

[126] Coglianese, Zeckhauser and Parson, 'Seeking Truth for Power', n. 123 above, 311.

regulators would be able to deliver regulation based on more accurate information if they would divide the decision-making process into different stages. As more information is produced in the first experimental phase, they could then adapt regulations accordingly.[127]

The regulation of innovative products and services is not only characterized by the lack of information but also by emergent risks and uncertainty that may be difficult to tackle. Gersen suggests the employment of temporary legislation (a concept that also includes sunset clauses and experimental legislation) as a means to tackle social, legal or economic problems or situations characterized by *uncertainty.*[128] This uncertainty can refer to the duration, complexity or effects of the problems. When little is known about these type of situations, a temporary legislative measure can be a safer option which provides an immediate remedy for a problem without putting the whole population at stake, and which, at the same time, can easily be extinguished. Sunset clauses and experimental legislation offer the required flexibility to deal with temporary problems or problems characterized by acute uncertainty, or to enact policies about which little is known and the risk of error is high.[129]

In addition, where experimental regulations are enacted in parts of the territory or smaller jurisdictions in the case of federalism, the risk inherent to the enactment of novel policies and laws can be limited and more time can be granted to the legislator to gather information as to their effects.[130]

In a similar context, Ginsburg, Masur and McAdams also argue that sunset clauses and experimental laws and regulations have the advantage of improving the efficiency gains of legislation since they are based on superior information.[131] Even if the enactment of a law is preceded by *ex ante* studies, there is still uncertainty as to its effects and the best legislative or regulatory approach to the problem in question. Only after the law has been in place for a reasonable period can lawmakers observe and evaluate these effects: laws that are ineffective can be discontinued after the sunset; and improvements can be added to an experimental

---

127 Zachary J. Gubler, 'Experimental Rules' (2014) 55 *Boston Law Review* 129.

128 Gersen, 'Temporary Legislation', n. 2 above, 248.

129 Questioning this argument, see Rebecca M. Kysar, 'Lasting Legislation' (2011) 159 *University of Pennsylvania Law Review* 101, 135.

130 Listokin, 'Learning through Policy Variation', n. 113 above, 514.

131 Tom Ginsburg, J. Masur and Richard H. McAdams, 'Libertarian Paternalism, Path Dependence, and Temporary Law' (2014) 81 *University of Chicago Law Review* 291.

law.[132] Lawmakers can therefore use sunset clauses and experimental legislation to gather information, and given this informational advantage, proceed to the correction of errors.

In Germany, Horn argues that experimental legislation can be particularly suitable to regulate novelties carrying certain dangers or risks, or when it is difficult to fully estimate the side-effects of a new law.[133] Rebecca Kysar, despite her critical position toward temporary legislation, acknowledges that sunset clauses have been used in the United States as an instrument to assess the risks and effects of a new policy, as well as to obtain more information about it during the interim period between the enactment and the sunset.[134] Sunset clauses are expected to prevail in policy contexts characterized by uncertainty, scarce or unreliable information, and the existence of a number of risks.[135]

As described in the German literature, sunset clauses and, particularly, experimental legislation can be regarded as the 'highest form of testing [the effectiveness] of laws', which can be particularly important when legislators have insufficient information regarding the effects of laws.[136] A similar perspective can be identified in Germany, where experimental legislation has typically been described as an instrument for gathering information, solving the so-called *Prognose* problems due to information asymmetries and minimizing risks.[137]

In the Netherlands, it has been suggested in the literature that sunset clauses can contribute to the reduction of uncertainty, especially when the latter results from potential risks (for example, latent harms to the environment, food safety, public health and other scenarios typically connected with the precautionary principle).[138] This 'precautionary' use of sunset clauses would mean that a novelty representing potential (but scientifically unproven) harms for the environment or society could be temporarily authorized and during this period the alleged risks could be

---

132 *Ibid.* 34.

133 Horn, *Experimentelle Gesetzgebung unter dem Grundgesetz*, n. 57 above.

134 Kysar, 'Lasting Legislation', n. 129 above, 135.

135 Finn, 'Sunset Clauses and Democratic Deliberation', n. 73 above, 451.

136 Böhret and Hugger, *Test und Prüfung von Gesetzentwürfen*, n. 91 above, 50.

137 Antonis Chanos, *Möglichkeiten und Grenzen der Befristung parlamentarischer Gesetzgebung* (Duncker and Humblot, 1999) 19.

138 Eijlander and van Gestel, *Horizonwetgeving: effectief middel in de strijd tegen toenemende regeldruk?*, n. 75 above.

further examined. This would be an alternative to an all-or-nothing approach.[139]

This 'information gathering' side of experimental legislation can be used not only for the regulation of innovative fields but also for the general improvement of the administration of justice. The latter was the subject of a study conducted in 1981 by the US Federal Judicial Center on the virtues of experimentation in law.[140] In question was not only experimental legislation but also the use of programme experiments and random assignment of laws. According to this report, a justice system can more easily attain its goals if it is flexible, willing to try out new methods of achieving justice and evaluate their effectiveness and compare these results with the existing alternatives.[141] As underlined by the Federal Judicial Center in the mentioned report, experimentation with innovations in law can resolve the uncertainties 'about whether the innovation in question, although promising in theory, will in fact produce the desired improvements without undesirable consequences'.[142]

The above described informational function of experimental legislation is, according to Hoffmann-Riem, one of the main features of this legislative instrument: the possibility to extract lessons from the experiment and use them to revise or revoke laws on the grounds of new and more effective ideas or legal instruments.[143] After having experimented with new rules, legislators will be able to make a more informed future choice between the existing rules and the ones tried on an experimental basis.

Notwithstanding the advantages mentioned above, the 'research' or 'information gathering' function of sunset clauses and experimental legislation has been criticized in the Netherlands. In the 2001 Bill regarding 'distance voting' (Experimentenwet Kiezen op Afstand), the Dutch Council of State inquired whether there was not an alternative method which could avoid using a statute as 'a research instrument'.[144] This institution refused to accept an abstract formulation of objectives

---

139 ZENC, *Horizonwetgeving Dichterbij*, n 38 above, 39.

140 Federal Judicial Center, Advisory Committee on Experimentation in the Law, *Experimentation in the Law* (Federal Judicial Center, 1981), available at www.fjc.gov/public/pdf.nsf/lookup/experlaw.pdf/$file/experlaw.pdf.

141 *Ibid.*

142 *Ibid.*

143 Hoffmann-Riem, 'Législation expérimentale en Allemagne', n. 63 above, 185.

144 Opinion of the Council of State of 9 November 2001, no. W04.01.0380/I, Voorstel van wet met memorie van toeliching houdende tijdelijke regels terzake

referring to the 'acquisition of experience or knowledge': if the experiment in question was to be used to learn about distance voting, it would be important to define beforehand exactly what type of 'experience', knowledge or information one aims to acquire from it.[145] The paradox between the minimum amount of information required to design an experiment and the need to experiment in order to gather the missing details is visible in this example.

In conclusion, experimental legislation and sunset clauses are not only meant to resolve uncertainties connected with difficult prognostics in innovative fields, but they can also and primarily be employed to gather information and ensure that legislators make decisions based on evidence.[146] It is important to question whether the enactment of these legislative instruments contributes to the improvement of the quality of legislation.

2.4.2 To Enhance the Quality of Legislation

The quality of legislation can be evaluated on the basis of legal criteria (democratic legitimacy, subsidiarity, proportionality, legal certainty and transparency of the legal procedure); factual criteria (ability of the law to respond and adapt to the real-life circumstances and its effectiveness); and, finally, the quality of the text in itself (clarity, coherence and simplicity of language).[147]

The standards of quality of legislation also imply that legislators consider social reality not only by implementing *ex post* evaluation schemes but also by enacting other types of laws which are more flexible with regard to the evolution of social and economic change. This is where sunset clauses and experimental legislation come in. These instruments can contribute to the improvement of the quality of legislation and

---

van experimenten in het kader van het project 'Kiezen op Afstand (Experimentenwet Kiezen op Afstand).

145 Voorstel van wet met memorie van toelichting tot wijziging van de Wet op het primair onderwijs, de Wet op de expertisecentra, de Wet op het voorgezet onderwijs en de Wet medezeggenschap onderwijs 1992 in verband met een verruiming van de bestedingsvrijheid voor scholen in het primair en voortgezet onderwijs, Advies van Raad van State en nader rapport, Kamerstukken II, 2002–2003, 28 762, no. A, 2–3.

146 Hoffmann-Riem, 'Législation expérimentale en Allemagne', n. 63 above, 177, 207.

147 A. Flückiger, 'Voter, élire et signer par Internet: le droit expérimental à l' épreuve de la sécurité' in M. Müller and A. Thomas (eds), *E-voting* (Bern, 2003) 107.

regulations for several reasons: first, these instruments can 'rationalize' the legislative process; secondly, they may be capable of reducing regulatory pressure by terminating unnecessary regulations; thirdly, both instruments require legislators to gather more information about the effectiveness of regulations and consider evidence-based information in the lawmaking process; fourthly, they convert the legislative process into an iterative learning process.

(a) Instruments to rationalize the legislative process

Although the legislative challenges described in Chapter 1 cannot be entirely solved by the enactment of experimental legislation or sunset clauses, these instruments have been used to rationalize the legislative process and, consequently, legislation as its end-product. This objective can be furthered by frequent legislative oversight, the gathering and consequent incorporation of new information, and the extinction of ineffective laws and regulations. Moreover, the rationalization of the legislative process is also enhanced by the fact that specified provisions or whole laws expire, whenever these are no longer necessary, or they are revised according to the observed social or economic changes.[148]

In the United States, sunset clauses have been regarded since the 1970s as instruments of rational decision-making, suitable to confer consistency, effectiveness and comprehensiveness on the lawmaking process.[149] In Germany, sunset clauses emerged in the debates concerning the rationalization of legislation, improvement of the quality of legislation and, more recently, together with experimental legislation, in the context of the discussion regarding the need to enhance the efficiency and effectiveness of public administration.[150] The Netherlands followed the same tendency.[151]

According to Horn, experimental legislation responds to the idea of developing laws sustained in multidisciplinary and empirically driven methodology (*Rechtsetzungsmethodik*).[152]

---

148 Robert Baldwin, 'Is Better Regulation Smart Regulation?' (2005) *Public Law* 499.

149 Sandra M. Vidas, 'The Sun Also Sets: A Model for Sunset Implementation' (1976) 26 *American University Law Review* 1170.

150 Stettner, 'Verfassungsbindungen des experimentierenden Gesetzgebers', n. 61 above.

151 See also ZENC, *Horizonwetgeving Dichterbij*, n. 38 above.

152 Horn, *Experimentelle Gesetzgebung unter dem Grundgesetz*, n. 57 above, 20–21.

(b) To reduce regulatory pressure

Sunset clauses emerged in the past decades in the political debate in Germany and in the Netherlands regarding the need to tackle bureaucracy and reduce regulatory pressure.[153]

In the Netherlands, sunset clauses emerged in the 1990s as an instrument at the service of deregulation and improvement of the quality of legislation and regulation. By the 1980s, the Dutch government had become aware of the need to introduce 'better regulation' strategies.[154] The Dutch government initiated a regulatory reform aimed at reducing and avoiding the enactment of excessive and deficient legislation.[155] Comprehensive regulation seemed to become rapidly obsolete since the legislator was not able to meet the expectations of a progressively more complex society characterized by rapid technological developments and globalization.[156] This perception led to an effort to proceed to substantial deregulation which, however, was not translated into a broad enactment of sunset clauses.[157]

It was only in the 1990s that a first connection between deregulation and temporary legislation emerged with a statute aiming to promote 'social renovation' ('*sociale vernieuwing*') in the context of the economic crisis.[158] This Act included a sunset clause and was presented as a flexible and simple instrument in the context of deregulation.[159] The

---

153 Bertelsmann Stiftung, 'Gutachten: Wirksamkeit von Sunset Legislation und Evaluationsklauseln' n. 79 above.

154 OECD, *Better Regulation in Europe: The Netherlands* (OECD, 2010) 15; OECD, *Regulatory Reform in the Netherlands* (OECD, 1999).

155 J.H. Van Kreveld, 'The Main Elements of a General Policy on Legislative Quality: Dutch Experiences' in Alfred E. Kellermann, Giuseppe Ciavarini Azzi and Rex Deighton-Smith (eds), *Improving the Quality of Legislation in Europe* (Kluwer Law International, 1998) 91.

156 G.W. van der Voet, *De kwaliteit van de WMCZ als medezeggenschapswet* (Erasmus Universiteit Rotterdam, 2005) 152–3, available at http://repub.eur.nl/res/pub/6920/.

157 See, as an example, the deregulation programme on environmental and urbanistic affairs of the Van der Grinten Committee, *Dereguleringsprogramma Ruimtelijke Ordening en Milieubeheer* (also 'DROM-rapport'), Kamerstukken II, 1982–1983, 17 931, no. 4. See the Geelhoed Committee report, *Deregulering van overheidsregelingen* also referred as *Eindbericht van de Commissie vermindering en vereenvoudiging van overheidsregelingen*, Kamerstukken II, 1983–1984, 17 931, no. 9.

158 Tijdelijke bepalingen ter stimulering en bekostiging van sociale vernieuwing, Kamerstukken II, Vergaderjaar 1992–1993, 23 052, no. 3.

159 In practice, there was little 'social renovation' to the mentioned statute and the suggested temporary regime was aimed, amongst others, at the reduction

sunset clause conferred the necessary flexibility to keep pace with the constant changes over time of policies. More recently, this instrument was employed in a framework designed to tackle overregulation and regulatory pressure;[160] to stimulate the enactment of effective laws and the periodic evaluation of legislative acts;[161] and to reduce the annual amount of laws[162] and the complexity of the lawmaking process. In the Netherlands, it has been discussed whether sunset clauses can contribute to a reduction of regulatory burdens. Periodic evaluations and termination of Acts would lead to the extinction of unnecessary burdens. Sunset clauses can be useful but they are not a panacea for regulatory pressure. Moreover, considering the US experience with sunsets in the 1980s, one can fear that the excessive enactment of sunset clauses can generate more bureaucracy than it eliminates.

In Germany, there has also been for several decades a growing awareness of the excessive number of laws and regulations.[163] New approaches and instruments have been sought to concretize the desired *Bürokratieabbaus*. It has been argued that sunset clauses can tackle excessive bureaucracy since they put an end to unnecessary policies. Policy termination is, according to the literature, an exception in Germany, which is used to tackle the issue of obsolescence of laws and regulations. The same can be verified in the United States[164] and in the Netherlands, where there appears to be a political attachment to enacted policies even when they are not producing the expected results (see Chapter 7). Although a broader use of sunset clauses has been suggested in the literature in this context, according to the OECD, Germany has not 'particularly encouraged sunset clauses or other devices that would trigger review of individual regulations'.[165] However, according to the same institution, sunset clauses could be used 'when a new approach is

---

of burdens for municipalities and their respective costs. Nevertheless, this was the first sign of the expansion of sunset clauses to other contexts and its entry into the debate on deregulation.

[160] Commissie Regeldruk Bedrijven, report available at www.rijksoverheid.nl/documenten-en-publicaties/brieven/2011/04/22/advies-toezicht-20-van-de-commissie-regeldruk-bedrijven.html.

[161] ZENC, *Horizonwetgeving Dichterbij*, n. 38 above.

[162] *Ibid.*

[163] See Jörg Steinhaus, *Gesetze mit Verfallsdatum: Ein Instrument des Bürokratieabbaus?* (Books on Demand, 2008).

[164] Peter deLeon, 'Afterward: The Once and Future State of Policy Termination' (2012) 20(12) *International Journal of Public Administration* 2195.

[165] OECD, *Better Regulation in Europe: Germany* (OECD 2010) 108.

being tested, or it is important to check what [happens] in practice'.[166] Despite this debate, up until now, there is no solid evidence indicating that a broader implementation of sunset clauses will necessarily result in a reduction of regulatory pressure.

(c) Gathering facts and considering evidence-based information

The enactment of experimental legislation can also improve the quality of legislation because it obliges the legislator to take into account evidence-based information. According to the literature, one of main political aims of experimental legislation is to influence the lawmaker to respond positively to the evidence resulting from the experiment.[167] In this context, Roth defined that experiments have a tripartite function: 'speak to theorists', 'search for facts' and 'whisper in the ears of princes'.[168] To wit, experimental results can provide a better cross-check for the analysis of new policy instruments than just an evaluation exclusively based on theoretical models.[169] Theoretical knowledge is the departing point ('speak to theorists' as formulated by Roth), but experimentation can provide the practical information ('search for facts') and thus the 'piece of advice' that lawmakers need to make a policy decision ('whisper in the ear of princes').[170] However, the quality of legislation will only improve if the exact 'facts' resulting from the experiment are whispered in the ear of the prince and the latter will indeed listen to them.[171]

(d) Legislative process converted into a learning path

Besides gathering evidence-based information, experimental legislation and sunset clauses can improve legislation because they enable a general strategy centred on a social and political learning process.[172] It is through

[166] *Ibid.* 114–15.

[167] A.E. Roth, 'Introduction to Experimental Economics' in J. Kagel and A. Roth (eds), *Handbook of Experimental Economics* (Princeton University Press, 1997).

[168] *Ibid.*

[169] Charles A. Holt, William M. Shobe and Angela M. Smith, 'An Experimental Basis for Public Policy Initiatives' in Alan S. Gerber and Eric M. Patashnik, *Promoting the General Welfare: New Perspectives on Government Performance* (Brookings Institution Press, 2006) 174–96.

[170] *Ibid.*

[171] See for a critical perspective, Donald T. Campbell, 'Reforms as Experiments' (1969) 24 *American Psychologist* 409.

[172] Manuel Eisner, 'Déterminants de la politique Suisse en matière de drogue. L'exemple du programme de prescription d'héroïne' (1999) 23 *Déviance et Société* 191.

experimenting that learning is enabled. 'Experiential education' or 'learning-by-doing' was first proposed by John Dewey in 1938.[173] The awareness that people remember more of what 'they do' (or experiment) than what 'they are told' has been further developed in different fields and supports the idea that learning should be based on active experimentation followed by a reflective observation.[174]

The virtues of the learning-by-doing process through experimentation have been acknowledged by public policy, justifying the incorporation of experiential learning programmes on social policies, such as immigration.[175] Political scientists have not remained indifferent to this approach to learning through experimentation. In this setting, it has been stated that 'experiments can be helpful in understanding the micro-foundations of human behavior'.[176] On the one hand, experimental laws, like scientific experiments, proceed to similar tests because they put into practice a legal solution in order to observe and rationally evaluate the response of citizens. On the other, experimental laws can have a double educational value since not only can politicians learn from their practical implementation but also citizens will to a certain extent be 'instructed' by their own legislation. Citizens may, at first, question experimental laws due to their inherent uncertainty and temporary duration; however, if a law is submitted to the test of reality, it might be recognized as a more efficient and legitimate law since evidence of its positive or negative implementation will be taken into consideration.[177]

---

[173] See John Dewey, *Experience and Education* (Kappa Delta Pi, 1938).

[174] Peter L. Gess and Nicole G. Sanders, 'Governing a Diverse Community: The Effect of Experiential and Cross-Cultural Learning on Georgia Local Government Officials' (2008) 40(2) *State and Local Government Review* 75, 77.

[175] This is the case, for example, of a pilot cross-cultural programme, which consisted of an experiential learning tour to Mexico for 18 local government officials from the State of Georgia (US). This programme aimed at assisting these officials to understand the economic, social and cultural differences and problems affecting the group of Mexican immigrants. See Gess and Sanders, 'Governing a Diverse Community', n 174 above: this study concluded that this experiential pilot programme produced a change in the participants' views and values towards immigration and assisted them in obtaining a better understanding of Mexican immigrants' problems.

[176] Gerry Stoker. 'Exploring the Promise of Experimentation in Political Science: Micro-Foundational Insights and Policy Relevance' (2010) 38 *Political Studies* 315.

[177] Koen van Aeken, 'Pushing Evaluation Forward: Institutionalization as a Means to Foster Methodological Growth of Legislative Ex Ante Evaluation' in

2.4.3 To Improve the Effectiveness of Public Administration

Sunset clauses were originally depicted as 'a cure-all to the ills of inefficient government'.[178] A general discontentment with the performance of government and the uncontrolled growth of administrative agencies was at the root of the enactment of sunset clauses. However, the United States was not the only country facing problems at this level.

Since the late 1980s, there has been a growing awareness of the multiple problems of the German public administration: excessive administrative burdens, budgetary problems and lack of transparency. A deep reform of the German public administration was put into practice, especially in the 1990s. There was an essential shift from the so-called 'control perspective' (strict legislative standards imposed on the public authorities and control by courts for the safeguard of individual rights) which prevailed in administrative law until that time, to a governance perspective (*Steuerung*).[179] According to this new insight, administrative law should provide public actors with the means and tools to effectively implement legal principles and rules and, at the same time, allow them to use their resources as efficiently and economically as possible.[180] This explained the emergence of the 'New Public Management'. In the German context, the practical implementation of this public administration management focused on the autonomous administration of municipalities.

In the 1990s, German municipalities (Kommunen) were facing two types of growing challenges: on the one hand, financial problems, and, on the other, increasing demands to develop a closer relationship with citizens.[181] The modernization of local municipalities conducive to more 'citizen-friendly', flexible and transparent policies was then required. The solution to the mentioned problems resided in an enhancement of local autonomy, in other words, municipalities could administrate their own finances according to their needs. The Neues Steuerungsmodell, as a new

---

Jonathan Verschuuren, *The Impact of Legislation: A Critical Analysis of Ex Ante Evaluation* (Martinus Nijhoff Publishers, 2009) 111.

178 Chris Mooney, 'A Short History of Sunsets' (2004) *Legal Affairs* 67.

179 Matthias Ruffert, 'The Transformation of Administrative Law as a Transnational Methodological Project' in Matthias Ruffert (ed.), *The Transformation of Administrative Law in Europe* (Sellier, 2007) 10–11.

180 *Ibid.*

181 Beck and Schürmeier, 'Die kommunalrechtliche Experimentierklausel als Reforminstrument' n. 61 above.

output-oriented model based on the self-government of municipalities, was suggested in this context.[182]

Two experimental legislative instruments were used by municipalities in Germany to proceed to experiments: *Experimentierklauseln* and *Standardöffnungsklauseln*.[183] Municipalities highly in deficit opted for these dispositions, which, in most cases, exempted them from observing stricter rules or legal standards contained in state regulations and gave them more leeway to determine their own policies.

The use of experiments at the local level aimed at diminishing the burdens faced by private actors and improving the relationship between the local administration and citizens. An example can be found in Brandenburg: the Standard-erprobungsgesetz of this state was designed to reduce the administrative burdens faced by citizens and companies, and tackle the excessive bureaucracy and inefficiency of public administration.[184] This Act allowed municipalities to derogate from state regulations and experiment with new forms of executing state standards. They were still bound by the state goals but not by the means to achieve them. By granting this possibility to municipalities, it was expected to spur entrepreneurial action and stimulate business start-ups.[185] Budgetary problems have been one of the grounds for the enactment of experimental legislation, not only in Germany but also in other countries. It is thus important to explain how and why these experiments have performed an important role in this context.

The choice of experimental legislation has not always been unreservedly accepted in Germany. Former Minister of Justice of Saxony, Steffen Heitmann, once stated that deregulation and the reform of public administration did not require the use of temporary laws, because unnecessary laws could just as easily be abolished without deadlines. According to Heitmann, this 'deadline' inserted in temporary laws would inevitably damage legal certainty and constituted a considerable threat to

[182] *Ibid.* 489.

[183] Thomas Freund, *Kommunale Standardöffnungs- und Experimentierklauseln im Lichte der Verfassung* (WVB, 2003) paras 16-18, 25–32.

[184] Heinrich Plückelmann, 'Mit zum Experiment – Das Standarderprobungsgesetz des Landes Brandenburg' (2009) 5 *Themenschwerpunkt – AWV-Informationen* 4.

[185] Christian W. Otto, 'Gesetz zur Erprobung der Abweichung von landesrechtlichen Standards in Kommunen des Landes Brandenburg' (2008) *Landes- und Kommunalverwaltung* 67.

the *Rechtsstaat.*[186] This objection will be further analyzed in Chapters 3 and 4 as two of the possible arguments against a broader use of experimental legislation.

German municipalities were not the only local authorities turning to experimentation in order to overcome their financial problems. The same tendency is being observed in the last decades in the United States. As illustrated in example 2.8, the adoption of charters by cities and county governments has granted them more autonomy and created more room for experimentation with the organizational instruments and programmes that fit their budgets and needs.[187]

EXAMPLE 2.8 EXPERIMENTS WITH OUTSOURCING PUBLIC ADMINISTRATION

In recent years in California, a number of municipalities have been trying to avoid bankruptcy by experimenting with outsourcing of traditional public services. This is the case of Maywood, which even outsourced its police department.[188] The aim of this experiment was not to verify whether outsourcing is 'a good idea', but rather to provide information on the possible functioning of small municipalities without public services.[189] This is an ongoing experiment which might potentially lead to an improvement in the quality of services such as police and education and to a reduction in the budgetary deficits of municipalities with financial problems.

---

[186] Ingo von München, 'Die Zeit im Recht' (2004) *Neue Juristische Wochenschrift* 4.

[187] Alvin D. Sokolow, 'The Limited and Contrary Uses of County Charter Reform: Two California Cases' (2004) 36(1) *State and Local Government Review* 7.

[188] David Streitfeld, 'A city outsources everything. Sky doesn't fall', *New York Times*, 19 July 2010, available at www.nytimes.com/2010/07/20/business/20maywood.html?pagewanted=all&_r=0.

[189] Chris Niccolls, 'The Maywood Experiment', in http://outsourcing.about.com/od/avoid/a/The-Maywood-Experiment.htm.

2.4.4 To Respond to Temporary Problems

Although the idea of 'permanence' appears to be traditionally associated with legislation, temporary phenomena such as wars, economic crises or extraordinary circumstances have always required temporary legislative measures.[190] Most of these older forms of temporary laws and regulations were labelled as 'emergency legislation', which, under a state of emergency, granted the possibility to introduce exceptional measures (often disregarding some fundamental rights) such as a curfew.[191] Public officials may be allowed to go outside the constitutional order, enacting 'extra-legal measures' to protect the nation if they are faced with calamities or grave dangers. According to Oren Gross, the adequate pursuit of these measures 'may strengthen rather than weaken, and result in more rather than less, long-term constitutional fidelity and commitment to the rule of law'.[192]

In times of crisis there may be a tension of 'tragic dimensions' between democratic values and responses to emergencies; often this tension is solved by introducing a sunset clause in emergency regulations.[193] In principle, experimental regulations *stricto sensu* should not easily be conceivable in this context since, as explained earlier, these legislative instruments are enacted to introduce a regulation for the future and not to respond to a temporary calamity.

Temporary legislation, including sunset clauses, is still nowadays used not only as a reaction to social or political emergencies or terrorist threats but also as a response to economic crisis, namely, to assist companies in need. In these scenarios of crises, it is difficult to draw the line between

---

[190] An example of the adoption of a temporary regulation in order to respond to an exceptional situation was Wet van 6 maart 2002 tot vaststelling van de tijdelijke wet voor de penitentiaire noodcapaciteit ten behoeve van drugkoeriers (tijdelijke wet penitentiaire capaciteit drugkoeriers), Stb. 2002, 124.

[191] Well-known examples of contested emergency laws are the Notstandgesetze enacted by the Bundestag on 30 May 1968. According to these emergency laws, in scenarios of a state of emergency, the legislative federal competences would be extended to permit the enactment of exceptional measures disregarding a number of constitutional rights such as the secrecy of correspondence. These emergency laws were a reaction to the social crisis of May 1968, which involved an ever-more turbulent period dominated by the terrorist activities in West Germany perpetrated by the Baader-Meinhof Group.

[192] Oren Gross, 'Chaos and Rules: Should Responses to Violent Crises Always be Constitutional?' (2003) 112 *Yale Law Journal* 1011, 1023.

[193] *Ibid.* 1028.

the broad concept of 'temporary law' and the sunset clauses introduced in the particular laws enacted for the purpose.

During periods of economic crisis, it is important to keep investing in research and innovation. Since the beginning of the global financial crisis in 2008, a serious economic downturn has been observed. Banks became risk-averse, which meant that businesses had increasingly more difficulties in gaining access to finance. In order to ensure that companies continue investing in R&D and consequently innovating, the European Commission adopted the Temporary Union Framework for State Aid Measures (see example 2.9).[194]

EXAMPLE 2.9 TEMPORARY UNION FRAMEWORK FOR STATE AID MEASURES

By introducing this common temporary framework, the European Commission opened temporary and exceptional possibilities to grant well-targeted state aid aimed at unblocking lending to companies and stimulating investment in the future.[195] This signified for the Member States that the Commission would temporarily consider certain types of state aid[196] justified and compatible with Article 107(3)(b) of the Treaty on the Functioning of the European Union. These temporary measures implied a more flexible approach to state aid rules or even a derogation from the existing framework.[197] Temporary support to companies in a time of crisis is also regarded as an essential means to ensure investment in a sustainable growth economy and avoid

[194] Communication from the Commission, Temporary Framework for State Aid Measures to Support Access to Finance in the Current Financial and Economic Crisis [2009] OJ C16/1.

[195] *Ibid.*

[196] The types of state aid allowed were subsidized loan guarantees for a limited period; granting of public or private loans at an interest rate defined by the European Commission; and aid in the form of an interest-rate reduction for investment loans for financing environmental friendly products or projects. See Communication from the Commission, Temporary Framework, n. 194 above.

[197] A temporary derogation from the Community guidelines on state aid to promote risk capital investment in small- and medium-sized enterprises was granted initially until 31 December 2010, and then extended for one year, see Communication from the Commission, Temporary Framework, n. 194 above.

jeopardizing the progress achieved in recent years in the environmental field.[198] This communication followed the 2008 Communication 'A European Economic Recovery Plan', which was already based on short-term measures to boost demand and 'smart-investment',[199] and the 2006 Community Framework for State Aid for Research and Innovation, which also contained provisions targeted on the investment in R&D.[200] The Temporary Union Framework for State Aid Measures expired on 31 December 2011. Evidence collected by the European Commission demonstrates that Member States substantially used these temporary possibilities under the temporary framework and that this proved to be a valuable instrument to ensure access to credit during the financial crisis.[201]

There are also examples of sunset clauses used to respond not only to temporary but also to lasting exceptional circumstances. This is the case of terrorism, which is not necessarily a temporary problem, but which is assessed at different levels of risk and might therefore require the adoption of exceptional stringent measures. The US Patriot Act[202] is an example of the use of sunset clauses to respond to a situation of higher level of terrorist threat (see example 2.10).

[198] Communication from the Commission,Temporary Framework, n. 194 above.

[199] Communication from the Commission to the European Council, COM(2008)800.

[200] European Commission, Community Framework for State Aid for Research and Development and Innovation [2006] OJ C323/1.

[201] Communication of the Commission, Temporary Union Framework for State Aid Measures to Support Access to Finance in the Current Financial and Economic Crisis [2011] OJ C6/5.

[202] Uniting and Strengthening America by Providing Appropriate Tools Required to Intercept and Obstruct Terrorism (US PATRIOT) Act of 2001, 18 USC 1, Public Law 107-56, 26 October 2001.

EXAMPLE 2.10 SUNSET CLAUSES IN THE US PATRIOT ACT

The US Patriot Act is one of the few federal examples of sunset clauses. It was enacted in 2001 as a response to the September 11 terrorist attacks. In the US Patriot Act, sunset provisions were included in order to limit the duration of measures constraining fundamental rights to a five-year period.[203] At the time, this was thought to be a response to a higher level of terrorist threat. This Act was, however, reauthorized several times in the following years.

In Germany and the Netherlands, sunset clauses have also been passed or discussed in the context of national security and counter-terrorism policies. In Germany, this was the case of the Terrorismusbekämpfungsgesetz which, in 2002, introduced several temporary limitations to fundamental rights on the ground of the need to safeguard national security.[204] A similar attempt was made in the Netherlands. The most commonly invoked reasons have been the need to limit extraordinary competences and assess periodically the necessity and proportionality *stricto sensu* of a law. Both reasons were argued by the Dutch Council of State in its opinion regarding a statute on national security which included extraordinary measures and competences to be used in the prevention of terrorist attacks (Wet Bestuurlijke Maatregelen Nationale Veiligheid).[205] The recommendation of the Council of State to include a

---

[203] Examples are the interception of communications, disclosure of communication, surveillance orders. US Patriot Act, s. 224 contained a sunset clause of five years. However, a number of sections were renewed (for example, regarding sharing of criminal information, single-jurisdiction search warrants).

[204] Gesetz zur Bekämpfung des internationalen Terrorismus (Terrorismusbekämpfung) vom 9 January 2002, Bundesgesetzblatt 2002, Teil I, No. 3, 361: according to art. 22 of this statute, the limitations of fundamental rights (on data privacy, grant of entry visas, identity control) introduced to the Bundesverfassungsschutzgesetz were only valid until 11 January 2007. A day before these measures would have expired, a new law extending these limitations was enacted: the Terrorismusbekämpfungsgesetz of 10 January 2007 introduced a package of 15 special laws, which again included the possibility to limit fundamental rights (for example, house searches at night).

[205] Regels inzake het opleggen van beperkende maatregelen aan personen met het oog op de bescherming van de nationale veiligheid en inzake het

sunset clause was not welcomed by the responsible Minister who refused to introduce it, asserting that 'terrorism cannot be regarded as a transitory problem'.[206] Terrorism is indeed a lasting problem. However, the introduction of a sunset clause in this context is not focused on the duration of the problem, but on the necessary limited duration of extraordinary measures and powers to be used in the prevention of terrorist attacks. The legislator cannot guarantee that by virtue of the mentioned legislative instruments, the sun will set on terrorism. However, a sunset clause can ensure that extraordinary powers are revisited after a previously determined period of time.

2.4.5 To Act as 'Consensus-Finders'

Legislation is the result of a compromise between political parties. However, this is far from being a simple task. Divided governments and significant political opposition are often reflected in legislative fragmentation and lack of provisions ensuring the continuity of laws or imposing future reconsiderations of laws.[207]

Experimental legislation and, particularly, sunset clauses create more room for political bargains and have been chosen as mechanisms to achieve a social or political consensus. Opponents to a specific law or provision within it may be more willing to pass it if there is a guarantee that the previously existing status quo will return after the sunset expires

---

weigeren of intrekken van beschikkingen met het oog op de bescherming van de nationale veiligheid (Wet bestuurlijke maatregelen nationale veiligheid), Advies van de Raad van State en nader rapport, Kamerstukken II, 2005–2006, 30 566, no. 4, 12.

[206] Regels inzake het opleggen van beperkende maatregelen aan personen met het oog op de bescherming van de nationale veiligheid en inzake het weigeren of intrekken van beschikkingen met het oog op de bescherming van de nationale veiligheid (Wet bestuurlijke maatregelen nationaal veiligheid), Advies van de Raad van State en nader rapport, Kamerstukken II, 2005–2006, 30 566, no. 4, 12–13: in the ministerial report, it was argued that an evaluation (instead of a sunset clause) would suffice to guarantee that the extraordinary competences would not remain for a longer period than necessary.

[207] Forrest Maltzman and Charles R. Shipan, 'Change, Continuity, and the Evolution of the Law' (2008) 52(2) *American Journal of Political Science* 255: in this study, these scholars argue that political conditions at the time of the enactment of a law, namely the existence of a divided government, can influence the probability that a law will be amended. Sunset provisions are described in this context as 'substantial vehicles for encouraging a law to be revisited … and build coalitions'.

or if the experiment fails.[208] This occurs, for example, when there is a conflict of multiple interests or when information as to the potential (negative) effects of law might be lacking. The adoption of sunset provision increases the probability that political opponents will support new laws due to the 'promise' of future evaluation or revision.[209] In the United States, it has been argued that this provides the experimentalist motivation which often underlies multiple sunset clauses.[210]

An example of a controversial Act, which would have gathered little consensus if it had been enacted as a permanent statute, is the so-called Kendra's Law (see example 2.11). In this case, a sunset clause was inserted in the Mental Hygiene Law imposing involuntary outpatient treatment.

EXAMPLE 2.11 KENDRA'S LAW

This law was passed by the State of New York following the death of a young woman brutally pushed under an oncoming train by a schizophrenic man just discharged from a psychiatric hospital.[211] As a result of the pressure to react to this incident, the New York State approved a law directed at people with mental illness who, in view of their medical history, cannot survive in the community without medical assistance and can be therefore submitted to involuntary outpatient treatment. It was not necessary to evidence that they constituted a real harm to society in general. The lack of compliance with this treatment plan would justify the involuntarily admission of the patient to hospital for a 72-hour evaluation period. The adoption of a

[208] Ginsburg, Masur and McAdams, 'Libertarian Paternalism, Path Dependence, and Temporary Law', n. 131 above, 42.

[209] Maltzman and Shipan, 'Change, Continuity, and the Evolution of the Law', n. 207 above, 255.

[210] Thomas Merrill, 'Showcase Panel IV: A Federal Sunset Law, The Federalist Society 2011 National Lawyers Conventions' (2012) 16 *Texas Review of Law and Politics* 339.

[211] Mental Hygiene Law, s. 9.60 Assisted outpatient treatment. New York State Kendra's Law (due to sunset in 2015). See Kathryn A. Worthington, 'Kendra's Law and the Rights of the Mentally Ill: An Empirical Peek Behind the Courts' Legal Analysis and a Suggested Template for the New York State Legislator's Reconsiderations for Renewal in 2010' (2009) 19 *Cornell Journal of Law and Policy* 213.

sunset clause was justified by the need to obtain more information on the implementation of this new system and due to its contentious character.[212]

Another example of the employment of sunset clauses to gather support for a controversial act was the Anti-Crime Act enacted by the US Congress in 1994. The Act prohibited the manufacture, sale and possession of particular assault weapons.[213] In this case, the legislature adopted a ten-year sunset clause.

Experimental legislation is also an adequate instrument to reach a compromise or to convince the opponents or sceptics of a certain rule as to its positive effects or absence of side-effects. In the Netherlands, Eijlander and Van Gestel mention the example of the statute on vehicle inspection (Wet Periodieke Autokeuring) which apparently only 'survived' the heavy parliamentary criticism thanks to its temporary enactment.[214] The lack of political consensus arises also in the context of complex issues about which little is known and where doubts arise as to possible legal, social and ethical implications. An example is the Dutch Embryowet on experiments with stem cells and embryos.[215] The introduction of a sunset clause in this Act was aimed at gathering consensus regarding any ethical problems arising in respect of this law.

The 'consensus-finding' function of temporary legislation can, in some cases, be seen as 'political manoeuvring'. This danger will be developed in Chapter 7.

2.4.6 To Facilitate the Regulation of Innovation

In the last three decades, several federal laws have been enacted in the United States with the mission of facilitating and stimulating technological advancement in the private sector, and, ultimately, fostering

[212] *Ibid.*

[213] Violent Crime Control and Law Enforcement Act of 1994, Pub. L. No. 103-332, 108 Stat. 1792. This law expired on 13 September 2004.

[214] Eijlander and van Gestel, *Horizonwetgeving: effectief middel in de strijd tegen toenemende regeldruk?*, n. 75 above, 17.

[215] Wet van 20 juni 2002 houdende regels inzake handelingen met geslachtcellen en embryo's.

innovation.[216] This has been a well-intended strategy but legislators and regulators are still far from mastering the 'art of regulating' emerging technologies and innovation in general. Highly innovative fields are characterized by lack of information, rapid changes, uncertainty and risks. Therefore, regulators will often be confronted not only with information asymmetries but also with an 'information vacuum' as to the most suitable regulatory instruments. The information regulators need often has not been produced or disclosed yet while the information they possess has become outdated due to the rapid changes of technology and society. As W. Scheuerman argued 'time has been socially [and technologically] accelerated … by science'.[217] On the one hand, technology has changed and accelerated society due to the emergence of the Internet, social networks and faster transportation; on the other, the demands of society have also put enhanced pressure on technology to develop improved and more efficient products. The law thus needs to keep up with this 'acceleration' in order to solve the consequently emerging social problems, control the risks which arise and safeguard the opportunities opened up by technological development. The rapid pace with which social and technological innovation occurs appears to call for frequently updated, flexible and often transitory legislative measures.[218] The traditional methods and instruments of the legislator do not suffice: they are often slow, costly and time-consuming.[219]

New administrative tools for a more adaptive and responsive regulation of these technologies have been suggested in the literature, notably by Gary Marchant and Lyn Gaudet.[220] Besides negotiated rulemaking, direct

---

[216] Wendy H. Schacht, *Cooperative R&D: Federal Efforts to Promote Industrial Competitiveness*, Report for Congress, Order Code RL33526, Congressional Research Service (2008). Examples of the Congressional initiatives are the National Cooperative Research Act; the National Cooperative Production Act; the Stevenson-Wydler Technology Innovation Act; the America COMPETES Act; and, more recently, the Competitiveness through Education, Technology and Enterprise Act of 2007.

[217] The concept of 'social acceleration of time' developed by William Scheuerman is here adapted. See William E. Scheuerman, *Liberal Democracy and the Social Acceleration of Time* (Johns Hopkins University Press, 2004).

[218] For a legal perspective on the regulatory challenges in the context of emerging technologies, see Roger Brownsword, *Rights, Regulation, and Technological Revolution* (Oxford University Press, 2008).

[219] Scheuerman, *Liberal Democracy and the Social Acceleration of Time*, n. 217 above, xiv.

[220] Lyn M. Gaudet and Gary Marchant, 'Administrative Tools for More Adaptive and Responsive Regulation' in Gary Marchant, Braden R. Allenby and

final rulemaking, e-rulemaking, the scholars also suggest temporary legislation as one of the magic keys to more flexible regulation. Marchant and Gaudet refer mainly to sunset clauses, however experimental legislation offers even more flexibility to regulators to address the problems of rapidly changing fields. The use of sunset clauses and experimental legislation in fields characterized by uncertainty is likely to facilitate the regulation of innovation for different reasons. First, these flexible instruments can ensure the adaptability of regulation to new social and technological developments, by incorporating new information in the regulatory process. Experimental legislation is a phased law and rule-making process that enables legislators and regulators to rethink and reshape the rules on the grounds of the obtained evidence. Secondly, both instruments avoid obsolete regulatory requirements turning into obstacles to the introduction of novelties in the market: the sun 'sets' on regulatory rules that are ineffective or superseded by the current state of technology. These positions have also been discussed in the literature.

Yair Listokin argues that adapting laws and regulations to the changing times and to new information can actually contribute to finding optimal policy solutions. Relying on Edmund Burke, Listokin claims that new policies should only be partially implemented, submitted to evaluations, changed if necessary or terminated.[221] Listokin argues that sunset clauses can be used to promote a continuous process of learning and ensure policy reversibility. The scholar explains that, by experimenting, policy-makers can learn from their own legislative acts and change these laws accordingly.[222] It is easier to draw lessons if policies are reversible. This reversibility can be created by introducing sunset clauses in legislative acts.[223] Although all policies have a certain degree of irreversibility as to their impact in society and economy; the introduction of this temporary disposition would ensure that the relevant policy would indeed terminate and be imperatively reassessed (see Chapter 2). The employment of a sunset clause also forces legislators and regulators to reassess the need of existing regulations and update them.

Terminating regulations by employing sunset clauses can be useful to ensure that rules keep up with the changes in technology and society. However, when there is little information as to the subject to be regulated or the outcomes of regulation are uncertain, experimenting with new

---

Joseph R. Herket (eds), *The Growing Gap Between Emerging Technologies and Legal Ethical Oversight: The Pacing Problem* (Springer, 2011) 167.

[221] Listokin, 'Learning through Policy Variation', n. 113 above, 485–6.

[222] *Ibid.* 485.

[223] *Ibid.* 485–6.

regulations may be a wiser response to the features of innovation. This should be accepted in principle by innovators, since according to the research carried out by Dyer, Gregersen and Christensen, 'the capacity to experiment' is one of the 'DNA elements' of innovation.[224] Experimentation is considered to be essential for businessmen to put into practice new processes and products conceived: the world is regarded as their laboratory. Therefore, it should not be surprising that innovation reflects this tendency towards experimentation. The European Commission advanced a similar idea in the context of the Innovation Union Flagship.[225] It results from this Communication that the use of experimentation can favour the establishment of a more innovation-friendly regulatory framework.

By experimenting and adapting regulations according to the results obtained, legislators and regulators can effectively respond to the demands and characteristics of innovation. Experimental regulations are compatible with the *uncertainty* inherent to innovation, responding to this challenge because they are temporary rules that can be tested in a part of the territory before they are extended to the whole country. Experimental laws and regulations can thus be enacted when little is known about the novelty to be regulated or the outcomes of its regulation are uncertain. Experimental legislation emerges here as a compromise between not legislating or delaying the legislative or regulatory process due to the lack of information, and 'legislating in the dark'.

A number of temporary legislative initiatives in innovative fields have attempted to remove barriers to technological development in the private sector and provide funding or economic incentives to stimulate innovative activities.[226] This is the case of the US Economic Recovery Tax of 1981.[227] The majority of these Acts were to sunset within a period of time established beforehand but, due to the popularity of the programmes created, most of them were renewed at least once. These attempts were particularly visible in the field of cooperative R&D, where numerous

---

[224] See Jeffrey Dyers, Hal Gregersen and Clayton Christensen, 'Het DNA'van innovatievermogen' (2010) 131 *Holland/Belgium Management Review* 23.

[225] Communication from the Commission to the European Parliament, the Council, the European Economic and Social Committee and the Committee of the Regions, Europe 2020 Flagship Initiative Innovation Union, COM(2010)546, 21.

[226] Schacht, *Cooperative R&D: Federal Efforts to Promote Industrial Competitiveness*, n. 216 above, 5.

[227] Economic Recovery Act of 1981, P.L. 97-34, see title II, amended by the Tax Reform Act of 1986.

laws were enacted in order to advance cooperation between industry and university and between industry and the federal R&D enterprise.

In the regulation/deregulation or re-regulation of innovative sectors, sunset clauses and, particularly, experimental legislation could be assuming an increasingly important role in the Netherlands. This appears to be the case in the use of an experimental provision included in article 18(1) of the 1998 Dutch Telecommunications Act.[228] In this article, the possibility to 'experiment and anticipate new developments' by derogating from existing standards was regarded by the literature as an adequate mechanism to allow (and assess) the introduction of innovative solutions on a small scale.[229] The idea was then to verify whether certain developments could promote the achievement of the statute's objectives. This was equally one of the objectives of the German experimental legislation on telecommunications and media (Kabelpilotprojekt- und andere Medienerprobungsgesetze). These legislative initiatives were designed to ensure the privatization of the sector and the development of a unified telecommunications policy.[230]

2.5 VALUE OF SUNSET CLAUSES AND EXPERIMENTAL LEGISLATION

Considering the multiplicity of functions that sunset clauses and experimental legislation can perform, these legislative instruments deserve the preference of legislators in various situations. The decision on whether to choose a lasting law or a temporary legislative instrument requires consideration of different elements and posing a number of questions.

2.5.1 Nature of the Problem or Sector

According to Daniel Farber, the nature of the underlying problem or the characteristics of the sector at stake determine to a great extent the choice of a permanent or a temporary legislative or regulatory instrument. If the circumstances and available information change slowly and sufficient information is available, then a permanent law or regulation will be more

---

[228] Telecommunicatiewet of 19 October 1998, Stb. 1998, 610.

[229] Ph. Eijlander, M. Lokin and W. Voermans, 'Delegatie van regelgevende bevoegdheid: de Aanwijzingen voorbij' (2001) 2 *RegelMaat* 69.

[230] Horn, *Experimentelle Gesetzgebung unter dem Grundgesetz*, n. 57 above, 68–9.

appropriate (for example, laws on land tenure).[231] However, a dynamic approach to legislation might be required to ensure constant adaption to social needs and technological innovation. This occurs, for example, in technologically innovative sectors such as telecommunications, or socially innovative fields like poverty reduction or integration of minorities. Under a scenario of limited and rapidly changing information, sunset clauses and particularly experimental legislation have been argued to be the most effective instruments.[232]

In Germany, the literature has also acknowledged that in rapidly changing sectors, including telecommunications, the uncertainty as to the effects of regulations justify the need to adopt experimental laws or regulations and grant regulators the competence to deviate temporarily from existing laws in order to experiment with regulatory solutions that advance innovation.[233] Rupert Stettner argues that in complex fields, where forecasting the effects of new regulations may seem particularly intricate, experimental laws and regulations would be valuable tools. These would help legislators 'define our future in a more rational and organized [way]'.[234] The scholar adds that this rationalization of the lawmaking process based on 'trial and error' and 'conjectures and refutations' pertain to the central task of the legislator.[235] This position is supported in the jurisprudence of the German Constitutional Court which acknowledges that legislators should be allowed to 'build legislation by incorporating gathered information and experience'.[236]

The argument that sunset clauses and experimental legislation should be employed in fast changing fields characterized by lack of information, risk and uncertainty has also been defended in the Netherlands. Here, Van Gestel and Eijlander argue that, under uncertain circumstances, the use of sunset clauses would not only be appropriate but would also contribute to the reduction of uncertainty, particularly when the latter derives from

---

[231] Daniel A. Farber, 'Environmental Protection as a Learning Experience' (1993) 27 *Loyola of Los Angeles Law Review* 791, 798.

[232] *Ibid.* 798.

[233] Holznagel, 'Innovationsanreize durch Regulierungsfreistellung vom Umgang mit neuen Diensten und Märkten im Medien und TK-Recht', n. 96 above.

[234] Stettner, 'Verfassungsbindungen des experimentierenden Gesetzgebers', n. 61 above, 812.

[235] *Ibid.* 812.

[236] Decision of the German Constitutional Court, 1 BvR 213/58, 27 January 1965, BVerfGE 18, 315.

risks such as potential harms to the environment or food safety.[237] The scholars refer to the use of sunset clauses on an experimental basis to limit the risks of the introduction of new regulations. They consider that, by 'precautionary' experiment with the regulation of new products, it would be possible to gather more information and evidence, and verify whether this regulation is effective.[238] This would enable legislators to protect the general public from regulatory risks, without depriving them of the benefits of potentially innovative products. It must be underlined that the use of sunset clauses or experimental legislation does not replace sufficient laboratory testing.

2.5.2 Legislative Goals

Besides the concrete circumstances and the characteristics of the sector, the goals to be attained with a legal disposition may also determine whether sunset clauses or experimental legislation (instead of permanent legislation) are the most suitable instruments in the situation at stake. To wit, if legislators intend to 'advance legal flexibility under rapidly changing market conditions', an experimental regulation will probably be the most appropriate instrument since it provides the possibility to observe the reactions of the market, learn from them and ensure that regulations keep up with the changing circumstances.

According to the Bertelsmann Stiftung, the employment of general sunset clauses is not advisable for a number of policy goals. Instead, sunset clauses should only be introduced here if they match the goals to be pursued. Their position is exemplified with the policy goal '(enhancement of) parliamentary supervision of government' which can be concretized by incorporating a sunset clause 'in any kind of delegated (subordinate) legislation'.[239] While it is true that sunset clauses enhance legislative oversight, this objective can also be achieved with an evaluation or review clause. In the context of sunset clauses, the central consideration refers to the fact that the goal to be pursued in a specific case can only adequately be achieved if a temporary character is conferred to the respective law or provision.

If the goal of a law or regulation is to deliver a rapid legislative response to an innovative problem or situation, then a sunset clause may

---

[237] Eijlander and van Gestel, *Horizonwetgeving: effectief middel in de strijd tegen toenemende regeldruk?*, n. 75 above, 23.

[238] *Ibid.* 23.

[239] Bertelsmann Stiftung, *Sunset Legislation and Better Regulation*, n. 31 above, 21.

be more adequate than a permanent law. In these cases, it is not required that the situation in question qualifies as an emergency, it can simply be a problem that puts the legislator under a great deal of pressure. This was the case of the Dutch Crisis- en herstelwet that aimed to accelerate the administrative decision-making procedure in respect of complex projects and was itself an example of a temporary and complex law enacted in less than seven months.[240] This law is a hybrid example of a temporary law with an apparent experimental character, which could be regarded as an alternative to an 'all-or-nothing' approach, avoiding a potential conflict between an acceleration of the legislative process and a precautionary approach to lawmaking.[241]

2.5.3 Forbidden Ground for Temporary Legislation?

There are also restrictions or precautions to be taken into consideration to avoid an excessive and inadequate enactment of sunset clauses and experimental legislation.[242] These legal restrictions are the topic of the second part of this book. Besides the need to observe higher law, including international and EU law (in the case of Germany and the Netherlands) and fundamental legal principles, it can be questioned whether some matters should simply be excluded from the scope of temporary legislation. This is the case of core legal institutions and concepts which, due to their relevance for the functioning of any state and society, should have a lasting character. This restriction on the enactment of temporary rules in these cases is supported by the case law of the German Constitutional Court on the requirements of transitory law. This Court affirmed that 'laws that are indispensable for the legal capacity and [normal] functioning of a state'[243] and the laws that are required for the concretization of fundamental rights guarantees (for example, media and broadcasting laws) are not compatible with a temporary or transitory nature. To avoid an unreasonable extension of the mentioned limitation, the expression 'indispensable for the legal capacity and normal functioning of a state' should be narrowly interpreted so as *only* to include the material core concepts of a legal order (for example,

---

240 See N. Verhey, 'The Fast and the Furious: de Crisis- en herstelwet' (2012) 27 *RegelMaat* 140.

241 J.F.L. Roording, 'Versnelling van wetgeving: over uiteenlopende ontwikkelingen en eigenwijze actoren' (2012) 27 *Regelmaat* 126–7.

242 V. Bouffier, 'Normprüfung: Modifizierung des hessischen Befristungskonzepts'(2012) *Zeitschrift für Rechtspolitik* 55.

243 See 1 BvR 79/70, 9 November 1976.

right granting access to justice) and *not* their procedural implementation (for example, experiment with new mechanisms to accelerate proceedings). Legislators should not be precluded from enacting a sunset clause or an experimental regulation in the mentioned legal context, but should only be allowed to enact it at a procedural level and as long as the underlying fundamental right or 'core institution' is not endangered. However, a casuistic analysis of the situation at stake should assist the legislator in deciding whether an instrument with legislative character is required.

2.6 CONCLUSION

Sunset clauses and experimental legislation are instruments with many faces and functions. Their historical background reveals that both instruments emerged to respond to a certain discontentment with the state of legislation and regulation. In the beginning, sunset clauses were primarily enacted to ensure that laws did not lag behind the evolution of society and to guarantee a renewed legislative oversight on regulations that increase the level of bureaucracy. Experimental legislation was traditionally used to assist the accommodation of diversity and try out novelties in the legal order. Nowadays, they still perform these functions and have been used for many more. As explained in this chapter, these instruments can be valuable tools to tackle uncertainty and risks; rationalize the lawmaking process; improve the quality of legislation and effectiveness and efficiency of public administration; obtain political consensus; and last but not least, facilitate the regulation of innovation.

Sunset clauses and experimental legislation may often perform similar functions; however, they should not be confused with each other since they represent two different legislative approaches. Contrary to sunset clauses, experimental legislation aims to prepare the legal order for the enactment of lasting and universally valid laws.[244]

In conclusion, it is precisely in the most complex, rapidly changing and uncertain fields that legislators may opt for temporary instruments: sunset clauses when termination of the underlying problem might be in sight; experimental laws or regulations when complex and new situations should be regulated and sufficient information is lacking but can be generated via an experiment. Caution should be exercised in the case of

---

[244] Bertelsmann Stiftung, 'Gutachten: Wirksamkeit von Sunset Legislation und Evaluationsklauseln', n. 79 above, 6.

'laws that are indispensable for the legal capacity and [normal] functioning of a state' and that are required for the concretization of fundamental rights guarantees: in such cases, the material core of these legal institutions and concepts may not always be compatible with temporary dispositions. The procedural concretization of the mentioned legal aspects might be open to experimental provisions as long as these contribute to the further concretization of the core legal principles and concepts and do not affect the essence of the those concepts. Thus, experimenting with different forms of training and educational programmes may be allowed as long as, for example, the right to free and compulsory primary education is guaranteed to all citizens. This issue may be particularly controversial in the case of electronic voting, where the procedural concretization of the right to vote may directly affect its essence. These legal concerns will be considered in the second part of this book, devoted to the constitutional limits of sunset clauses and experimental legislation.

3. Separation of powers, delegation and a legality framework

> It is one thing to be subordinate to the laws, and another [for the Executive] to be dependent on the legislative body. The first comports with, the last violates, the fundamental principles of good government; and, whatever may be the forms of the Constitution, unites all power in the same hands.
>
> Alexander Hamilton, Federalist No. 71, Federalist Papers (1788)

3.1 A DIFFERENTIATED APPROACH

The fundamental principles of law have often been described in the German literature as limits to the enactment of temporary legislation.[1] Is this also the case of the principle of separation of powers?

If we read the United States Constitution, we will not find a 'principle of separation of powers clause': it is one of its many unwritten principles that supplement and transcend the meaning of individual constitutional clauses.[2] As Jack Balkin explains 'it is a principle we derive … from how the various institutions and structures outlined in the constitutional text relate to each other'.[3] It is also a principle to be inferred from history and context that 'helps preserve political stability and keep the enterprise of governance going when people disagree strongly about what is just or unjust'.

The principle of separation of powers is not necessarily a constraint on both sunset clauses and experimental legislation. Instead, in the United States and in Germany, it has been argued that sunset clauses could be enacted to control the excessive powers of the executive. They are an

[1] See for example, Antonis Chanos, *Möglichkeiten und Grenzen der Befristung parlamentarischer Gesetzgebung* (Duncker and Humblot, 1999).

[2] Akhil Reed Amar, *America's Unwritten Constitution: The Precedents and Principles We Live By* (Basic Books, 2012) 6.

[3] Jack M. Balkin, *Living Originalism* (Harvard University Press, 2011) 14.

instrument of legislative oversight.[4] This explains why this principle is analyzed in Part I of this book and serves as a ground to plant a legal framework for sunset clauses and experimental legislation.

Before presenting a legal framework for experimental legislation and sunset clauses, this chapter is introduced by an analysis of the principle of separation of powers and principle of legality. As far as experimental legislation is concerned, it will first be examined how the principle of separation of powers constrains the enactment of this instrument (3.3). Since experimental legislation requires clear legality boundaries, a legality framework for the enactment of this instrument will be provided (3.4). None of the three countries under analysis possesses one. However, imposing a statutory basis for the delegation of the power to enact experimental provisions is not sufficient to fulfil legality requirements. Such statutory basis must contain specific elements (3.4). This chapter offers a differentiated approach to legality in the sense that it first sketches the theoretical relationship between the principle of separation of powers and experimental legislation (3.3) and then attempts to solve potential intricacies by suggesting a concrete and complete framework, which is built on different doctrines of delegation (3.5) and illustrated by examples (3.6).

3.2 SUNSET CLAUSES AND SEPARATION OF POWERS

In the United States, the principle of separation of powers has been referred to in the light of the concepts of modern government and the role of administrative agencies (the so-called 'fourth branch' of government),[5] and less in the context of the traditional Montesquieuian separation of powers. While the principle of separation of powers or the guarantee of 'checks and balances' should be present in any *Rechtsstaat*, 'the line of division is nevertheless somewhat indefinite, since in many cases the legislature may designate the agents for the execution of its enactments'.[6] In the case of federal and state agencies – key actors in the enactment of

---

4 See also Katherine R. Williamson (ed.), *Revisiting and Evaluating the Congressional Review Act* (Nova Science Publishers, Inc., 2009).

5 H.H. Bruff, 'Separation of Powers under the Texas Constitution' (1990) 68(7) *Texas Law Review*. 1337.

6 Thomas M. Cooley and Andrew C. McLaughlin, *The General Principles of Constitutional Law in the United States of America* (Little, Brown and Company, 1898) 45.

sunset clauses and experimental regulations in the United States – the three classical powers overlap.[7] However, this overlap has not always been peacefully accepted, explaining the need for new oversight instruments.

In the 1980s, state agencies had become so numerous and powerful that the widespread idea that 'elected officials [had] lost control over bureaucrats who really [ran] things' enhanced the citizens' distrust in these agencies.[8] In the United States, sunset clauses emerged as a tool to balance the uncontrolled growth of administrative agencies. This legislative instrument was designed to strengthen legislative oversight on these agencies and ensure that those that had become superfluous due to the accomplishment of their regulatory missions would be extinguished.[9] As explained in Chapter 2, sunset clauses in Germany and in the Netherlands have not primarily been enacted to review agencies, but, in some cases, they have been introduced to tackle the process of excessive bureaucracy, regulatory pressure, and to guarantee frequent legislative oversight.[10] In the United States, sunset clauses were (and still are, though in a more limited way) parliamentary instruments of control of executive activities, more specifically, of administrative agencies.[11]

In conclusion, sunset clauses have been used as instruments to advance the separation of powers, by guaranteeing a periodic legislative oversight of agencies and regulations, and ensuring that the executive does not exceed its powers.

3.3 SEPARATION OF POWERS AND EXPERIMENTAL LEGISLATION

The study of the principle of separation of powers in the setting of experimental legislation has been particularly visible in the German literature. In this country, the traditional separation of powers directed at avoiding despotism and 'power monopoly' has been replaced by the

---

[7] Bruff, 'Separation of Powers under the Texas Constitution', n. 5 above, 1345.

[8] Dan R. Price, 'Sunset Legislation in the United States' (1978) 30(3) *Baylor Law Review* 406.

[9] Richard C. Kearney, 'Sunset: A Survey and Analysis of the State Experience' (1990) *Public Administration Review* (January/February) 55.

[10] Jan Funke, *Bürokratieabbau mit Hilfe zeitlich befristeter Gesetze: zu den Erfolgsbedingungen der Sunset-Gesetzgebung* (AVM, 2011) 43.

[11] *Ibid.* 43.

functional approach to this principle developed by the German Constitutional Court.[12] According to Lindner, experimental regulations diverge from the traditional distribution of competences between the legislator and executive (*'parlamentarische Grundsatzentscheidung/executive Konkretisierung'*) since experimental regulations imply a division of the controlling and administrative competence (*Steuerungskompetenz*) between the legislator and the executive.[13] Lindner argues that in the case of experimental regulations, much more than the further elaboration of details and execution is delegated. In fact, the executive can enact and implement on an experimental basis a legal regime which differs from the existing one.[14] However, as this scholar explains, legislators must always remain the 'master' of this controlling process since they should grant the authorizations for the implementation of experiments, define their duration and scope, and decide on their extinction.[15]

Brüning disagrees with Lindner, arguing that experimental dispositions do not grant the executive a true 'legislative task' but only the decision to apply (or not) national legal standards previously adopted.[16] This is not, however, entirely true because although in Germany many experimental clauses provide for the experimental disapplication of hierarchically higher rules (see Chapter 2), other clauses are true experiments which introduce new rules in the legal order. However, the question whether there is a divergence from the principle of separation of powers implies determining if the experiment refers to essential or adjacent elements of the law (*'Kern- oder Randbereich'*) (see 3.4 and 3.5). Brüning adds that no breach of the principle of separation of powers will occur because any experimental regulation must be based on a formal law.[17] Although this is true, much more must be said on the legality requirements to be fulfilled by any experimental regulation: only a clear legality framework where the legislator remains 'the master of the experiment' can ensure that the principle of separation of powers is not endangered.

---

[12] A. Groth, *Kommunalrechtliche Experimentierklauseln* (Lorenz-Von-Stein-Institut für Verwaltungswissenschaftem an der Christian-Albrechts-Universität zu Kiel, 2005) 170.

[13] J.F. Lindner, 'Experimentelle Rechtssetzung durch Rechtsverordnung – Am Beispiel des Hochschulrechts' (2007) *Die öffentliche Verwaltung* 1004.

[14] *Ibid.* 1006.

[15] *Ibid.* 1006.

[16] C. Brüning, 'Die kommunalrechtlichen Experimentierklauseln' (1997) *Die öffentliche Verwaltung* 278, 286.

[17] *Ibid.* 287.

A clear legal framework guiding the legislator at the legality level is lacking in the three jurisdictions under analysis. Since experimental legislation implies derogation from existing law and extensive delegation powers, this legislative instrument raises more normative concerns than sunset clauses. This justifies the need to devote more attention to this legislative instrument than to the latter. The design of a clear legality framework can avoid experimental regulations eroding the limits of legislative delegation and exceeding the original parliamentary objectives. These legality concerns date back to the New Deal legislation and have even been admitted by vehement supporters of experimental regulations. The imperative to respect constitutional limitations and legislative primacy even in spite of 'the nation's need' to limit private property – or in the case of this study, to stimulate innovation – was expressed by Brandeis in *Louisville Joint Stock Land Bank* v. *Radford*.[18] In the absence of a framework for experimental legislation, the risk of arbitrariness might lurk around the corner and it is questionable whether excessively broad delegations to experiment would be in observance with the principle of legality. This is one of the issues to be addressed in the context of a framework for the enactment of experimental laws. Moreover, the definition of explicit goals and a transparent framework can make it more difficult for politicians to usurp or relegate the results of evaluation reports of sunset clauses or experimental regulations without a solid motivation for such decisions. This framework could enhance the transparency and accountability of the decision-making procedure as far as experimental regulations are concerned.

3.4 A LEGALITY FRAMEWORK FOR EXPERIMENTAL LEGISLATION

3.4.1 Principle of Legality

The principle of legality is a corollary of the principle of separation of powers. It constitutes a safeguard against arbitrary government action but, at the same time, it should not frustrate the actions expected from the modern public administration:[19] it is not up to the legislator to fulfil a 'research function' experimenting with the best approaches to new

---

[18] *Louisville Joint Stock Land Bank* v. *Radford*, 295 U.S. 555 (1935).

[19] W. Voermans, 'Legaliteit als middel tot een doel' in NJV, *Handelingen der Nederlandsche Juristen-Vereeniging, Controverses rondom legaliteit en legitimatie* (Kluwer, 2011) vol. 141(1), 3.

problems. Such a time- and resource-consuming task does not match the legislator's role. However, at the same time, citizens should be protected from far-reaching interventions in fundamental rights which, on an experimental basis, can substantially modify or withdraw benefits or impose upon them additional burdens. The main concern here is that experimental regulations do not become an unwarranted delegation mechanism for areas reserved to the legislator which can be used to severely restrict fundamental rights. To avoid such a scenario, the legislator should remain the master of experiments with laws.

It is important to underline that 'to fulfill its promise, democratic government must be democratic as well as effective'.[20] Therefore, legislative delegation (not only for the purposes of experimental regulations) is one of the basic foundations of public administration: in Germany, the United States, the Netherlands, and even in the European Union, it is inconceivable, undesirable, inefficient and physically impossible to leave all regulatory tasks to Parliament.[21] Since the 1980s there has been a tendency towards the enhancement of this mechanism of transferring legislative and administrative competences in order to 'revitalize' the public administration and respond to the exigencies of the modern state.[22] Delegation promotes, amongst others, legislative flexibility and efficiency since regulations can be rapidly enacted and modified; and advances decentralization by authorizing actors who are closer to the problems to be regulated, and more informed about them, to undertake the regulation.[23] This explains why the 'modern nation-state could not exist without delegation'.[24]

Notwithstanding the broad acceptance and employment of delegation, this instrument can distort to a certain extent the original meaning of the principle of legality.[25] This is not a surprising finding or original claim

---

[20] W.C. Müller, T. Bergman and K. Strøm, 'Parliamentary Democracy: Promise and Problems' in W.C. Müller, T. Bergman and K. Strøm (eds), *Delegation and Accountability in Parliamentary Democracies* (Oxford University Press, 2003) 3.

[21] A.H.M. Dölle, *Mandaat en delegatie* (W.E.J. Tjeenk Willink 2000) 1.

[22] Hermann Punder, 'Democratic Legitimation of Delegated Legislation: A Comparative View on the American, British and German Law' (2009) 58 (2) *International and Comparative Law Quarterly* 353–4.

[23] W. Voermans, *Toedeling van bevoegdheid* (Boom Juridische Uitgevers, 2004) 39.

[24] A. Lupia, 'Delegation and its Perils' in W.C. Müller, T. Bergman and K. Strøm (eds), *Delegation and Accountability in Parliamentary Democracies* (Oxford University Press, 2003) 32.

[25] Voermans, *Toedeling van bevoegdheid*, n. 23 above, 39.

but it translates a general observation: 'by transferring rulemaking competences to the executive, namely to the government, ministries and even administrative agencies, the direct participation of the parliament in the establishment of rules [can be] endangered'.[26]

The expansion of delegation and of 'the regulatory state', not only in the different legal systems but also at the EU level, has raised many questions as to the need to secure democratic legitimacy. According to Majone, this legitimacy will be at stake when important policy-making powers are delegated to non-majoritarian institutions, notably agencies.[27] This scholar suggests enhanced accountability structures as the solution to this problem. Legislative delegation implies in fact that the administrative organ exercising the delegated legislative competence will do so on its own behalf and responsibility. It has been underlined in the Dutch literature that it is exactly this responsibility or, more precisely, accountability that partially compensates for the 'loss' in democratic legitimacy.[28]

A clear intervention of Parliament in the delimitation of an experimental provision would aim to respond to the mentioned challenges. In addition, an active intervention of the legislator at this level enhances the democratic legitimacy of the experiment, which can potentially attenuate the intellectual reluctance towards experimental laws and regulations and improve their acceptance.

To resolve the above-mentioned legality intricacies, the legality framework for experimental legislation suggested below (3.4.2) will be inspired by the German theory of essentiality (*Wesentlichkeitstheorie*) and interpreted in the sense that the 'essential elements' of an experimental legislative instrument should be predetermined by Parliament. This legality framework aims to provide the answer to, or guidance on, diverse enigmas: does experimental legislation endanger the reservation of parliamentary law (*Parlamentsvorbehalt*) and can the respective prohibition to delegate (*Delegationsverbot)* be circumvented with an experiment? If the legislator is entitled to delegate, how far can the legislator go in delegating the competence to experiment? These questions are relevant in the Netherlands, Germany and in the United States

---

26 *Ibid.* 39.

27 Giandomenico Majone, 'The Regulatory State and its Legitimacy Problems' (1999) 22 *West European Politics* 1; see also Giandomenico Majone, 'The Rise of the Regulatory State' (1994) 17 *West European Politics* 77; Giandomenico Majone, 'Regulatory Legitimacy' in G.D. Majone (ed.), *Regulating Europe* (Routledge, 1996) 284.

28 Voermans, 'Legaliteit als middel tot een doel', n. 19 above, 1, 43.

and are inevitable dilemmas in 'a modern constitutionalism whose theoretical justifications presuppose regarding government as a concatenation of confined lines of attribution, and whose practices reside in a systematic probing of the title, purpose, scope, and outer legal limits of each exercise of power'.[29] Section 3.5 elaborates on the theories of delegation behind this framework and the definition of 'essential elements', while section 3.6 provides an explanation and illustration of these elements.

3.4.2 Legality Framework

Experimental regulations can in principle be enacted in a number of fields but their enactment must be bound by the principle of legality and grounded on a clear legal basis. Depending on the subject matter, the constitutional requirements in a given legal system, the nature of the underlying problem or situation at stake or desired experimental intervention, the experimental legislative instrument might require that 'the essential decisions' are taken by Parliament. This is important for the safeguarding of the principle of legality, particularly for jurisdictions that do not possess a Constitutional Court (such as the Netherlands) which can control *ex post* the constitutionality of these essential decisions or their omission.

The US Supreme Court and the German Constitutional Court (see German Constitution, article 93) are entitled to review statutes for consistency with the Constitution, principles of law and other statutes, and in the German case, with EU law as well. The power to proceed to judicial review is not explicitly mentioned in the US Constitution but it results clearly from the scope, text and history of the Constitution. An important document in this context is Federalist Paper No. 78 by Hamilton where the courts are described as 'the intermediate body between the legislator and the people' whose duty 'must be to declare all acts contrary to the manifest tenor of the Constitution void … [because] no legislative act … contrary to the Constitution can be valid'.[30]

In the Netherlands, there is no court comparable to the German Constitutional Court nor does the Supreme Court (Hoge Raad) have the competence to review acts of Parliament in the light of the Constitution

[29] B. Iancu, *Legislative Delegation: The Erosion of Normative Limits in Modern Constitutionalism* (Springer, 2012) 1.

[30] Alexander Hamilton (Publius), Federalist Paper No. 78, *Independent Journal*, 14 June 1788, available at http://avalon.law.yale.edu/subject_menus/fed.asp.

or unwritten principles (Dutch Constitution, article 120). A superficial analysis of article 120 of the Dutch Constitution, which forbids such judicial review,[31] would bring us to the immediate conclusion that there is no *ex post* control of sunset clauses or experimental laws in breach of the Constitution or unwritten principles of law.[32] This is not, however, entirely true. First, since the case of *Pothuis* in 1864, it has been acknowledged that ordinary courts can control the constitutionality and legality of regulations.[33] Secondly, in the light of article 94 of the Dutch Constitution, statutes (or acts of Parliament) which are enacted in breach of international treaties will not be applied (but they cannot be declared unconstitutional).[34] Thirdly, regulations can be subject to judicial review and most experimental acts are in fact regulations (secondary legislation), which means that they can be judicially reviewed in all the three countries under analysis. This judicial review refers not only to the appreciation of the consistency of regulations with the Constitution, EU law and international treaties (Dutch Constitution, article 94), but also, since the 1986 HR *Landbouwvliegers* case, the conformity with unwritten principles of law.[35]

A legality framework for the enactment of experimental legislation requires the following:

(1) Depending on the subject matter, the constitutional requirements in a given legal system, the nature of the underlying problem or situation at stake or desired experimental intervention, the experimental legislative instrument might require that 'the essential decisions' are made by Parliament.
(2) 'Essential decisions' will be in question when:

---

[31] In the Netherlands, there is a long-standing belief that laws (statutes) are absolute and inviolable. This was expressed in the expression '*de wetten zijn onschendbaar*' which was included in the original version of art. 131 of the Dutch Constitution of 1848. In art. 120 of the current Dutch Constitution (version as of 2013) it is stated that 'the constitutionality of Acts of Parliament and treaties shall not be reviewed by the court' ('De rechter treedt niet in de beoordeling van de grondwettigheid van wetten en verdragen').

[32] See HR, 14 April 1989, NJ 1989, 469 (*Harmonisatiewetarrest*).

[33] Hoge Raad, 6 March 1864, W2646 (*Pothuis).*

[34] Dutch Constitution, art. 94 reads: 'Binnen het Koninkrijk geldende wettelijke voorschriften vinden geen toepassing, indien deze toepassing niet verenigbaar is met een ieder verbindende bepalingen van verdragen en van besluiten van volkenrechtelijke organisaties'.

[35] HR, 16 May 1986, NJ 1987, 251 (*Landbouwvliegers*).

(i) an experimental regulation or provision is susceptible of affecting to a considerable extent the concretization of fundamental rights;
(ii) the experiment may hinder the materialization of a fundamental constitutional principle;
(iii) the experiment interferes with the granting of substantial benefits or implies the imposition of considerable burdens on citizens;
(iv) the Constitution explicitly reserves the subject to the legislator;
(v) in the case of EU Member States, the implementation of EU law may be put at stake.

On essential elements reserved to Parliament, no delegation is allowed. These essential decisions can be concretized in a myriad of elements that should be exclusively and explicitly determined by the legislator in the statutory basis delegating the competence to experiment:

(a) *the goal(s) of the experiment*: the legislator should formulate as unambiguously as possible its intent and the need for the experiment. The definition of goals does not exclude the possibility to employ indeterminate concepts, particularly when the experimental regulation aims to assist the legislator in gathering more information regarding a new approach to a new problem. However, guidance as to the interpretation of these indeterminate concepts should be provided in order to avoid granting excessive discretion to administrative organs;
(b) *the 'direction' and 'extent' of the experiment*: the term 'direction' refers to the type of delegation to be executed. This means the legislator should be explicit about whether authorization is given to *derogate* from existing laws enacting parallel experimental rules applicable to a part of the population or rather exempt or *waive* a number of rules or standards for a determined period. In addition, the 'extent' of the experiment should be defined, notably by including an explicit list of the articles or sections of a law that the experimental regulation can waive or derogate from;
(c) *the duration of the experiment*;
(d) *the evaluation criteria and deadline to submit the public evaluation report of the experiment to Parliament*: if possible and adequate to the situation in question, the institution performing this evaluation and the auxiliary expert commissions assisting the evaluation

should also be mentioned. Ethical commissions[36] can be of great assistance when socially and ethically controversial regulations are at stake;[37]

(e) *a reasonable deadline for the institution implementing the experiment to decide on the evaluation report*: the establishment of internal sanctions in case of the violation of this deadline or the obligation to decide could ensure that this framework is respected. This possibility depends, however, on national rules regarding delegation, notably the possibility of parliamentary or judicial scrutiny of legislation. In some cases, statutory dispositions are derogated from by experimental secondary legislation because the legislator wishes to verify whether these new dispositions would be more effective than existing law. Should this be the case, it is up to Parliament to consider the results of this experiment and decide whether the statute should be amended according to the information obtained.

3.5 LEGALITY FRAMEWORK AND THEORIES OF DELEGATION

Although the theory of essentiality constitutes the main source of inspiration for the legality framework presented above, the American non-delegation theory and the Dutch literature on delegation have also played an important role in the design of the above-suggested legality conditions. These three doctrines are here extensively described and analyzed in an attempt to identify the 'essential elements' of any experimental legislative act that may be common to these three jurisdictions.

3.5.1 Theory of Essentiality (*Wesentlichkeitstheorie*)

In the German literature, the areas reserved to Parliament (*Vorbehalt des Gesetzes*), the traditional intervention in 'freedom and property' (*Eingriffe in Freiheit und Eigentum*), do not encompass the possibility to delegate the competence to experiment with essential decisions. This

---

36 W. Hoffmann-Riem, 'Les lois expérimentales en Allemagne' in C. Morand (ed.), *Évaluation législative et lois expérimentales* (Presses Universitaires d'Aix-Marseille, 1992).

37 See Chapter 2 for examples on the temporary law on experiments with embryos and stem cells.

traditional concept has been expanded in the last decades and reinterpreted by the German Constitutional Court as the imperative that 'the essential decisions for the concretization of fundamental rights' should be made by the legislator (*Gesetzgeber*).[38] It is on these grounds that the first part of the suggested legality framework will be explained:

(1) Depending on the subject matter, the constitutional requirements in a given legal system, the nature of the underlying problem or situation at stake or desired experimental intervention, the experimental legislative instrument might require that 'the essential decisions' are taken by Parliament.

This part of the legality framework raises the following questions: what type of underlying problems or situations should be considered here? What are the essential elements that should be reserved to the formal legislator and, therefore, excluded from legislative delegation?

The answer to the first question is inspired by the doctrine of the parliamentary reservation (*Gesetzesvorbehalt*) and the criteria of the 'theory of essentiality' (*Wesentlichtkeitstheorie*). This section develops their concretization so as to distinguish between the elements that should be determined by the formal legislator and those that can be delegated. The parliamentary reservation and the theory of essentiality derive from the *Rechtsstaatsprinzip* and the *Demokratiegebot*, which require that no delegation of decisions on essential aspects of the concretization of fundamental rights – not even on an experimental basis – should occur. This is, however, far from being a rigid rule of thumb, instead further clarification and illustrations are required.

In the light of the *Wesentlichkeitstheorie*, the greater the relevance for or the interference of a regulation with fundamental rights (*Grundrechtsrelevanz*), in other words, the interference with the fundamental rights in the sphere of stakeholders, the more necessary the intervention of the Parliament will be.[39] According to the German Federal Administrative Court, the enactment of legal provisions on 'the benefits granted to civil servants, judges and elderly beneficiaries' is reserved to the formal legislator.[40]

---

38 H. Schulze-Fielitz, *Theorie und Praxis parlamentarischer Gesetzgebung – besonders des 9. Deutschen Bundestages (1980–1983)* (Duncker and Humblot, 1988) 158–63.

39 *Ibid.* 164.

40 BVerwG ZBR 2005, 42. See C. Tegethoff, 'Verwaltungsvorschriften und Gesetzesvorbehalt' (2005) *Juristische Arbeitsblätter* 794.

In the case of experiments, it must be determined how relevant the experimental rules will be *in concreto* for citizens: the greater the relevance, the more accurate the legislative dispositions on the experiment should be. This theory is based on democratic concerns: democratically elected legislators should be the ones issuing the essential decisions that affect the citizens' fundamental rights because of their democratic legitimacy.[41] Therefore, the first criterion to determine whether an element is essential and points in the direction of the *Wesentlichkeitstheorie* is its 'fundamental rights' relevance (*Grundrechtsrelevanz*), in other words, its significance for the materialization of fundamental rights.[42]

The main concretizations of the so-called *Grundrechtsrelevanz* have been: (a) the 'intensity of the affected fundamental rights' which can be measured by the individual or collective long-term effects of the regulations enacted; and (b) the proximity of the possible interdependency of the law and the intervention in the fundamental rights, in other words, 'essential elements' will only be the immediate and direct intended effects of a rule.[43] An Act of Parliament will not be required when the relation between the experiment to be enacted and the intervention in fundamental rights is not immediate but rather the result of a chain of actions. This theory is of particular importance, for example, in the field of education where it is widely accepted that regulations with a direct and immediate interference with fundamental rights should be determined by the parliamentary legislator.[44]

A second criterion to determine 'what is essential' refers to decisions that are significant for other founding principles of the Constitution and their materialization. This is the case of the *Rechtsstaatsprinzip* and the principle of separation of powers, namely, the independence of the judiciary.[45]

---

[41] J. Staupe, *Parlamentsvorbehalt und Delegationsbefugnis: Zur 'Wesentlichkeitstheorie' und zur Reichweite legislativer Regelungskompetenz, insbesondere im Schulrecht* (Duncker and Humblot, 1985) 149–50.

[42] M. Dombert, 'Gesetzesvorbehalt und Breitbandkabel' (1986) *Neue Zeitschrift für Verwaltungsrecht* 277.

[43] Schulze-Fielitz, *Theorie und Praxis parlamentarischer Gesetzgebung – besonders des 9*, n. 38 above, 165–6.

[44] P. Becker, 'Der Parlamentsvorbehalt im Prüfungsrecht' (1990) *Neue Juristische Wochenschrift* 273.

[45] R. Brinktrine, 'Organisationsgewalt der Regierung und der Vorbehalt des Gesetzes – zur Reichweite der "Wesentlichkeitstheorie" am Beispiel der Zusammenlegung von Justiz- und Innenministerium in Nordrhein-Westfalen' (2000) 3 *Jura* 123, 126.

A third category of essential decisions in the organizational or administrative sector is connected with the elements that are fundamental for the performance or grant of state subsidies or benefits and that are not unilateral and exclusively reserved to the executive.[46]

In light of the mentioned criteria developed by the German Constitutional Court, it is possible to name clear examples of 'essential decisions' that should exclusively be taken by the Parliament: decisions on war and peace involving the concrete and verifiable expectation of the involvement of German soldiers in armed conflicts;[47] or decisions on the absolute requirements constraining the admission and choice criteria ('numerus clausus') at public universities.[48] In contrast, decisions concerning the execution of benefits, rather than their attribution, can be left to the executive.

According to the German Constitutional Court 'only the legislator has a prerogative of evaluation to assess the actual developments ... and react to the changed circumstances'.[49] The measure in which the legislator should 'determine the guidelines necessary for [the situation at stake] depends on its relation to fundamental rights'.[50] The constraint of fundamental rights cannot be derived from general duties, for example, under civil service law or of other public nature; instead, and as demonstrated in example 3.1, an explicit statutory basis should be provided.

EXAMPLE 3.1 PROHIBITION TO WEAR HEADSCARVES

In this case, a constitutional complaint was made against a decision of the Stuttgart Higher School Authority, considering that the petitioner could not be appointed as a civil servant as a teacher at German primary schools on the grounds of her

[46] *Ibid.* 126.

[47] 2 BvE 1/03 of 7 May 2008, 38, 57, 58, 92.

[48] 1 BvL 32/70 and 25/71 of 3 May 1972: the German Constitutional Court considered that a disposition of the Hamburg University Law was unconstitutional on the grounds that 'der Gesetzgeber seinerseits für den Fall absoluter Zulassungsbeschränkungen keine Bestimmungen über Art und Rangverhältnis der Auswahlkriterien getroffen hat' ['in this case the legislator had not adopted absolute limitations regarding the nature or ranking of the selection criteria'].

[49] BVerfG, 2BvR 1436/02 of 24 September 2003, 66.

[50] *Ibid.* 67.

declared intention to wear a headscarf. The German Constitutional Court affirmed that in this case 'the necessary and sufficiently determined statutory basis [did] not exist to decide that teachers of the Islamic faith [wearing headscarves] lack aptitude for service at the primary school and non-selective secondary school and thus to restrict their fundamental right under Article 4 of the Basic Law'. The German Constitutional Court affirmed that a restriction on the freedom of religion (German Basic Law, article 4(1) and (2)) – a fundamental right which is unconditionally guaranteed – required 'a sufficiently definite statutory basis'.[51] The Court explicitly recognized the possibility for the legislator to introduce the lacking statutory basis, namely, on the grounds of the 'social change' associated with 'the increasing religious plurality'. In this context, the Court declared that 'the provision that one of the duties of a teacher is to refrain in class from wearing a headscarf or any other indication of religious conviction is a material [essential] (*wesentlich*) provision in the [sense] of the case law on the requirement of parliamentary reservation'.[52]

The *Wesentlichkeitstheorie* is equally applicable to experimental restrictions on fundamental rights: any direct and substantial restriction of these rights, either on a permanent, temporary or experimental basis, should have a clear and definite statutory basis.

As to the definition of 'essential decisions', it is important to underline that the fact that there is a political controversy connected with an element does not convert it into 'an essential one'.[53] Nevertheless, whenever serious interventions in fundamental rights are at stake, the participation of Parliament, if possible associated with a form of demonstrated public opinion, should be required so as to obtain sufficient social support. In the cases where experimental legislative instruments are used to seek political consensus (more than in other areas), the legislator is thus advised to be clear and explicit as to the determination of the essential elements, instead of leaving them to the discretion of the

[51] See *ibid.* 38, 57–61, 66–70.

[52] *Ibid.* 70.

[53] See 1 BvR 1640/97 of 14 July 1998: in this case, the constitutionality of a regulation introducing new spelling rules in German schools was challenged. The German Constitutional Court considered that this task could be derived from the laws on education and did not lack a statutory basis.

executive.[54] Although the *Wesentlichkeitstheorie* guarantees that the formal legislator does not lose sight of the legislative process on essential matters, the expansion of this doctrine by state constitutional courts has been criticized for constraining the leeway of the executive of adopting innovative organizational forms.[55] This doctrine has equally been criticized for its lack of clarity, indeterminacy and unpredictability,[56] it even being affirmed that 'wesentlich ist, was das Bundesverfassungsgericht hält'.[57]

All in all, the reference to the *Wesentlichkeitstheorie* serves the purpose of enhancing the legitimacy of experimental laws and regulations. Parliament remains the institution that translates the people's sovereignty and, as such, constitutes the greatest source of legitimacy due to its central role in the representation of the people.[58]

3.5.2 Non-delegation Theory in the United States

The departure from the German perspective does not mean that the limits for legislative delegation have not been discussed in the United States or that these legality questions are not relevant.[59] The discussion in the US literature has also played a role in the design of the above-described framework. On the other side of the Atlantic, it has been equally visible that with an increasingly more diverse and changing society, Congress has been forced to delegate 'the duty of doings things which in the

---

[54] M. Dombert, 'Gesetzesvorbehalt und Breitbandkabel' (1986) *Neue Zeitschrift für Verwaltungsrecht* 277.

[55] Brinktrine, 'Organisationsgewalt der Regierung und der Vorbehalt des Gesetzes', n. 45 above, 131–2.

[56] Schulze-Fielitz, *Theorie und Praxis parlamentarischer Gesetzgebung – besonders des 9*, n. 38 above, 171.

[57] ['Some elements are essential just because the German Constitutional Court says so']. Ulrich Karpen, 'Gesetzgebungslehre und Rechtsprechungslehre' in W. Hoppe, W. Krawietz and M. Schulte (eds), *Rechtsprechungslehre, Zweites Internationales Symposium Münster 1988* (Heymanns, 1992) 29, 52. For an overview of the criticism to the *Wesentlichkeitstheorie*, see U.R. Haltern, F.C. Mayer and C.R. Möllers, 'Wesentlichkeitstheorie und Gerichtsbarkeit: Zur institutionellen Kritik des Gesetzesvorbehalts' (1997) 3 *Die Verwaltung* 51.

[58] M. Morlok and C. Hientzsch, 'Das Parlament als Zentralorgan der Demokratie. Eine Zusammenschau der einschlägigen parlamentsschützenden Normende' (2011) *JuS* 1.

[59] In the United States, the delegation of policy-making authority and legislative power to the courts has also been discussed, see for example, M.H. Lemos, 'The Consequences of Congress's Choice of Delegate: Judicial and Agency Interpretations of Title VII' (2010) 63 *Vanderbilt Law Review* 363.

inception of the government it might well have done itself'.[60] This has been mainly executed through legislative delegation. The growing use of 'big waivers'[61] to update law, introduce innovations in the market and encourage experimentation,[62] justifies the need to discuss the boundaries of legislative delegation in this country.

The most traditional non-delegation doctrine prohibits the legislator to delegate its legislative power to another branch of government. In the past there were examples of statutes being struck down by the US Supreme Court when the legislator delegated power to agencies without providing sufficient standards to delimitate these agencies' discretion.[63]

The leading cases are *Panama Refining Corp.* v. *Ryan*[64] and *A.L.A. Schechter Poultry Corp. v United States*[65] from the 1930s where, in the New Deal context, the US Supreme Court invalidated a Congressional delegation of legislative powers. Although the federal or state Constitutions do not explicitly forbid legislative delegation, the arguments against broad delegation have been based on article I of the (Federal) Constitution which consecrates the doctrine of separation of powers.[66] The interpretation of this article has diverged in the US literature and varied between the mentioned non-delegation doctrine and the 'exclusive delegation' doctrine which advocates that 'an administrative agency's power to promulgate legislative regulations is limited to the authority delegated by Congress', in other words, 'only the Congress' may delegate lawmaking power.[67]

According to the US Supreme Court interpretation of 'delegation of legislative power', there is no unconstitutional delegation as long as the agency's discretion has been confined by an 'intelligible principle' laid down by the Congress. In *Yakus* v. *United States*, the US Supreme Court expressed the need to set criteria for evaluating legislative standards that guide an administrative agency through the execution of the legislator's

---

60 J.B. Cheadle, 'The Delegation of Legislative Functions' (1917) 27 *Yale Law Journal* 892.

61 See Chapter 2 for a definition of 'waiver'.

62 D.J. Barron and T.D. Rakoff, 'In Defense of Big Waiver' (2013) 113 *Columbia Law Review* 265.

63 G.J. Greco, 'Standards or Safeguards: A Survey of the Delegation Doctrine in the States' (1994) 8 *Administrative Law Journal of the American University* 567.

64 *Panama Refining Corp.* v. *Ryan,* 293 U.S. 388 (1935).

65 *A.L.A. Schechter Poultry Corp. v. United States*, 295 U.S. 495 (1935).

66 Greco, 'Standards or Safeguards', n. 63 above.

67 Thomas W. Merrill, 'Rethinking Article I, Section I: From Nondelegation to Exclusive Delegation' (2004) 104 *Columbia Law Review* 2097.

will.[68] In the above-described framework, more than just this 'intelligible principle' is required as a statutory basis for experimentation.[69]

In the past decades, both the US Supreme Court and state courts have followed the different trend of upholding broad delegations of legislative power. This doctrine will only be briefly explained, since in practice it has not been used by the US Supreme Court as the grounds to strike down an act of Congress since the New Deal *A.L.A. Schechter Poultry Corp.* v. *United States* case.[70] The non-delegation doctrine is considered to be nowadays 'effectively unenforceable'[71] and even a 'dead letter'.[72] Nonetheless, this doctrine remains useful at the state level, although it might have lost its importance as far as Acts of Congress are concerned.[73] In addition, the Supreme Court sometimes refers to the non-delegation doctrine when interpreting broad statutes or explains its reasoning in the light of this doctrine.[74]

The idea that the legislator should make the *fundamental political choices* underlies the non-delegation doctrine. Although it could be argued that the agencies' legitimacy to take decisions resides in their expertise, the fundamental 'political decisions involve values and there are no real values experts'.[75] Thus agencies and other administrative authorities to whom powers have been delegated (should) make statutorily constrained choices.[76] This is equally true in the case of experimental regulations, only here agencies will limit the scope of application of this choice.

Alexander and Prakash argue that if Congress is allowed to delegate its lawmaking power (article I, section I, conventional delegations), then it is also possible to claim that this institution could also delegate other

---

[68] *Yakus* v. *United States*, 321 U.S. 414 (1944).

[69] See *J.W. Hampton, Jr and Co.* v. *United States*, 276 U.S. 394, 409 (1928); see more recently *Whitman* v. *American Trucking Ass'ns*, 531 U.S. 457, 472 (2001).

[70] *A.L.A. Schechter Poultry Corp.* v. *United States*, 295 U.S. 495 (1935).

[71] Merrill, 'Rethinking Article I, Section I: From Nondelegation to Exclusive Delegation' n. 67 above, 2099.

[72] See *Mistretta* v. *United States*, 488 U.S. 361 (1989).

[73] Carl McGowan, 'Congress, Court, and Control of Delegated Power' (1977) 77 *Columbia Law Review* 1119, 1128.

[74] Peter H. Aranson, Ernest Gelhorn and Glen O. Robinson, 'A Theory of Legislative Delegation' (1982) *Cornell Law Review* 1, 12.

[75] Alfred C. Aman, Jr, 'Administrative Law in a Global Era: Progress, Deregulatory Change, and the Rise of the Administrative Presidency' (1988) 73 *Cornell Law Review* 1101, 1221.

[76] *Ibid.* 1222.

Congressional powers, notably the power to propose amendments or approve treaties.[77] Although both scholars acknowledge the far-reaching effects of such an extensive interpretation, they wish to draw attention to the dangers of unconstrained delegations.[78] US Constitution, article I, section I does not, however, forbid legislative delegation, and although there are arguments for both non-delegation and exclusive delegation, there is no strong evidence that the Framers did not admit a certain degree of overlap between the legislative and executive powers.[79] There are thus less strict positions regarding legislative delegation in the United States, which have served as inspiration for the above-described framework.

Interpreting the US Constitution and the non-delegation doctrine, Lawson claims that Congress can assign a function to another actor or authorize that actor to make a decision that Congress could have also made; however, 'the real question is whether Congress is attempting to authorize another actor to exercise power that exceeds that actor's enumerated constitutional powers': making 'ancillary decisions about the operation and meaning of a statute' is far from doing so.[80] Although the 'theory of essentiality' is not present in the US literature, the mentioned position brings us to similar conclusions.

The questions that remain unresolved are how far these actors may go, and how their discretion should be limited so that their acts are traceable to the power originally granted by Congress. Different positions have been put forward in the United States. It has been argued in the literature that although state courts apply the (non-) delegation doctrine, states implement different material criteria varying from 'strict' standards and safeguards to 'loose standards'.[81] In the first cases, delegations of legislative power will be upheld if they are constrained by a statutory basis containing 'adequate standards of policy or an intelligible principle

---

[77] Larry Alexander and Saikrishna Prakash, 'Delegation Really Running Riot' (2007) 93 *Virginia Law Review* 1035.

[78] *Ibid.* 1058–79.

[79] Merrill, 'Rethinking Article I, Section I: From Nondelegation to Exclusive Delegation', n. 67 above, 2128.

[80] Gary Lawson, 'Delegation and Original Meaning' (2002) 88 *Virginia Law Review* 327, 359.

[81] Greco, 'Standards or Safeguards', n. 63 above, 580–99: the scholar distinguishes a third category of non-material criteria but procedural standards. There is a third category of state court that will uphold broad legislative delegations as long as administrative agencies adopt adequate procedural safeguards. Examples of the states applying this approach are Oregon, Washington and California.

for the agency to follow'.[82] Among the states striking down broad delegations depleted of guiding standards are notably Ohio, Oklahoma, Pennsylvania, New York and Texas. The second category of states authorizes broader legislative delegations as long as the statute contains general guidelines to be followed by administrative agencies. These guidelines can be materialized in general standards, procedural safeguards or a blend of both.[83] Examples of states implementing this second approach are Indiana, Georgia, New Jersey and Minnesota. The question to be raised in this context is: which of these paths should be chosen for the legislative delegation in the case of experimental regulations?

It results from the above-presented framework that not only broad guidelines and fundamental political and policy decisions should be attributed to the parliamentary legislator, but also other material elements, such as duration and evaluation criteria, must not be left to the executive. This is not a plea for strict rules, but rather for a clear delimitation of the path to be followed and its limitations. However, it is up to the executive to decide how it will cover it. Despite the non-existence of a theory of essentiality in the United States, it seems that also in this jurisdiction the most 'important' decisions should be made by the legislator.

3.5.3 Delegation in the Netherlands

Legislative delegation in the Netherlands is presumed to be prohibited unless the Constitution explicitly grants this option to the formal legislator.[84] A specific terminology referring to the possibility to 'regulate' ('*bij of krachtens de wet*', '*regels*' '*regelen*' or '*regeling*') indicates whether the formal legislator can delegate its legislative competence.[85] Parliament[86] has, on the grounds of article 81 of the Dutch Constitution, a general competence to legislate but, as mentioned earlier, this does not mean that this organ is always allowed to delegate about any subject.[87] In

---

[82] Greco, 'Standards or Safeguards', n. 63 above, 580–81.

[83] *Ibid.* 588.

[84] Dölle, *Mandaat en delegatie*, n. 21 above, 23, 28–9.

[85] Gert-Jan Veerman, *Over wetgeving: principes, paradoxen en praktische beschouwingen* (2nd edn, SDU, 2009) 56; Sjoerd E. Zijlstra *et al.*, *Wetgeven: Handboek voor de centrale en decentrale overheid* (Kluwer, 2012) 254.

[86] The 'formal legislator' in the Netherlands is composed by the two chambers of the Parliament (Staten-General) and the government as laid down in Dutch Constitution, art. 81.

[87] M.C. Burkens, H.R.B.M. Kummeling, B.P. Vermeulen and R.J.G.M. Widdershoven, *Beginselen van de democratische rechtsstaat: Inleiding tot de grondslagen van het Nederlandse staats- en bestuursrecht* (Kluwer, 2012) 76–7.

order to ensure this, it is not sufficient to impose this obligation to refer to the statutory ground but to provide adequate guidance while leaving enough discretion to the executive.

Just as in Germany, the constitutional prohibition to delegate does not mean that administrative actors are not allowed to regulate in the fields covered by such prohibition but rather that the 'essential provisions concerning the subject in question must be legislated by an Act of Parliament (*wet in formele zin*)'.[88]

The interpretation of instructions 22, 23 and particularly 24 of the Instructions for Legislative Drafting (*aanwijzingen voor de regelgeving*) provides more information as to what should be defined by Parliament and what should be understood as an 'essential' or 'main' element. The choice as to 'which elements should be in the statute and which ones can be delegated' should be guided by the primacy of the legislator.[89] This primacy does not mean that Parliament should define all elements of a statute, but rather the most important legal-political choices that should be included in it.[90] According to the explanatory note to instruction 22 'essential elements' are the 'scope', 'the structural elements of the regulation' and, when applicable 'the main permanent norms'. Van Gestel argues that this note is misleading since it further reads that 'in the interest of accessibility, it may be advisable not to include substantive norms in an Act of Parliament, but to leave it to a subordinate legislative authority to draw up an integrated substantive regulation'.[91] The mentioned scholar considers that this part appears to 'undermine the whole idea behind the primacy of the parliamentary legislator'.

According to instruction 23, whenever the Constitution requires the intervention of the formal legislator, this should be interpreted as a prohibition to delegate. As in Germany, in the areas reserved to Parliament, the 'essential elements' (*wezenlijke elementen*) should be defined by the formal legislator. In the Netherlands, this concept is less concretized and almost leads us to a word game: 'the main elements of a

---

[88] Voermans, 'Legaliteit als middel tot een doel', n. 19 above, 1, 45.

[89] See R.A.J. Van Gestel, 'The Deparliamentarisation of Legislation: Framework Laws and the Primacy of the Legislator' (2013) 9 *Utrecht Law Review* 106.

[90] W.J.M. Voermans, 'Toekomstperspectieven voor het primaat van de wetgever' (1998) 1 *RegelMaat* 35.

[91] Van Gestel, 'The Deparliamentarisation of Legislation', n. 89 above, 112.

regulation are the structural elements of a regulation, which should constitute the essential provisions with reference to the subject at stake'.[92]

According to Zijlstra, since delegation, broadly considered, implies the transference of a competence which will be directly exercised by the delegatee, the legislator is not allowed to provide the former with instructions regarding the execution of the delegated competences.[93] Nonetheless, this does not mean that, in the case of legislative delegation, the legislator cannot explicitly declare whether the enactment of regulations on an experimental basis should be allowed. Instead, as demonstrated in the context of the analysis of German and US literature and case law, the decision to delegate the possibility to enact experimental regulations must be explicitly stated in the statutory basis. Moreover, a close connection between delegation and experimental regulation should be expected, since in the words of Eijlander, Voermans and Lokin, delegation is the appropraite mechanism to 'experiment and anticipate new developments' which also means diverging from the existing legal standards and allowing (and assessing) the introduction of innovative solutions on a small scale.[94] The authors quote the example of article 18(1) of the Telecommunications Act which foresaw the enactment of rules in deviation from it.[95] The idea was then to test if certain developments could promote the achievement of the statute's objectives.

The executive is usually not obliged to experiment with rules, but it can do so. The legislator must, however, find it 'necessary' to grant this possibility, which may at first convey the idea that experimental regulations should not be a first choice. Such conclusion can be drawn from the Instructions for Legislative Drafting (*aanwijzingen voor de regelgeving*): instruction 10a provides an explicit legality framework for the enactment of experimental regulations. This instruction provides a ground of delegation for experimental regulations, specifying that 'a [hierarchically] lower regulation can diverge from a [hierarchically] higher regulation on an experimental basis'. Nevertheless, in the higher act, it should be listed from which provisions or parts this derogation is allowed. The lower and experimental regulation should refer to the ground of delegation.

---

[92] R.J.N. Schlössels and S.E. Zijlstra, *Bestuursrecht in de Sociale Rechtsstaat* (Onderwijseditie, Kluwer, 2010) vol. 1, 259.

[93] *Ibid.* 151.

[94] Ph. Eijlander, M. Lokin and W. Voermans, 'Delegatie van regelgevende bevoegdheid: de Aanwijzingen voorbij' (2001) 2 *RegelMaat* 69, 73.

[95] Telecommunicatiewet of 19 October 1998, Stb. 1998, 610.

Instruction 10a(2) of the Dutch Instructions for Legislative Drafting contains further guidelines for the divergence from a statute: only a governmental decree (*algemene maatregel van bestuur*) can deviate from the rules laid down in a statute (see example 3.2). The instruction also adds that 'subdelegation' may be allowed if a more detailed implementation is required.

3.5.4 Delegation Doctrines: Preliminary Conclusion

'In a time of increasing technological progress … and complex technological and economic development, broad delegation to the Executive is a characteristic of the modern state'.[96] Therefore, the above-described doctrines on the *Wesentlichkeitstheorie*, non-delegation theory and considerations on delegation in Dutch law should seek the balance between guaranteeing this 'modern state' and ensuring that the 'essential elements' capable of affecting the realization of fundamental rights are still in the hands of a democratically elected legislator. History has also shown us that uncontrolled broad delegations in the name of economic development can have tragic ends. Open-ended delegations in the case of experimental legislation are therefore to be avoided.

Although Germany, the United States and the Netherlands appear to advocate different delegation doctrines, a number of common aspects can be identified. First, the 'essential' decisions related to the important political choices or direct and substantial intervention in fundamental rights should be made by the legislator. In the three jurisdictions at stake, it should be the legislator deciding on legal change as well, even if its implementation is left to the executive. Although in the United States less strict standards are applied, the discretion of administrative actors should still be constrained according to the guidelines provided by the legislator. In the following subsection, the contents of the delegation basis are discussed: these contents are the main guidelines that the executive should take into consideration when enacting and implementing an experimental regulation.

---

[96] Jan S. Oster, 'The Scope of Judicial Review in the German and U.S. Administrative Legal Systems' (2008) 9 *German Law Journal* 1267.

3.6 ELEMENTS OF THE LEGALITY FRAMEWORK: CLARIFICATION

The statutory delegation basis enabling the enactment of an experimental regulation should contain, at a minimum, *the contents, objective and extent* of the latter. These elements should be explicit and sufficiently specific.

According to the Dutch *Fluoridering* case, the required statutory basis for delegation should be 'sufficiently specific' considering 'the nature and contents of the subject to be regulated'.[97] A 'specific statutory basis' means in the Netherlands not only that 'the circumstances will be concretized as much as possible … but also that the statutory basis will determine if the executive has the freedom to enact a regulation or it is obliged to [do so]'.[98] In the mentioned case, the executive proceeded to a serious intervention without any support on an explicit statutory basis.

The statutory basis referring to the possibility to enact experimental regulations will usually be indicated in a separate article or section of the statute. This is, for example, required by Instruction 10b of the Dutch Instructions for Legislative Drafting which determines that on the delegation ground it should be decided on the maximum duration of the experimental regulations and how the evaluation will take place.[99] Example 3.2 provides an illustration of the legality requirements implemented in practice. This example will be used to analyze and explain the different elements of the legality framework suggested above, including the definition of the goals of the experiment; the clarity of the legislative

97 HR, 22 June 1973, NJ 1973, 386 (*Fluoridering*).

98 S.E. Zijlstra, T.C. Borman, S.A. J. Munneke, F.J. Van Ommeren, A.E. Schilder and E. Steyger, *Wetgeven: Handboek voor de centrale en decentrale overheid* (Kluwer, 2012) 252.

99 The original text of instruction 10b reads: '1. De wettelijke regeling die de grondslag biedt voor een experimentele regeling of een experiment bepaalt de maximale geldingsduur van de op basis daarvan vast te stellen experimentele regelingen of uit te voeren experimenten.2. In de toelichting bij een experimentele regeling wordt aangegeven hoe evaluatie van de regeling plaatsvindt. Indien een experimentele regeling een evaluatiebepaling bevat wordt het volgende model als uitgangspunt genomen:

> 'Onze Minister van/voor … zendt (in overeenstemming met Onze Minister van/voor …) drie maanden voor het einde van de werkingsduur van een algemene maatregel van bestuur als bedoeld in artikel … /dit besluit aan de Staten-Generaal een verslag over de doeltreffendheid en de effecten van het experiment in de praktijk, alsmede een standpunt inzake de voortzetting van die maatregel/dit besluit, anders dan als experiment'.

intent; the 'direction' or 'extent' of the experiment; duration; and evaluation criteria. Example 3.2 will be complemented by other examples of dispositions authorizing the enactment of experimental regulations or provisions.

3.6.1 Elements of the Statutory Basis: An Example

In example 3.2, the Dutch legislator appears to have been concerned not only with fulfilling the normative condition of providing a specific statutory basis, but also with methodological aspects, notably drawing attention to the need to reflect on the selection of participants.

EXAMPLE 3.2 DUTCH ELECTRICITY LAW

Wet van 2 juli 1998, houdende regels met betrekking tot de productie, het transport en de levering van elektriciteit (Elektriciteitswet 1998).[100]

Article 7a [artikel 7a]
1. It is possible to derogate [from these provisions] on an experimental basis by virtue of this law by governmental decree, considering the decisions of the Council of the European Union, the European Parliament together with the Council or of the European Commission. [Bij algemene maatregel van bestuur kan, met inachtneming van bindende besluiten van de Raad van de Europese Unie, van het Europees Parlement en de Raad gezamenlijk of van de Europese Commissie, bij wege van experiment worden afgeweken van het bepaalde bij of krachtens deze wet.]
2. The first section of the article can exclusively be applied when the experiment contributes to improvements in the field of the production, transport and distribution of decentralized generated and sustainable electricity, or electricity generated in an installation for combined heat and power and fits within the responsible financial context of the state. [Er kan uitsluitend toepassing worden gegeven aan het eerste lid indien het experiment bijdraagt aan ontwikkelingen op het gebied van de productie, het

[100] Wet van 2 juli 1998, houdende regels met betrekking tot de productie, het transport en de levering van elektriciteit (Elektriciteitswet 1998), Stb.1998, 427; as amended 28 February 2013, Stb. 2013, 102.

transport en de levering van decentraal opgewekte duurzame elektriciteit, of elektriciteit opgewekt in een installatie voor warmtekrachtkoppeling en past binnen verantwoorde financiële kaders van het Rijk.]
3. The rules on experiments will be enacted by governmental decree as defined in the first section, where it will be determined [Bij de algemene maatregel van bestuur, bedoeld in het eerste lid, worden regels gesteld over experimenten als bedoeld in het eerste lid, waarbij in elk geval wordt bepaald]:

(a) which disposition(s) of this law can be derogated from [welke afwijking of afwijkingen van deze wet zijn toegestaan];
(b) to what categories of [electricity] users the derogations will be applied and the definition of the group for which the derogation will be valid [voor welke categorieën afnemers de afwijkingen gelden en de omvang van de groep afnemers waarvoor een afwijking geldt];
(c) the maximum authorized duration allowed for the [mentioned] derogations [de ten hoogste toegestane tijdsduur van die afwijking of afwijkingen];
(d) the number of situations for which a divergence is authorized; and [het aantal situaties waarin een afwijking is toegestaan; en]
(e) the criteria according to which it is decided whether an [experimental] derogation has fulfilled its objectives and whether the duration for [the accomplishment of such objective] requires adjustments [de wijze waarop wordt vastgesteld of een afwijking aan haar doel beantwoordt, en of de tijdsduur daarvan aanpassing behoeft].

4. The Minister will make a report on the effectiveness and the effects of the experiment three months after its termination to the House of Representatives, including an opinion on its continuation other than as an experiment. [Onze Minister zendt uiterlijk drie maanden na de beëindiging van een experiment een verslag over de doeltreffendheid en de effecten ervan, alsmede een standpunt inzake de voortzetting ervan anders dan als experiment, aan de Tweede Kamer der Staten-Generaal.]

3.6.2 Goals of the Experiment

The above-described framework implies that the legislator sets 'the goal(s) of the experiment, translating as unambiguously as possible the intent of the legislator' (see above). The definition of goals does not exclude the possibility to employ indeterminate concepts, particularly when the experimental regulation aims to assist the legislator in gathering more information regarding a new approach to a new problem. The use of indeterminate concepts should not, however, open the doors to excessive discretion. The legislator must thus set *explicit goals* which should be as concrete as possible. In addition, guidance as to the meaning of these goals should be provided, notably in the form of an explanation of the reasons behind the decision to elect experimental regulation as a means to concretize the described goals.

In example 3.2, it was made explicit in the statute that experiments should aim to contribute to 'improvements in the field of the production, transport and distribution of decentralized, generated and sustainable electricity, or electricity generated in an installation for combined heat and power', without imposing excessive costs. This goal is broadly defined. Since a myriad of interpretations of 'improvements' are admissible in this context, this goal should be strictly interpreted to avoid excessive discretion. The executive should limit itself to the concretization of the legislative intent. The definition of 'goals' reflects at the same time flexibility and stringency: flexibility because it allows the legislator to set goals employing indeterminate concepts, when little is known about the best legislative means to achieve the goal; stringency because these goals should not open the door to unlimited discretion and vague regulations.

The legislator must have determined *the need* for an experiment, even if it delegates to the executive the competence to design and execute it. The definition of the goals of experimental regulation is crucial to the success of the experiment, but it is also one of the most challenging tasks for the legislator in the context of the implementation of a legislative instrument.[101]

First, the definition of a problem implies acknowledging that a legislative solution for a problem can be found and that this can result from an experiment.[102] Nevertheless, not all members of society might

[101] David R. Mayhew, 'Congress as a Problem Solver' in A.S. Gerber and E.M. Patashnik, *Promoting the General Welfare: New Perspectives on Government Performance* (Brookings Institution Press, 2006) 219.

[102] *Ibid.* 220.

share this conclusion or agree with the delimitation of a problem in itself. Secondly, defining a problem (for example, economic crisis) and a respective single-policy goal to be pursued in this context (for example, to stimulate technological innovation through *x* or *y*) is not a realistic option in a world where legislators are meant to pursue multiple policy goals. These goals are often legitimate, but there is the risk that they will be contradicted by other existing goals (for example, environmental protection).[103] When inserted in a complex and lengthy agenda, these goals can be difficult to reconcile with each other.[104] Thirdly, policy goals evolve over time with the change of social and technological circumstances.[105] Although the delimitation of a problem and the policy goals to be pursued are complicated tasks, legislators should try to define these goals with the available information and adapt them to the knowledge obtained through the evaluation of experimental legislation.

The mentioned challenges regarding the definition of objectives should not serve as excuses not to enact these legislative instruments; instead under uncertain conditions, experimental legislation might even be the wisest choice for legislators. If there is little consensus as to the defined problem or its solutions, experimenting with them on a small-scale basis might produce evidence to prove the opposition wrong and eliminate controversies (see Chapter 2). As simplistically argued by John Dewey, ‘science is isomorphic to democracy’ since both search for solutions.[106] The former will try out new solutions in laboratories; while the latter might ‘achieve a satisfactory system of governance through seeking and sharing information in an ascending learning curve’.[107] This means that

---

[103] M. Wiktorowicz and R. Deber, ‘Regulating Biotechnology: A Rational-Political Model of Development’ (1997) 40 *Health Policy* 118.

[104] Linda Cohen and Matthew Spitzer, ‘Term Limits’ (1992) 80 *Georgetown Law Journal* 477, 486.

[105] Wim Timmer, *Het doel wel gesteld: een praktijkonderzoek naar de toepassing van doelregelgeving* (Boom Juridische uitgevers, 2011) 33. The problems mentioned with regard to the definition of goals in the context of sunset clauses and experimental legislation are, to a certain extent, also present in so-called ‘goal regulation’. For a critical analysis of this type of regulation, see Pauline C. Westerman, ‘De onmogelijkheid van deregulering’ (2006 (3)81 *Nederlands Juristenblad* 132; Pauline C. Westerman, ‘Een nieuwe stijl van reguleren’ (2006) 3 *Recht der Werkelijkheid* 33; Pauline C. Westerman, ‘The Emergence of New Types of Norms’ in L.J. Wintgens (ed.), *Legislation in Context: Essays in Legisprudence* (Ashgate, 2007) 117.

[106] Mayhew, ‘Congress as a Problem Solver’, n. 101 above, 220. See John Dewey, *The Public and its Problems* (Swallow Press, 1954).

[107] See Dewey, *The Public and its Problems*, n. 106 above.

both democracy and science can use the experimental method in their pursuit for the best solutions.

The determination of the goals is also decisive for the successful implementation and *ex post* evaluation of experimental legislation. In order to avoid arbitrariness regarding the implementation of this legislative instrument, the 'fate' of experimental regulations should be dependent on the attainment of these goals. The predetermined evaluation criteria should be used to assess the successful and effective attainment of the goals of the experiment.

The mere setting of broad goals has been criticized in the literature. In the United States, Schoenbrod has argued in the context of the non-delegation doctrine, that 'a valid statute must set forth a rule of conduct and not merely a goal or set of goals towards which executive or judicial actors must strive. The act of legislation is not completed simply by announcing an ambition; the Constitution requires the legislator to specify how and to what extent those ambitions should be realized'.[108] Defining detailed rules may, however, be increasingly difficult in a complex and evolving society and this explained the tendency towards goal-based legislation and framework directives briefly mentioned in Chapter 2. The definition of broad goals instead of rules has also been criticized in the European context. Pauline Westerman claims that due to this tendency, legal interpretation and the concretization of broad goals have become highly dependent on (non-legal) expert knowledge.[109] Notwithstanding this criticism, the above-suggested framework fulfils the minimum requirements suggested by Schoenbrod: the delegation basis for experimental regulation should indeed specify why an experiment is necessary but also how and to what extent it should be implemented.

Example 3.2 on Dutch experiments in the energy sector is an illustration of a specific delegation basis where the legislator defines more than just an 'ambition', but where there is still room to discuss what the

[108] D. Schoenbrod, 'The Delegation Doctrine: Could the Court Give It Substance?' (1985) 83 *Mich. L. Rev.* 1223, 1227; G. Lawson, 'Delegation and Original Meaning' (2002) 88 *Va. L. Rev.* 327, 373.

[109] Pauline C Westerman, 'Arguing about Goals: The Diminishing Scope of Legal Reasoning' (2010) *Argumentation* 211; Pauline C. Westerman, 'Governing by Goals: Governance as a Legal Style' (2007) *Legisprudence* 57. For the challenges of legislating in the modern *Rechtsstaat*, including the need to tackle the excessive amount of information and to take into account expert knowledge, see WRR, *De toekomst van de nationale Rechtsstaat* (WRR, 2002). For the difficulty in 'communicating' the intended goals of the legislator, see Willem Witteveen, *Het wetgevend oordeel* (Boom Juridische uitgevers, 2010).

legislator meant by 'improvements'. One could question whether the legislator could and should have provided additional guidelines. One 'could' but need not do so in this context: the interpretation of the concept of 'improvements' in the fields defined in the statutory basis can here rightly be left to the executive. This is, however, a judgment that can only be pronounced in light of specific circumstances.

3.6.3 Unambiguous Legislative Intent

The requirement that the delegation basis translates as *unambiguously* as possible the *intent* of the legislator is to a certain extent inspired by the *Chevron* case, more specifically by the so-called '*Chevron* step one'.[110] In this case, the US Supreme Court was requested to review the Environmental Protection Agency's interpretation of the term 'stationary source' in the context of the Clean Air Act.[111] This case refers to the limits of judicial review of agencies' decisions. Nonetheless, the suggested test should be used in this context not necessarily to determine whether agency interpretations should be deferred but rather as a guideline to avoid misunderstandings as to the formulation of the goals of an experiment and the underlying legislative intent.

Considering the statutory text, statutory structure, legislative purpose and history, 'step one of the *Chevron* test' analyzes whether 'Congress has directly spoken to the precise question at issue'. In order to avoid misinterpretations by agencies or other levels of the executive, it is essential that the legislative intent is unequivocal. Textualism plays here a decisive role. If the statute is unambiguous as to the legislative intent, then it is not necessary to proceed to step two, which refers to whether the agency's interpretation is reasonable and permissible. The *Chevron* test implies that although Congress delegates the competence to interpret to agencies, it is always the former that must decide on the fundamental questions, namely, whether to regulate or not and what to leave to the agency's margin of appreciation (see above).[112] In the case of experimental regulations, this is concretized by formulating unequivocal goals that leave no margin of doubt as to the legislative intent.

---

[110] *Chevron USA, Inc.* v. *Natural Resources Defense Council*, 467 U.S. 837 (1984).

[111] Jan S. Oster, 'The Scope of Judicial Review in the German and U.S. Administrative Legal Systems' (2008) 9 *German LJ* 1267.

[112] *Ibid.*

3.6.4 'Direction' and 'Extent' of the Experiment

The suggested framework requires that the 'direction' of the experiment is explicit. The legislator should be explicit as to whether authorization is given to derogate from existing laws, enacting a parallel system applicable to a part of the population, or rather to exempt a group of citizens from rules or standards. From the examples provided throughout this study, one is left with the impression that there is a tendency for the Dutch legislator to allow the enactment of experiments through the derogation from existing laws (see example 3.2); for the US legislator to grant waivers (see example 3.3); and for the German legislator to do both (see Chapter 2).

It is worth noting that in the United States, the legislator defines under what conditions a waiver may be granted, but states must apply for it. This is illustrated in example 3.3, where the responsible Secretary decides the state's application for a waiver according to the requirements laid down by the legislator.

EXAMPLE 3.3 PATIENT PROTECTION AND AFFORDABLE CARE ACT

Patient Protection and Affordable Care Act, 42 USC s. 18052, Waiver for State Innovation[113]

(a) Application

(1) In general: A State may apply to the Secretary for the waiver of all or any requirements described in paragraph (2) with respect to health insurance coverage within that State for plan years beginning on or after January 1, 2017. Such application shall –

(A) be filed at such time and in such manner as the Secretary may require;

---

[113] Patient Protection and Affordable Care Act, Waiver for State Innovation, 42 USC s. 18052. An amendment of this Act is currently pending before the US Congress and Senate. The Bill for the State Leadership in Health Care Act has been suggested to 'provide for an earlier start for State health care coverage innovation waivers under the Patient Protection and Affordable Care Act'. This would imply replacing the date '1 January 2017' with '1 January 2014'. For the full text and status of the Bill, see www.govtrack.us/congress/bills/113/hr1841.

(B) contain such information as the Secretary may require, including –
   (i) a comprehensive description of the State legislation and program to implement a plan meeting the requirements for a waiver under this section; and
   (ii) a 10-year budget plan for such plan that is budget neutral for the Federal Government; and
(C) provide an assurance that the State has enacted the law described in subsection (b)(2).

...

(6) Definition: In this section, the term 'Secretary' means –

(A) the Secretary of Health and Human Services with respect to waivers relating to the provisions described in subparagraph (A) through (C) of paragraph (2); and
(B) the Secretary of the Treasury with respect to waivers relating to the provisions described in paragraph (2)(D).

(b) Granting of waivers

(1) In general: The Secretary may grant a request for a waiver under subsection (a)(1) only if the Secretary determines that the State plan –

(A) will provide coverage that is at least as comprehensive as the coverage defined in section 18022(b) of this title and offered through Exchanges established under this title ... as certified by Office ... of the Actuary of the Centers for Medicare & Medicaid Services based on sufficient data from the State and from comparable States about their experience with programs created by this Act and the provisions of this Act that would be waived;
(B) will provide coverage and cost sharing protections against excessive out-of-pocket spending that are at least as affordable as the provisions of this title ... would provide;
(C) will provide coverage to at least a comparable number of its residents as the provisions of this title ... would provide; and
(D) will not increase the Federal deficit.

...

(c) Scope of waiver

(1) In general: The Secretary shall determine the scope of a waiver of a requirement described in subsection (a)(2) granted to a State under subsection (a)(1).
(2) Limitation: The Secretary may not waive under this section any Federal law or requirement that is not within the authority of the Secretary.
...

(e) Term of waiver

No waiver under this section may extend over a period of longer than 5 years unless the State requests continuation of such waiver, and such request shall be deemed granted unless the Secretary, within 90 days after the date of its submission to the Secretary, either denies such request in writing or informs the State in writing with respect to any additional information which is needed in order to make a final determination with respect to the request.

The legislator determines the direction and the extent of the divergence or exemption, listing with which provisions or parts of them the regulator is authorized to experiment. The legislator may, in some cases, provide a greater leeway to the executive as to the extent of the experiment (see example 34), namely, by allowing the former to decide by decree on how, for how long and from which articles the divergence on an experimental basis should be allowed. In such cases, it is important that this divergence does not go beyond the articles listed by the legislator in the statutory basis.

In example 3.3 on the Waiver for State Innovation in the context of the Patient Protection and Affordable Care Act, the legislator not only defines the direction ('waiver') and the extent ('all or any requirements described in paragraph (2) with respect to health insurance coverage within that State for plan years beginning on or after January 1, 2017') but also establishes the limits of the exemptions granted: they should provide a 'comparable coverage, be as comprehensive and affordable' as the federal provisions. Hence, states may be exempted from complying with a number of provisions as long as states enacting experiments guarantee the same level of protection. The idea of waiving federal requirements cannot be regarded as a mere authorization to experiment *contra legem*. As long as the federal objectives determined by Congress are included, the former does not need to be controversial: in the United States, experimental waivers are often authorized to allow states to pursue their own policies and to innovate within the general aims of the statute. This brings us to the already mentioned metaphor of 'states-as-laboratories' (see Chapter 2). Experimental regulations entail not implementing a statute as it is, but rather regulating, in many cases, *contra legem,* by enacting and implementing regulations that deviate from statutory provisions.

While in the context of regular delegation, the executive further develops the details of a statute which are necessary for its implementation, in the case of an experiment, divergent provisions are enacted and implemented on an experimental basis. At first sight, this appears to contradict the logic behind delegation, but in fact it does not. The executive experiments with new solutions in order to find out what the most effective provisions are and to draw valuable lessons from them. The legislator cannot execute this task on its own.

Experimental regulations may go further than 'regular delegations' but they do so in the name of learning purposes. The legislator should, however, set the tone for these experimental derogations and exemptions in order to guarantee that these experiments do not endanger the implementation of essential elements defined in the statute or exceed the legislative intent (see example 3.4).

EXAMPLE 3.4 LAW ON WORK AND SOCIAL WELFARE

Wet van 9 oktober 2003, houdende vaststelling van een wet inzake ondersteuning bij arbeidsinschakeling en verlening van bijstand door gemeenten (Wet werk en bijstand)[114]

Article 83. Innovation [artikel 83. Innovatie]

In order to research the possibilities to implement this law more effectively in relation to labour integration and financing, it is allowed to derogate on an experimental basis the provisions laid down in or by virtue of articles 6 to 10 (inclusive), 31(2) and

[114] Wet van 9 oktober 2003, houdende vaststelling van een wet inzake ondersteuning bij arbeidsinschakeling en verlening van bijstand door gemeenten (Wet werk en bijstand), 9 October 2003, Stb. 2003, 375; last amendment on 22 December 2011, Stb. 2011, 650 (several amendments pending, see www.wetten.nl).

paragraph 7.1 by governmental decree. [Bij algemene maatregel van bestuur kan bij wijze van experiment, met het oog op het onderzoeken van mogelijkheden om deze wet met betrekking tot de arbeidsinschakeling en de financiering doeltreffender uit te voeren, worden afgeweken van het bepaalde bij of krachtens de artikelen 6 tot en met 10, 31, tweede lid, en paragraaf 7.1. Bij toepassing van de eerste volzin wordt bij algemene maatregel van bestuur geregeld op welke wijze en gedurende welke periode van welke artikelen van de wet wordt afgeweken.]

3.6.5 Duration

The duration of an experiment should be sufficient to ensure that it produces meaningful results. The duration of an experiment can thus be the passport to success or failure of an experiment. Since the duration is a structural element of every experimental disposition, it should be determined by the legislator. As illustrated in example 3.5, this does not eliminate the possibility for the executive to apply for a renewal as long it justifies the need to prolong the experiment.

EXAMPLE 3.5 DURATION WAIVER FOR STATE INNOVATION

Protection and Affordable Care Act, 42 USC s. 18052, Waiver for State Innovation

(e) Term of waiver

No waiver under this section may extend over a period of longer than 5 years unless the State requests continuation of such waiver, and such request shall be deemed granted unless the Secretary, within 90 days after the date of its submission to the Secretary, either denies such request in writing or informs the State in writing with respect to any additional information which is needed in order to make a final determination with respect to the request.

The duration of the experiment should be defined according to the objective pursued and the characteristics of the sector, notably the speed of social or technological change and of the expected subjects' response to the introduction of new laws. As mentioned earlier, experiments in social fields (for example, education, integration of minorities in the labour market) would intuitively require longer periods than experiments designed to assess the impact of new regulations in technological sectors (for example, telecommunications, media). In the latter, the objectives of experiments can be attained within one or two years.

3.6.6 Evaluation Criteria and Transparency

One of the main criticisms (presented in Chapter 7) refers to the risk that the results of experiments will be disregarded and put at the service of politicians' interests. The acceptance and reputation of experimental legislation, as well as the validity of the experimental results, could be endangered if there is a widespread perception that this type of legislative instrument is never satisfactorily evaluated. Clear criteria known beforehand, periodic evaluations, the participation of stakeholders, and the granting of a public character to this process can enhance the transparency and accountability of the enactment and implementation of experimental regulations. The attempt to confer more transparency on this process is visible in example 3.6, where the public is involved through public hearings. As stated below, the intervention of the public should be organized so as to guarantee that stakeholders can provide meaningful input. The involvement of stakeholders before the experiment is initiated can also be desirable when socially controversial experiments are in question.

EXAMPLE 3.6 PUBLIC PARTICIPATION: WAIVER FOR STATE INNOVATION

42 USC s. 18052, Waiver for State Innovation

(4) Waiver consideration and transparency

(B) Regulations

Not later than 180 days after March 23, 2010, the Secretary shall promulgate regulations relating to waivers under this section that provide –

(i) a process for public notice and comment at the State level, including public hearings, sufficient to ensure a meaningful level of public input;

(ii) a process for the submission of an application that ensures the disclosure of –
  (I) the provisions of law that the State involved seeks to waive; and
  (II) the specific plans of the State to ensure that the waiver will be in compliance with subsection (b);

(iii) a process for providing public notice and comment after the application is received by the Secretary, that is sufficient to ensure a meaningful level of public input and that does not impose requirements that are in addition to, or duplicative of, requirements imposed under the Administrative Procedures Act, ... or requirements that are unreasonable or unnecessarily burdensome with respect to State compliance;

(iv) a process for the submission to the Secretary of periodic reports by the State concerning the implementation of the program under the waiver; and

(v) a process for the periodic evaluation by the Secretary of the program under the waiver.

(C) Report

The Secretary shall annually report to Congress concerning actions taken by the Secretary with respect to applications for waivers under this section.

A transparent periodic evaluation, as laid down in example 3.6 would be beneficial to the three jurisdictions under analysis.

Experimental legislation is a learning instrument, and as such, one would expect that valuable lessons can be learned and employed to improve the quality of legislation and regulation. If the information obtained in the context of these experiments is valuable, then one can legitimately expect that it will be used: after all, good 'information is the lifeblood of regulatory policy, effective governance ... and decision-making'.[115] The demand for information motivates a number of experiments, pilot programmes and the development of administrative

[115] M.C. Stephenson, 'Information Acquisition and Institutional Design' (2011) 124 *Harvard Law Review* 1422–3; Cary Coglianese, R. Zeckhauser and E. Parson, 'Seeking Truth for Power: Informational Strategy and Regulatory Policymaking' (2004) 89 *Minnesotta Law Review* 277–9.

procedures focused on evaluating *ex ante* and *ex post* the outcomes of new laws and policies. The effort put into gathering this information should not be wasted due to the lack or insufficiency of the evaluation.

The assessment of the information gathered in the context of an experiment and the decisions made cannot be value-free or exempt from technocratic or political influences. However, the final decision should mainly be determined by the quality and content of the mentioned information.[116] While political rationality is an inevitable part of the lawmaking process (see Chapter 7), experimental legislation should be enacted so as to be taken as seriously as possible. As stated by the US Court of Appeals (District of Columbia): 'fundamental to the concept of any experiment is the assumption that the data developed from the experience thereunder will be subjected to *meaningful review, analysis, and evaluation* before the experimental practice is allowed to continue or to become institutionalized as a more permanent procedure'.[117] These requirements can be fulfilled by including transparent criteria in the delegation basis.

Alongside the already mentioned periodic obligations to report and evaluate, an evaluation commission can be designated to ensure the carrying out of an independent evaluation of the results. Although it might not always be possible to appoint an independent evaluation commission for this purpose – experimental regulations are often internally evaluated – it may be desirable to ensure that the work of evaluation commissions is assisted by expert committees. This is the case with ethical commissions who may be of added value in socially controversial fields.[118] The intervention of ethical commissions does not guarantee that it will be easier to determine the results of experimental regulations, but that additional points of view will be taken into consideration.

Finally, the risk that the results of experiments will be captured by politicians can be diminished if the evaluation reports are made public. Some of these reports are already public in the countries under analysis.[119] However, it would be important to guarantee more pro-active

---

[116] Stephenson, 'Information Acquisition and Institutional Design', n. 115 above, 1423–4.

[117] *Public Service Commission for the State of New York* v. *Federal Power Commission*, 167 U.S. App. D.C. 100, 511 F.2d 338 (1974).

[118] Hoffmann-Riem, 'Législation expérimentale en Allemagne', n. 36 above, 177.

[119] See for example, the evaluation report of the earlier mentioned experiment with unemployment benefits (s. 6c SGB II), available at www.bmas.de/

openness of government as far as the results of experimental regulations are concerned. If lawmaking and regulation tend towards greater transparency, than a solution would be to ensure that legislators and regulators 'provide reasons for their policies and … base their decisions on an administrative record that is available to the public as well as to courts and members of Congress'.[120] A solution for the countries under analysis would be to implement this idea of a public 'administrative record', possibly published on online platforms where other ministerial or agency documents are already currently uploaded. It is not only important to ensure that experimental regulations are evaluated but also that the evaluation results are incorporated in lawmaking. This brings us to the next element of the framework.

3.6.7 Follow-up Decision

The results of experimental regulations are often not taken seriously due to the gap between the evaluation of the experimental regulation and decision on 'what should happen next'. Even if the delegation basis imposes an obligation on the delegatee to report periodically to the delegator, nothing is said about the final decision to be taken once the experiment is terminated. However, the legislator can in principle state what should happen with determined results and within which period a decision must be made. This is also suggested in the framework suggested in this chapter. A number of questions may arise in this context: does the legislator have a deadline to take a follow-up decision on the subject? Should the legislator automatically proceed to an incorporation of the lessons learned? There are exceptions, as illustrated in example 3.7, but very often nothing is said about 'what happens next'.

SharedDocs/Downloads/DE/PDF-Publikationen/forschungsbericht-f362.pdf?__blob=publicationFile.

[120] Coglianese, Zeckhauser and Parson, 'Seeking Truth for Power', n. 115 above, 336.

EXAMPLE 3.7 DUTCH DECREE ON ENVIRONMENTAL SUBSIDIES, FOLLOW-UP DECISION

Besluit van 8 december 1998, houdende regels ter stroomlijning van de opzet van milieusubsidies (Besluit milieusubsidies)[121]

Article 17 [artikel 17]

3. Within one year after the termination of the experiment, the Minister will decide whether an amendment of this decree is necessary. [Binnen een jaar na afsluiting van het experiment beslist Onze Minister of een wijziging van dit besluit naar zijn oordeel noodzakelijk is.]

The legislator should be bound by a deadline to make a reasoned follow-up decision while considering the following: first, the renewal of the experimental period or a broadening of the sample group should only occur when further testing is necessary in order to clarify the results obtained up to that moment; secondly, the decision to terminate the experiment, re-establish the status quo (in so far as possible) and discard the obtained results should be sufficiently justified and should evidence why the results are not valid or cannot justify legislative changes; thirdly, the decision to proceed to a revision of existing law on the grounds of the experimental regulation should reflect not only the results obtained but also their evaluation. Although the legislator has the last word, experimental regulations should determine the revision of laws when it is possible to demonstrate that the tested rules pursue to a great extent (or even achieve) the goal(s) that motivated their enactment; do not produce undesirable side-effects; and are effective and efficient. A default disposition should also be included in order to restore the status quo for the group for which experimental dispositions were implemented.

The definition of transparent criteria and the public character of the evaluation report cannot be interpreted as a way of strictly binding legislators and regulators to the obtained results. Legislators retain a margin of appreciation to decide on the enactment of an experimental law

[121] Besluit van 8 december 1998, houdende regels ter stroomlijning van de opzet van milieusubsidies (Besluit milieusubsidies), Stb. 1998, 720, as amended 25 June 2009, Stb. 2009, 267.

and on its conversion into a permanent legislation. However, whenever legislators and regulators decide to deviate from the evidence produced, they should be under an enhanced duty to justify their choice. This point of view is inspired by the position adopted by the US Court of Appeals of the District of Columbia in *Public Service Commission for the State of New York* v. *Federal Power Commission*.[122] The court found that the federal agency in question did not perform a meaningful review of the results obtained in the context of the experimental regulation, and did not present solid evidence to diverge from the evidence obtained. In conclusion, if the objective determined by the legislator is attained by an experimental regulation introducing novel and apparently 'better' rules in the legal order, the legislators or regulators in charge of the 'follow-up' decision must have strong arguments to justify the rejection of the truth of the facts. A valid argument, for example, could be the inefficiency of the new (experimental) regulation.

In *Public Service Commission for the State of New York* v. *Federal Power Commission*, the US Court of Appeals of the District of Columbia criticized the administrative agency for not having engaged in a meaningful review, analysis and evaluation of the experience obtained in the experiment on advance payments. The court found that 'the data provided by the Commission as a justification of its repeated extensions of the advance payments program [provided] an inadequate basis from which to determine whether its justifying objectives are being satisfactorily met at an acceptable level of ultimate economic cost of the nation's gas consumers'. The court remanded the case for 'further evidence and consideration by the Federal Power Commission'.

3.7 CONCLUSION

The principle of separation of powers is not necessarily at odds with sunset clauses and experimental legislation. In fact, the first legislative instrument can even contribute to the advancement of this principle, by guaranteeing a periodic legislative oversight. In the case of experimental legislation, the principle of separation of powers and legality, as its corollary, here provide an important limit to its enactment.

The legality framework sketched in this chapter ensures that the legislator remains the 'master of the experiment' and the executive is clearly aware of the main 'rules of the game'. The framework developed

---

[122] *Public Services Commission for the State of New York* v. *Federal Power Commission*, 167 U.S. App. D.C. 100, 511 F.2d 338 (1974).

in this chapter attempts to find the balance between the legality and delegation aspects and the need to adapt constitutionalism to the fast-changing administrative state[123] we live in. As mentioned in the German literature, this might even require a relativization of the reservation of parliamentary law (*Relativierung des Parlamentsvorbehalts*),[124] but it should not prevent Parliament from assuming its responsibility for legislation on decisive subjects. It was therefore suggested in this chapter that the legislator should always define the 'essential elements' of any experiment, including the goals, direction, extent, evaluation criteria and terms of the follow-up decision.

A clear legal framework may not, however, suffice if the legislative instruments under analysis are still regarded as threats to other fundamental principles. Part II will provide us with a clearer insight into what constitutional sunsets and experimental regulations are or should be.

---

[123] E.L. Rubin, 'Law and Legislation in the Administrative State' (1989) 89 *Colum. L. Rev.* 369.

[124] Staupe, *Parlamentsvorbehalt und Delegationsbefugnis*, n. 41 above, 149.

PART II

Legal framework

Seen with the naked eye, the idea of a statute or regulation including a sunset clause that determines its expiration after a fixed period or allows its renewal depending on the results of an evaluation may cause a certain 'legal discomfort'. A 'worse case' scenario lurks behind the door: an experimental regulation, which derogates from an existing statute, and is only applicable to a small group of citizens. At first sight, these legislative instruments appear to challenge a number of fundamental principles. However, appearances are often misleading. In this second part of the book, it will be examined whether the principles of legal certainty, equal treatment and proportionality seriously constrain the enactment of sunset clauses and experimental legislation, or whether they 'shape' and provide guidance to these legislative instruments.

4. The principle of legal certainty

Law must be stable and yet it cannot stand still.

Roscoe Pound[1]

4.1 MEANING AND DIMENSIONS OF LEGAL CERTAINTY

Over the years, legislators have tried to deliver a perception of legal certainty as a synonym of continuity, determinacy and, above all, predictability. The legal relevance of legal certainty can be inferred from the principles that make up the rule of law, notably 'the capacity of legal rules, standards, or principles to guide people in the conduct of their affairs', 'efficacy' and 'stability'.[2] Legal certainty has been pursued by avoiding *ex post facto* laws; respecting acquired rights; adopting permanent laws; and seeking textual clarity and intelligibility. Lasting laws meant 'to govern perpetually' have been regarded as the standard or the 'normal' form of legislation.[3] The attachment to the symbolic value of legislation and its continuity is particularly strong in civil law countries. However, does it still make sense in a complex and unstable world of constant change? Do we want to live in a system obsessed with stability meaning that laws should endure while reality changes? Or in a system where stability stems from the consent of the governed,[4] freely given by those who see and support laws which reflect the current reality? And what happens when the reality is so uncertain that legislators cannot offer

---

[1] Roscoe Pound, *Interpretations of Legal History* (Cambridge University Press, 1923) I.

[2] Richard H. Fallon, Jr, 'The Rule of Law as a Concept in Constitutional Discourse' (1997) 97 *Columbia Law Review* 1.

[3] Frank Fagan, 'After the Sunset: The Residual Effect of Temporary Legislation' (2011) *European Journal of Law and Economics* (online), 2 February 2011.

[4] Diane P. Wood, 'The Rule of Law in Times of Stress'(2003) 70 *University of Chicago Law Review* 455, 468.

more than temporary rules? Can the disease of legal uncertainty be treated with controlled 'doses' of its own venom?

This chapter starts with a quotation from Roscoe Pound: a pragmatist, a scholar who believed that 'law was made up of adjustments or compromises'.[5] Pragmatists do not content themselves with static legal certainty. Instead, they adopt a casuistic approach to law and seek a balance between conflicting societal interests. What does this pragmatic adaptability mean for law? Is this perspective compatible with the rule of law? Are sunset clauses and experimental legislation the right instruments to give voice to a dynamic perspective of legal certainty?

The first step towards the analysis of the influence of the principle of legal certainty on the enactment of sunset clauses and experimental legislation is the study of the diverse dimensions of this principle and its foundation in the *Rechtsstaat* or the rule of law.

4.1.1 Different Forms and Dimensions of 'Legal Certainty'

In civil law countries, the principle of legal certainty has been traditionally associated with the ideas of durability, continuity and stability of law, and, therefore, regarded as a shield against legal surprises and a synonym of the calculability of law.[6] Nowadays, the principle of legal certainty cannot be reduced to the continuity of laws. Rather, it goes beyond this perception since it has been interpreted by the Dutch and German literature as a 'multidimensional' concept,[7] a true polyhedron which cannot be reduced to the continuity aspect. In addition, it has also been argued that legal certainty can only be achieved by discontinuing laws or introducing legal change.[8] For the purposes of this study on sunset

---

[5] A. Miller, *Toward Increased Judicial Activitism: The Political Role of the Supreme Court* (Greenwood Press, 1982) 39. Beau James Brock and Antonin Scalia, 'A Renaissance of Positivism and Predictability in Constitutional Adjudication' (1991) 51(3) *Louisiana Law Review* 623, 628.

[6] Wilhelm Herschel, 'Rechtssicherheit und Rechtsklarheit' (1967) 23/24 *Juristenzeitung* 728; Jörg Lücke, *Vorläufige Staatsakte, Auslegung, Rechtsfortbildung und Verfassung am Beispiel vorläufiger Gesetze, Urteile, Beschlüsse und Verwaltungsakte* (Mohr Siebeck, 1991) 352.

[7] See H.A. Oldenziel, *Wetgeving en rechtszekerheid: een onderzoek naar de bijdrage van het legaliteitsvereiste aan de rechtszekerheid van de burger* (Kluwer, 1998); Lücke, *Vorläufige Staatsakte, Auslegung, Rechtsfortbildung und Verfassung am Beispiel vorläufiger Gesetze,* , n. 6 above, 352; Paul E. Loving, 'The Justice of Certainty' (1994) 73 *Oregon Law Review* 746.

[8] See Patricia Popelier, *Rechtszekerheid als beginsel van behoorlijke wetgeving* (Intersentia, 1997).

clauses and experimental legislation, the most relevant dimensions of legal certainty to be analyzed are stability (or continuity), reliance or security of expectations and predictability, in other words, material legal certainty, rather than formal legal certainty.

In the United States, legal certainty also means predictability and consistency but it plays a different role than in civil law countries. It is a principle that assumes particular importance in the context of private law as a guarantee for business activity and the calculation of legal risks.[9] Here, legal certainty is not immediately associated with the continuity of legislation. However, doctrinal stability may matter in deciding legal cases since parties might rely on existing doctrine and laws to plan their affairs. Reliance more than continuity at all cost is an important dimension of legal certainty that should not be disregarded when analyzing the principle of legal certainty. In the United States, (legal) certainty is 'near the top rung in the hierarchy of law's social values'; however, legal certainty does not have the same meaning there as in Europe, where it can even be qualified as a general principle of European Union law.[10] In the United States, Americans 'are resigned to a high level of legal indeterminacy [meaning] that the law does not always determine the answer to a legal question'.[11] Legal certainty in the sense of determinacy requires notably that laws should be definite, intelligible and clear so that those subject to the law know by which rules they must abide.[12] The continuity of laws will in principle contribute to this goal of determinacy, but the latter is broader and includes the foreseeability of judicial decisions, limitation of retroactivity, and use of precise language. In the three countries under analysis, a certain degree of continuity of laws will be expected. In Germany and in the Netherlands, this expectation will be higher and refer to the possibility of identifying legal results

---

9 Diane Lourdes Dick, 'Legal Ethics, Commercial Practice, and the Certainty Imperative: A Cautionary Note' (2013) 40 *Northern Kentucky Law Review* 279; Shawn J. Bayern, 'Against Certainty' (2012) 41 *Hofstra Law Review* 53.

10 For a thorough analysis of the principle of legal certainty in the case law of the European Court of Justice, see Juha Raitio, *The Principle of Legal Certainty in EC Law* (Kluwer Academic Publishers, 2003).

11 James R. Maxeiner, 'Legal Certainty: A European Alternative to American Legal Indeterminacy?' (2006) 15 *Tulane Journal of International and Comparative Law* 541.

12 Takis Tridimas, *The General Principles of EU Law* (Oxford University Press, 2006); James R. Maxeiner, 'Legal Certainty: A European Alternative to American Legal Indeterminacy?' (2006) 15 *Tulane Journal of International and Comparative Law* 541, 549.

and decision-makers, and predicting the application of rules in the context of judicial and administrative decisions.[13]

In Europe, legal certainty is both a principle of good lawmaking[14] and a principle of good public administration.[15] As a principle of good lawmaking, two dimensions can be distinguished: material and formal legal certainty. The former relates to the revision of legal rules and decisions and the limitation of (disadvantageous) retroactive decisions (material legal certainty). Formal legal certainty refers to the doctrine of vagueness: laws must be accessible, intelligible and clear since lack of textual certainty may open the door to discretionary enforcement. As a principle of good administration, legal certainty means that citizens should be able to foresee the results of their acts and feel safeguarded against arbitrary decisions. A full understanding of legal certainty implies an interaction between both levels, since, as Oldenziel explains, the principle of legal certainty holds that the citizen should be able to know her legal position and rights attached not (only) in abstract but especially when placed in a specific situation.[16]

As formulated by the German Constitutional Court, the principle of legal certainty should stand for a guarantee that 'citizens subject to the law will not be disappointed in their trust in the reliability of the legal order by the retroactive alteration of acquired rights'.[17] Should such happen, reference should be made to the limitation of disadvantageous retroactivity of laws and administrative decisions, which assessment depends both in Germany and in the Netherlands on the concrete circumstances of the case.[18]

---

[13] Maxeiner, 'Legal Certainty', n. 11 above, 559–61.

[14] Popelier, *Rechtszekerheid als beginsel van behoorlijke wetgeving*, n. 8 above.

[15] See, for general information, H.F. Pennarts, *Beginselen van behoorlijk bestuur* (Maklu, 2008); A.J.C. de Moor-van Vugt, *Algemene beginselen van behoorlijk bestuur en buitenlandse equivalenten* (W.E.J. Tjeenk Willink, 1987); J. in't Veld, *Beginselen van behoorlijk bestuur* (W.E.J. Tjeenk Wilink, 1985).

[16] H.A. Oldenziel, *Wetgeving en rechtszekerheid: een onderzoek naar de bijdrage van het legaliteitsvereiste aan de rechtszekerheid van de burger* (Kluwer, 1998) 10–16.

[17] German Constitutional Court, 2 BvR 2661/06, 6 July 2010, Abs.81 (non-literal translation of the author): 'Der rechtsunterworfene Bürger soll nicht durch die rückwirkende Beseitigung erworbener Rechte in seinem Vertrauen auf die Verlässichkeit der Rechtsordnung enttäuscht werden'.

[18] R.J.N. Schlössels and S.E. Zijlstra, *Bestuursrecht in de sociale rechtsstaat* (Deel I, Onderwijseditie, Kluwer, 2010) 439–41.

Legal certainty implies predictability but this should not impede law from accommodating 'changed societal conditions'.[19] Lawyers must accept the impossibility and undesirability of achieving absolute stability and predictability. A system (possibly a totalitarian one) where those values are pursued does not abide by a rule of law, but by a rule of foolish men: society evolves, and so do laws. In fact, the German Constitutional Court has pointed out that the legislator, when challenged with the need to regulate new phenomena, should not be constrained by existing and traditional precedents that do not reflect modern society and its common interests. Instead, the legislator should ensure a timely modification of regulations in order to incorporate these changes.[20]

4.1.2 Legal Certainty and the *Rechtsstaat* or the Rule of Law

Legal certainty is a recent principle which can be derived from the rule of law or, in civil law countries, the *Rechtsstaat*.[21] In Germany, legal certainty and the *Rechtsstaatlichkeit* have been conceived as two sides of modern statehood.[22] Throughout the last century, legal certainty has been regarded as a shield against the arbitrariness of public administration.[23] However, there is space for concretization: the rule of law and legal certainty constantly take different forms in concrete situations but their core of predictability remains intangible.[24] In this section, some reflections on this central idea are made in order to understand whether sunset clauses and experimental legislation are compatible with a dynamic concept of legal certainty.

Uncertainty is, in principle, an enemy of the rule of law, particularly nowadays. According to Justice Scalia 'as laws have become more numerous ... we can less and less afford protracted uncertainty regarding

---

[19] Loving, 'The Justice of Certainty', n. 7 above.

[20] German Constitutional Court, 2 BvF 1/01, 24 October 2002, paras 210–16: case on the regulation of geriatric care.

[21] Popelier, *Rechtszekerheid als beginsel van behoorlijke regelgeving*, n. 8 above, 35.

[22] Uwe Volkmann, 'Sicherheit und Risiko als Probleme des Rechtsstaats' (2004) 14 *Juristenzeitung* 696.

[23] Patricia Popelier, 'Five Paradoxes on Legal Certainty and the Lawmaker' (2008) II *Legisprudence* 53.

[24] Popelier, *Rechtszekerheid als beginsel van behoorlijke regelgeving*, n. 8 above, 81–2.

what the law may mean. Predictability, or as Llewellyn put it, "reckonability" is a needful characteristic of any law worthy of the name'.[25] For Scalia, a rule of law is a 'law of rules': predictable rules and not discretionary standards. Experimental legislation implies, however, the formulation of these standards (see Chapter 3) often in the form of goals and the need to treat two groups differently. 'People may not have the patience to understand the nuances of the differences between cases in a discretionary regime', Scalia argues. Does this mean that the rule of law cannot be compatible with a 'law of experimental rules'? Would people be better off with 'bad rules'?

In a comment on Scalia's 'rule of law', David Strauss argues that 'the best rules … are the product of an evolutionary process of trial and error, and they continue to evolve after they have been announced'.[26] What Justice Scalia appears to refuse is that this evolution should be operated by courts, rather than by Congress. In *Carden* v. *Arkoma Associates*, judging a case involving the application of a rule more than 150 years old, Justice Scalia applied the rule, justifying this by stating that 'this decision was not the failure to accommodate the changing realities … but [involves] leaving that to the people's elected representatives'.[27]

Due to the constant changes in society, economy and technology, 'law cannot stand still' and it is up to the legislator to ensure the incorporation of change in the legal order. For the sake of legal certainty, the assimilation of legal change should be clearly justified and its integration should involve as little detriment to other values as possible. This is the legislator's task, so the rule of law could, in theory, be a 'law of sunset and experimental rules', as long as both offer sufficient certainty. Laws are instruments that offer determinability as to the citizens' rights and duties *in concreto*, but this certainty can only endure if laws remain permeable to future possibilities of change.[28] However, the incorporation of these legal changes implies a strict observance of the principle of legal certainty, namely, by granting enough time between the publication of the law and the date on which it comes into force, enacting transitory

---

[25] Antonin Scalia, 'The Rule of Law as a Law of Rules' (1989) 56 *University of Chicago Law Review* 1175.

[26] David A. Strauss, 'On the Origin of Rules (with Apologies to Darwin): A Comment on Antonin Scalia's the Rule of Law as a Law of Rules' (2008) 75 *University of Chicago Law Review* 997.

[27] *Carden* v. *Arkoma Associates*, 110 U.S. 1015, 1022 (1990).

[28] Popelier, *Rechtszekerheid als beginsel van behoorlijke regelgeving*, n. 8 above, 115.

regulations and, when appropriate, awarding a proportional compensation for possible damages.[29]

Legal certainty should not be a goal in itself. Legal certainty seeks fairness in the application of law, which also means that it accepts that a better law should replace an old one. The rule of law implies the existence of fixed and prospective rules, in other words, rules that guide individuals and governmental conduct so that planning and foreseeability are possible. Temporary rules as such do not seem to be contrary to the principle of legal certainty and the *Rechtsstaat* or the rule of law. Should these temporary rules be disadvantageous or in any way onerous for citizens, additional caution must be taken to guarantee that citizens are not 'caught off guard'.

Law should have a minimum of stability but reducing law either to a state of 'absolute stability' or to an 'instrument of change' seems too simplistic.[30] Some level of legal stability is desired since a high mutability of law could endanger the planning benefits that flow from the rule of law.[31] Law has an ambivalent relationship with time: the rule of law must have enough stability and be set 'beyond the ravages of time' but, in order for law to rule, 'it must be responsive and indeterminate, capable of extending to the infinite variety that confronts it'.[32] Briefly, the rule of law 'must be saturated in temporality', concludes Fitzpatrick. This core of stability does not change the fact that if law is meant to fulfil its function as a supreme instrument of social order, it has to respond to social change and adapt to it.[33] For example, while constitutional dispositions safeguarding the inalienable right to vote should be left unchanged, the regulation of the different forms of voting, like e-voting, should be frequently adapted to the evolution of technology.

As Hart describes, legal systems must find the middle ground between the need for certain rules, which can be safely applied by private individuals, and 'the need to leave open for later settlements by an informed, official choice, issues which can only be properly appreciated

---

29 *Ibid.* 116.

30 François Ost, 'L'instantané ou l'institué? L'institué ou l'instituant? Le Droit a-t-il pour vocation de durer?' in F. Ost and M. Van Hoecke (eds), *Temps et Droit* (Bruylant, 1998) 14.

31 Katie R. Eyer, 'Administrative Adjudication and the Rule of Law' (2008) 60 *Administrative Law Review* 647, 666.

32 Peter Fitzpatrick, 'Law in the Antinomy of Time: A Miscellany' in François Ost and M. Van Hoecke (eds), *Temps et Droit* (Bruylant, 1998) 185.

33 Wolfgang Gaston Friedman, *Law in a Changing Society* (University of California Press, 1959) ix.

and settled when they arise in a concrete case'.[34] This shows the difference between evolving from general and abstract legal statements, which are meant to last; and specific rulings which, as Stefano Bertea explains, 'are bound to remain out of reach [because] we will not know them in advance even within legal settings shaped by the principle of legal certainty'.[35]

Rigid laws and excessive normative certainty can result in uncertainty at the concrete level; therefore, a better alternative includes providing law with a reasonable amount of flexibility that guarantees that laws can adapt, in concrete, to changing circumstances, while still guaranteeing, in abstract, the predictability and foreseeability of law. As Patricia Popelier underlines, these are exactly the dimensions which might call for adjustments and provide room for innovation.[36] Finding the balance between the required flexibility for innovation and legal certainty was precisely one of the challenges discussed in Chapter 1.

In conclusion, the principle of legal certainty cannot be reduced to imperatives of mere continuity or stability of law; rather, it is a multidimensional concept that gains its significance when perceived *in concreto*. This multidimensional concept of legal certainty appears to leave the door open for the enactment of flexible legislative instruments that respond to changing circumstances and allow progressive and experimental legal innovations to enter the legal order. The following sections examine the relationship between the principle of legal certainty and sunset clauses and experimental legislation: are these legislative instruments and this principle 'friends' or 'foes'?

4.2 LEGAL CERTAINTY AND SUNSET CLAUSES

4.2.1 A 'Foe' to Legal Certainty

Sunset clauses determine the periodic termination of laws. At first sight, this might sound contrary to the minimum stability level required by a sound investment strategy. To wit, entrepreneurs base their investment decisions on legislation that will in principle be extinguished within a limited number of years, but can only expect to recover their investments

---

[34] Herbert Hart, *The Concept of Law* (Oxford University Press, 1961).

[35] Stefano Bertea, 'Towards a New Paradigm of Legal Certainty' (2008) II *Legisprudence* 25, 37.

[36] Popelier, 'Five Paradoxes on Legal Certainty and the Lawmaker', n. 23 above, 53–4.

over a long time span. According to Max Weber, legal certainty is fundamental to capitalism since without legal security the investment of capital will be reduced.[37] A capitalist system requires predictable and calculable laws, but these are not a synonym of absolute stability. Uncertain rules have the perverse effect of leaving private actors unsure about their rights and duties while affording unconstrained discretion to official decision-makers.[38]

In the United States, it has also been inquired whether the employment of sunset clauses can produce a negative effect on investment policies. Nevertheless, this will particularly occur when legislators establish sunset periods which do not take into consideration the development cycles of the regulated sector.[39] This was the case of the production tax credits which were designed to stimulate investment in renewable energy and hence advance clean energy innovation. These tax credits were subject to a sunset, which could be renewed for the period of one to three years. However, it takes three to seven years to develop a wind farm, which produced a feeling of uncertainty regarding the renewal of the tax credit that slowed down long-term investment.[40] Nonetheless, other scholars in the United States have argued that sunset clauses as such are not harmful for investment and they may even stimulate long-term investment.[41] In the cases involving taxes, a sunset may accelerate investment because taxpayers might fear losing tax benefits. Reluctance to invest in these cases is not unexpected. However, 'a calculable legal system' as desired by entrepreneurs, does not necessarily mean that private actors expect that legal systems will solely be inhabited by lasting, clear and unambiguous bright-line rules.[42] There is a discrepancy between the certainty pursued by lawyers, and the one pursued by economic parties. The latter are mainly interested in the certainty regarding their contractual

---

37 Max Weber, *Economy and Society* (University of California Press, 1978) 883.

38 Anthony D'Amato, 'Legal Uncertainty' (1983) 71(1) *California Law Review* 3.

39 Erin Dewey, 'Sundown and You Better Take Care: Why Sunset Provisions Harm the Renewable Energy Industry and Violate Tax Principles' (2011) 52 *Boston College Law Review* 1105.

40 *Ibid.*

41 George K. Yin, 'Temporary-effect Legislation, Political Accountability, and Fiscal Restraint' (2008) 84 *New York University Law Review* 174.

42 Offer Raban, 'The Fallacy of Legal Certainty: Why Vague Legal Standards may be Better for Capitalism and Liberalism' (2010) 19(2) *Public Interest Law Journal* 182–3.

rights and duties – the consequences of their actions.[43] Lawyers, on the contrary, identify legal certainty with the predictability of applying legal rules to specific cases. While lawyers may prefer clear, precise and determinate legal rules; entrepreneurs might often be satisfied with broad legal standards as long as they can allow them to calculate the consequences of their actions.[44]

As explained in Chapter 2, sunset clauses have been employed in recent years in Germany as a tool to reduce regulatory pressure and indirectly create better conditions for investment. However, these legislative instruments do not abound in this country. In Germany, the proposal of general sunset clauses,[45] in other words, clauses that determine that a set of acts or regulations will be extinguished, raised a number of legal questions in different states. The literature has questioned whether a temporal limitation of all laws and regulations would not weaken the exercise of the central functions of the state, such as the safeguarding of freedom and state authority.[46] This is nevertheless a criticism strongly focused on the introduction of a general sunset clause, which can indeed pose a threat to the continuity of law. All-embracing sunset clauses have not been introduced at the federal level in Germany. In the United States, a seven-year sunset rule was proposed in 1995 for agencies, but never saw the light.[47] In the Netherlands, the introduction of general sunset clauses for all new regulations was suggested in the political context, but this proposal did not gather sufficient consensus either.[48]

---

43 *Ibid.* 189–90.

44 *Ibid.* 190.

45 Sunset clauses determine the extinction of a specific statute or a number of its dispositions. 'General sunset clauses' impose the extinction of a large number of statutes or regulations.

46 Peter Zimmermann, 'Reform der Staatstätigkeit durch generelle Befristung von Gesetzen – Aspekte einer Problembewältigung mit verfassungswidrigen Mitteln' (2003) 22 *Die öffentliche Verwaltung* 943. For a more extensive analysis of this objection, see Sofia Ranchordás, 'Sunset Clauses and Experimental Legislation: Blessing or Curse for Legal Certainty' (2014) *Statute Law Review* (online), 11 February 2014 doi:10.1093/slr/hmu002.

47 Congressional Quarterly CQ Almanac, Vol. LI, 1995, 3–7; Chris Edwards, '"Sunsetting" to Reform and Abolish Federal Agencies' (2002) 6 *Cato Institute Tax and Budget Bulletin*, available at www.cato.org/sites/cato.org/files/pubs/pdf/tbb-0205-6.pdf.

48 See Advies van de Raad van Economische Adviseurs, 'De wetten en de regels die drooom en daad verstoren. Bureaucratisering en overregulering', Kamerstukken II 2004–2005, 30 123, no. 2. Arguing that a general sunset clause

General sunset clauses, as opposed to specific sunset provisions, can cause uncertainty and produce a negative influence on investment since they are indiscriminately enacted in the legal order. As explained in Chapter 2, sunset clauses serve multiple functions, but this does not mean that all laws can be rendered temporary. Instead, the duration of the law should be adapted to the reality that the latter intends to regulate. Still, in the United States, (regular) sunset clauses have been criticized for creating uncertainty in the legislative process; these provisions impede private actors from predicting and arranging their financial affairs since they often do not know when provisions will sunset.[49] These effects are particularly visible in tax legislation. This uncertainty does not result from sunset clauses as such, but can be explained by other factors that may affect the predictability of these rules. This is the case of the pressure exercised by lobbies and interest groups who may play a role in the successive renewals or sudden termination of sunset clauses (see Chapter 7).[50]

4.2.2 A 'Friend' to Legal Certainty

Some elements of the literature in the three countries under analysis have been sceptical as to the broad enactment of sunset clauses and their impact on legal certainty. Is this scepticism justified? The arguments of the advocates of sunset clauses can be reduced to two main points of view: first, under uncertain conditions sunset clauses may provide more legal certainty than permanent legislation; secondly, sunset clauses constitute an instrument to tackle legal uncertainty caused either by the unknown effects of a new regulation or by changed circumstances or new information.

---

would be counter-productive, Ph. Eijlander and R.A.J. Van Gestel, *Horizonwetgeving: effectief middel in de strijd tegen toenemende regeldruk?* (Ministerie van Binnenlandse Zaken, 2006), available at www.portill.nl/articles/Eijlander/Horizonwetgeving.pdf.

[49] Manoj Viswanathan, 'Sunset Provisions in the Tax Code: A Critical Evaluation and Prescriptions for the Future' (2011) 8 (2) *New York University Law Review* 657, 671–2.

[50] For a critical perspective on sunset clauses in tax legislation, see Rebecca M. Kysar, 'Lasting Legislation' (2011) 159 *University of Pennsylvania Law Review* 101.

(a) Sunset clauses as a source of certainty

In Germany, Chanos argued that the alleged uncertainty caused by sunset clauses is merely potential, since sunset clauses do not introduce more uncertainty in the legal order than permanent legislation does.[51] It is often forgotten that the legislator can at any time introduce changes, revise or extinguish permanent laws. Although these revisions imply sufficient political consensus and are submitted to democratic control, citizens are not in principle given any guarantees that permanent legislation will not be revised to fit the wishes of a new majority in Parliament. This argument is even acknowledged by sceptics of sunset clauses in the United States who agree that 'permanent legislation [merely] creates a certainty illusion, whereby taxpayers are not mindful of the frequent changes of legislation'.[52] Moreover, citizens are normally not previously warned about the intention of the legislator to revise laws, and this 'surprise effect' can in abstract interfere with the principle of legal certainty.

The German literature has clearly underlined that laws containing a sunset clause will in principle not be changed before the sunset date. Any changes or revisions should only be accepted on extraordinary grounds and should only occur when required by the public interest.[53] These temporary legislative instruments contain a certain continuity guarantee, thus any change or a possible extinction before the set deadline should be categorically refused.[54] Sunset clauses provide citizens with a time framework on which they can rely.[55] In Germany, this framework refers normally to a period of five years, so during this time-span citizens are provided with some certainty as to the inalterability of their rights and duties.[56] In this light, the principle of legal certainty would not be put at stake by sunset clauses, but instead it could function as an impediment to

---

[51] Antonis Chanos, *Möglichkeiten und Grenzen der Befristung parlamentarischer Gesetzgebung*, (Duncker and Humblot, 1999) 71.

[52] Dewey, 'Sundown and You Better Take Care', n. 39 above.

[53] Jan Funke, *Bürokratieabbau mit Hilfe zeitlich befristeter Gesetze: zu den Erfolgsbedingungen der Sunset-Gesetzgebung* (AVM, 2011).

[54] Chanos, *Möglichkeiten und Grenzen der Befristung parlamentarischer Gesetzgebung*, n. 51 above, 71.

[55] *Ibid.* 71.

[56] Alexander Tot, *Befristung von Gesetzen*, Seminar Moderne Rechtsetzung, Speyer, DHV, available at www.dhv-speyer.de/HILL/Lehrangebot/Wintersemester-2005/Moderne_Rechtsetzung/Referate/Tot,%20Alexander/Seminararbeit.pdf.

abrupt and unjustified changes before the sunset occurs. In the Netherlands, this perception of sunset clauses has not been extensively developed, but it appears to be accepted in the literature that this sunset period should in principle be respected.[57]

The argument that sunset clauses can provide for more legal certainty than regular legislation has also been supported by research. In an empirical study conducted by the Bertelsmann Stiftung, it was underlined that sunset clauses are adequate to fulfil the policy goal of providing for 'more legal flexibility'. These provisions can notably be introduced, first, in regulations with uncertain effects, namely, in the context of new or risky policy areas; or secondly, to take account of changes in relevant circumstances.[58] In these scenarios, the employment of sunset clauses help to tackle uncertainty.

(b) Sunset clauses can tackle uncertainty

Legal certainty is often presented as a synonym of continuity of lasting legislation due to the belief that law tends towards greater certainty.[59] However, as time goes by, the effectiveness of a rule may diminish due to the evolution of social circumstances; the discovery of new elements or information; the emergence of new complex conducts; or the consequent creation of room for novel legal disputes that were not originally comprehended by its scope. In addition, the deterrent effect of rules may equally diminish as potential litigants discover ways to readjust their conduct in order to avoid the application of this specific rule.[60] This increasing reduction of the effectiveness of rules constitutes a ground for claiming the need for legislative change. Supported by Calabresi, D'Amato suggests that a (judicial) sunsetting of statutes comparable to the amendment of precedents performed by courts would increase legal certainty and ensure that legislation is updated.[61] Hence, the need to take into account a change in circumstances can be regarded as a ground for admitting or even imposing a periodic revision of legislation: laws that are disconnected from the real world cannot provide for effective legal

---

57 Eijlander and Van Gestel, *Horizonwetgeving: effectief middle in de strijd tegen toenemende regeldruk?*, n. 48 above.

58 Bertelsmann Stiftung, *Sunset Legislation and Better Regulation: Empirical Evidence from Four Countries* (Bertelsmann Stiftung, 2010) 21.

59 This is the case of Ronald Dworkin, *Taking Rights Seriously* (Harvard University Press, 1977) 286.

60 Anthony D'Amato, 'Legal Uncertainty' (1983) 71(1) *California Law Review* 1.

61 *Ibid.* 47.

protection and, though they might be stable, they do not allow citizens to predict their rights and duties.

The fact that legislators revise rules, drawing benefits such as a tax exemption so as to ensure that new relevant circumstances are taken into account, is not contrary to the principle of legal certainty. This was notably ruled by the European Court of Justice (CJEU) in the *Plantanol*[62] case:

> In the context of Directive 2003/30 on the promotion of the use of biofuels or other renewable fuels for transport, it is not, in principle, contrary to the general principles of legal certainty and the protection of legitimate expectations for a Member State, with regard to a product composed of a blend of vegetable oil, fossil gas oil and specific additives, to withdraw, before the expiry date initially laid down in the national rules, the tax exemption scheme which applied to that product. In any event, such a withdrawal does not require the presence of exceptional circumstances. However, it is for the national court to consider, in the context of an overall assessment in the specific case, whether those principles have been observed by taking account of all relevant circumstances.

The CJEU affirmed that 'the principle of legal certainty does not prohibit legislative amendment, imposing rather, that the legislator takes account of the particular situations of traders and provides, where appropriate, adaptations to the application of the new legal rules'. In this case, the German law under analysis (Law on Taxation of Energy, article 50(1)(1)) did not include a sunset clause. In any case, should legislators be able to foresee a rapid change of circumstances, the introduction of this provision (or alternatively a review clause) can give a sign to private actors that laws and regulations might need to be terminated or reviewed. If the CJEU admitted that amending a law to fit the circumstances does not violate the principle of legal certainty, then 'announcing' that this amendment might take place within two or three years will not either. Sunset clauses may even ensure that legislators will proceed to a reconsideration of all relevant circumstances.

Sunset clauses may be equally important when the effects of a new regulation are unknown, requiring their evaluation as more information as to the regulation's effectiveness is gathered. Such uncertainty can be found in socially or ethically controversial laws or regulations. The evaluation criteria used here should be focused on the assessment of the

---

[62] *Plantanol GmbH and Co. KG* v. *Hauptzollamt Darmstadt*, Case C-201/08, Judgment of the Court (Third Chamber), 10 September 2009 [2009] ECR I-08343.

effects and side-effects of the regulation in question. In addition, uncertainty has been suggested as a ground or a justification for the use of sunset clauses.[63] This legislative strategy to guarantee the enactment of policies characterized by risk and uncertainty is, for example, visible in the German and US federal anti-terrorism laws mentioned earlier (see Chapter 2). The choice of sunset clauses was partially based on the uncertainty regarding the duration of the high terrorist threat.

In addition, the introduction of sunset clauses in controversial and uncertain laws, followed by an adequate evaluation, can increase their social acceptance because it reveals that regulators are willing to compromise and are open to review of regulations should these produce undesirable effects.[64]

In conclusion, sunset clauses do not endanger the principle of legal certainty, instead this legislative instrument can be a valuable tool to enable legal changes; to provide temporary (legal) certainty; and to respond to situations characterized by acute uncertainty, risks, lack of information and decreasing effectiveness of rules.

4.3 LEGAL CERTAINTY AND EXPERIMENTAL LEGISLATION

While sunset clauses can conflict with a static perception of legal certainty interpreted as a synonym of continuity, experimental legislation poses an augmented challenge. First, termination is not the only possible destiny of experimental regulations: these may be terminated at the end of the period determined beforehand; extended to a larger part of the territory or group; or converted into a permanent law. Secondly, legal uncertainty can equally result from the lack of clarity or determinativeness of the objectives and implementation of experimental rules. Similarly to sunset clauses, experimental laws and regulations can be regarded as 'friends' or 'foes' to the principle of legal certainty.

---

[63] See Frans Jan Douglas and Tessa van den Berg (ZENC, study commissioned by ACTAL), *Horizonwetgeving Dichterbij: onderzoek naar horizonwetgeving en regeldrukvermindering voor bedrijven* (ZENC, 2010).

[64] Funke, *Bürokratieabbau mit Hilfe zeitlich befristeter Gesetze*, n. 53 above, 57.

4.3.1 Experimental Legislation: A 'Foe' to Legal Certainty

The Dutch Council of State has expressed on numerous occasions its apprehension as to a potential tension between experimental legislation and the principle of legal certainty.[65] This institution has not been the only one to do so. In the context of parliamentary discussions, there has equally been reference to the risk of uncertainty arising from experimental regulations.[66] In Germany, the use of experimental legislation has also been criticized and there have been voices in the literature calling for a return to the traditional paradigms of continuity and constancy of law for the sake of the protection of the principle of legal certainty.[67] This was the case with Walter Leisner, who in the 1980s called for a reinforcement of the '*Zukunftssicherheit der Gesetze*' (the future certainty of laws), which should include a prohibition on experimenting with legislation and the enactment of temporary laws.[68] Although the European Union does not play a central role in this study, the scepticism of the jurisdictions under analysis may also be visible in EU policy and rulemaking documents. Example 4.1 on the experimental Directive on VAT rates on labour-intensive services illustrates the potential uncertainty caused by the enactment of experimental rules and their impact on citizens.

---

[65] An example of this objection was the Opinion of the Council of State of 8 June 2009, No. W13.09.0098/I, Voorstel van wet tot wijzing van de Drank- en Horecawet met het oog op de terugdringing van het alcoholgebruik onder met name jongeren, de voorkoming van alcoholgerelateerde verstoring van de openbare orde, almede ter reductie van de administratieve lasten.

[66] This is the case of the discussion of the 1998 Telecommunications Law in the Dutch Senate, see Eerste Kamer, Telecommunicatiewet, Wet van 19 oktober 1998, Toelichting op artikel 18.1 lid (Kamerstuk 25 533, no. 3, blz. 135). It is explicitly affirmed that legal certainty should be taken into account when enacting experimental laws/regulations which derogate from the existing regime.

[67] See Walter Leisner, 'Gesetz wird Unsinn ... Grenzen der Sozialgestaltung im Gesetzesstaat' (1981) *Deutsches Verwaltungsblatt* 849. See also Walter Leisner, *Staatsrenaissance. Die Wiederkehr der guten Staatsformen* (Duncker and Humblot, 1987).

[68] Leisner, 'Gesetz wird Unsinn ...', n. 67 above, 855.

EXAMPLE 4.1 EXPERIMENTAL REDUCED VAT RATES

In the EU context, the relationship between experimental legislation and the principle of legal certainty has not always been peaceful. It has been claimed that the uncertainty inherent to experimental legislation can produce negative effects on private actors who may decide to delay investment decisions until the permanent law is enacted. For example, in the EU experiment with reduced VAT rates on labour-intensive services, in the Dutch evaluation report it was stated that the lack of impact of the reduced rate on consumer prices was partially explained by the 'uncertainty as to whether the measure would be made permanent (35%)'.

The uncertainty allegedly caused by experimental legislation does not produce the same impact on entrepreneurs who are in principle endowed with better means of making prognoses regarding future legislative changes and complying with them. The average citizen might find exposure to temporal laws inconvenient; however, an experimental law or regulation does not expose her to a 'bare uncertainty' concerning future legislative developments. This argument was put forward (and accepted) by a German county (Landkreis) before the Berliner Gerichte für Arbeitssachen in a case involving an experimental clause (see example 4.2).[69]

EXAMPLE 4.2 EXPERIMENTAL CLAUSES AND 'BARE UNCERTAINTY'

In this case, the parties were disputing the effectiveness of the provisional employment contract of the petitioner. The influence of an experimental clause on the duration of the labour contract was one of the main legal issues under analysis. This experimental clause was incorporated in section 6a SBG II which

[69] LAG Berlin-Brandenburg, *Berliner Gerichte für Arbeitssachen*, Judgment of 25 August 2011, 14 Sa 977/11, BeckRS 2012, 70177.

conferred on municipalities, on an experimental basis, the competence to grant unemployment benefits. This power used to pertain to employment agencies. The experimental period was six years and it imposed a restructuring of the services of the defendant (the Landkreis). The court decided that when the petitioner signed her labour contract, she was not exposed to 'bare uncertainty' regarding the termination of her contract in 2010 (sunset of the experimental clause). The Berlin court pointed out that at the time of the signature of the labour contract, it was unclear what the legislator would do at the end of the experiment. Therefore, the petitioner could not count on an extension of her contract beyond the experimental period, because the results of the experiment were not then known. Should the defendant be given the competence to grant employment benefits, it would be required to maintain the current number of employees, otherwise some of them would have to be dismissed.

In the case described in example 4.2, the defendant argued that the enactment of an experimental regulation introducing alternatives to the existing rules on the reintegration of job-seekers should be regarded as an appropriate technique for gaining experience and knowledge, which being clearly limited to a five-year period does not expose the citizen to 'bare uncertainty'.[70] The employment of experimental clauses was not criticized by the Berlin court.

The argument that private actors might be hesitant to invest due to the lack of trust generated by experimental legislation has not been sufficiently proven and remains at the theoretical level. Entrepreneurs do not expect to encounter absolute certainty: uncertainty is 'part of the innovative business' and is inherent to doing business. Under uncertain circumstances and constant changes caused by rapid technological developments, sunset clauses and experimental regulations may be regarded as regulatory options that grant the greatest 'planning certainty' to private actors. This has been argued in Germany in the context of the regulation of access networks in the field of telecommunications.[71] In this

---

[70] *Ibid.*

[71] Christian Kirchner and Thorsten Käseberg, '§9a Neue Märkte' in Klaus-Dieter Scheurle and Thomas Mayen (eds), *Telekommunikationsgesetz: Kommentar* (C.H. Beck, 2008) 123, 125.

context, experimental regulations can be regarded as 'a friend' rather than a 'foe' to legal certainty.

4.3.2 Experimental Legislation: A 'Friend' to Legal Certainty

Although it has never been claimed in the literature that experimental legislation should be regarded as a companion to legal certainty, there appear to be numerous arguments in favour of the view that there is at least no general incompatibility between them. First, experimental regulations will not violate the principle of legal certainty as long the *Bestimmtheitsgebot* (imperative of determinacy) and legality dimensions are respected; and the contents, objective and scope of regulatory experiments are as precisely and extensively defined as possible.[72] The *Bestimmtheitsgebot* demands that citizens are aware of the goal to be achieved with experiments and the direction that these experiments will take.[73] Should these requirements be fulfilled, then the principle of legal certainty will not be endangered, even when undetermined concepts are employed. According to the German Constitutional Court, the use of these legal concepts may be necessary to facilitate 'flexible legislative reactions to changing social circumstances and to possible evasion tendencies'.[74] The adoption of experimental dispositions in Germany to enable the 'advancement of the local self-government' ('*Weiterentwicklung der kommunalen Selbstverwaltung*') or the implementation of the 'new public management' ('*Neues Steuerungsmodell*') are illustrations of the use of undetermined concepts.[75]

Secondly, the enactment of experimental legislation can also be justified by the imperative to keep up with 'technical advancements and improvements in the modes of communication so that the benefits of new inventions and developments may be made available' to the public.[76] This was acknowledged by the US Court of Appeals (District of Columbia) in

72 Thomas Freund, *Kommunale Standardöffnungs- und Experimentierklauseln im Lichte der Verfassung* (WVB, 2003) 100–101.

73 *Ibid.* 103.

74 German Constitutional Court, 2 BvL 1/57, 12 November 1958, BVerfGE 8,274 (326). See A. Groth, *Kommunalrechtliche Experimentierklauseln,* Kiel: Lorenz-Von-Stein-Institut für Verwaltungswissenschaftem an der Christian-Albrechts-Universität zu Kiel, 2005, Arbeitspapier No. 72, 117.

75 *Ibid.* 120–24.

76 *United Telegraph Workers* v. *Federal Communications Commission*, 141 U.S. App. D.C. 190, 436 F. 2d 920.

1970, which held that considering 'the congressional desire that [administrative agencies] encourage technological innovation' and the relevance of the implementation of experimental regulation for 'informational input that makes such an innovation possible', the court would only strike down an experiment in the presence of 'a compelling showing of legislative prohibition'.[77]

Thirdly, the enactment of experimental laws or regulations containing novel dispositions or new approaches to new social problems can prevent the abrupt introduction of changes in the legal order, hence safeguarding legal certainty. It could be argued that transitory law is originally meant to ensure these legislative transitions. However, experimental legislation can be useful in contexts of uncertainty, when legislators need to gather further information as to the most effective regulation of a new social problem or a technological novelty. Experimental regulations go beyond transitory law, guaranteeing, on the one hand, a subtle transition between 'old' and 'new' rules; and on the other, shaping the content and implementation of the latter, filling the verified knowledge gaps.

In the German literature, experimental laws have been described as 'preliminary' legislative acts that are meant to generate knowledge and experience and by this means reduce the uncertainty connected with the effects of new legal rules.[78] By experimenting and consequently evaluating these new rules, the legislator prepares the legal order for the incorporation of change and creates a solid ground for the enactment of permanent rules.[79] In this context, experimental legislation can be qualified as an evidence-based lawmaking instrument since it submits new legislation to a reality test and assists the generation of new information.[80]

77 *Ibid.*

78 Funke, *Bürokratieabbau mit Hilfe zeitlich befristeter Gesetze*, n. 53 above, 48.

79 *Ibid.*

80 A. Seidman and R.B. Seidman, 'ILTAM: Drafting Evidence-based Legislation for Democratic Social Change' (2009) 89 *Boston University Law Review* 435; R.A.J. Van Gestel and G. Van Dijck, 'Better Regulation through Experimental Legislation' (2011) 17(3) *European Public Law* 539; R.A.J. Van Gestel, 'Evidence-based Lawmaking and the Quality of Legislation: Regulatory Impact Assessments in the European Union and the Netherlands' in H. Schaffer and J. Iliopoulos-Strangas (eds), *State Modernization in Europe* (SIPE, Bruylant, 2007) 139.

In the 2001 *Dangerous Dogs* judgment, the German Constitutional Court adopted a favourable position towards the incorporation of evidence in the lawmaking process,[81] arguing that it was the task of the legislator to support theoretical assumptions on available facts. Since there appeared to be scientific evidence that the dangerousness of dogs did not solely depend on genetic characteristics but also on other elements, legislators should ensure that legislation would be revised in accordance with the acquisition of new information on this subject.

The importance of considering new information and scientific knowledge in lawmaking is particularly important in the regulation of new products and services. The German Constitutional Court acknowledged that in this case experimental legislation could be a particularly valuable instrument to gather information. In a case regarding the regulation of geriatric care, the Karlsruhe court affirmed:

> The experimental clause employed in the law (s. 4 para 6 AltPflG) is necessary because it creates space for temporary testing of integrated and generalist training models with new content and career-related specializations. The results of these pilot projects will be systematically monitored and evaluated in order to come closer to the long-term goal of a single professional field of 'care'.[82]

The introduction of an experimental clause was essential in this context to test integrated forms of education and training in the relatively new field of geriatric care. The German Constitutional Court here regarded experimentation as an uncontroversial form of testing novelties and improving the long-term objective of the law: guaranteeing uniformity in the provision of geriatric care.

Fourthly, a static concept of legal certainty makes little sense in the twenty-first century. In the last decades, the concept of legal certainty has evolved and so has the awareness that in a fast-changing society, laws are unable to keep pace with social and technological developments and

---

[81] German Constitutional Court, 1 BvR 1778/01, 16 april 2004, BVerfGE 110, 141, see paras 72–90.

[82] Translation of the author. See German Constitutional Court, 2 BvF 1/01, 24 October 2002, para. 383. The original text reads: 'Der in das Gesetz aufgenommene Experimentierklausel (§ 4 Abs. 6 AltPflG) ist erforderlich, weil sie Raum schafft zur befristeten Erprobung von integrierten und generalistischen Ausbildungsmodellen mit neuartigen Inhalten und berufsfeldbezogenen Spezialisierugen. Die Ergebnisse dieser Modellvorhaben sollen systematisch beobachtet und ausgewertet werden, um dem langfristigen Ziel eines einheitlichen Berufsfelds "Pflege" näher zu kommen'.

foresee all the phenomena to which they potentially apply.[83] Legal dispositions should be adapted to both social reality and the increasing amount of knowledge gathered on a certain topic. Therefore, legal certainty has to be dynamically interpreted so that laws can remain 'certain' in the light of the available information and the dynamic phenomena they regulate. This dynamism can be guaranteed through the adaptability of a legal system, since the more innovative and adaptable a legal order is, the easier it will be for it to respond to a changing environment and allow private actors to explore new opportunities in the market.[84] In this context, the principle of legal certainty should not be regarded as 'an obstacle in reforming norms', but rather 'as an instrument that consolidates the liberty of the legislator',[85] enabling it to adapt laws to the social reality and the judge to interpret them in conformity with the existing precedent.[86]

4.4 PRINCIPLE OF LEGAL CERTAINTY: PRELIMINARY CONCLUSION

An interpretation of the principle of legal certainty as an obstacle to change does not match a time of complex and constant changes. Legislators cannot guarantee a static perception of laws; citizens do not expect it; and entrepreneurs would see it as a potential hurdle to their investment plans. Laws should instead be permeable to change. This permeability can minimize legislative entrenchment and ensure that lawmaking is more 'future-oriented' and our lawmakers evolve from their

---

[83] Popelier, 'Five Paradoxes on Legal Certainty and the Lawmaker', n. 23 above.

[84] Katharina Pistor, Yoram Keinan, Jan Kleinheisterkamp and Mark D. West, 'Innovation in Corporate Law' (2003) 31 *Journal of Comparative Economics* 676.

[85] Maria Elena Lauroba Lacasa, 'The Principle of Juridical Certainty and the Discontinuity of Law' (2003) 63 *Louisiana Law Review* 1243.

[86] In this chapter, the principle of juridical certainty and the doctrine of *stare decisis* (principle of stability and standard of legislative questions) have not been examined since the study of the possible constraint exerted by the principle of legal certainty on the enactment of sunset clauses and experimental legislation is the main object under analysis, and not the change in interpretation by the judges of existing norms.

role as 'Epimetheus ("the one who reflects after the fact") to Prometheus ("the one who foresees")'.[87]

As long as private actors are able to know their rights and duties in a concrete situation, the temporary certainty granted by a sunset clause or an experimental regulation should be 'certain enough'.

The temporary certainty conferred by sunset clauses and experimental legislation is more meaningful than the illusion of certainty that most permanent laws provide. Furthermore, as the US Court of Appeals (District of Columbia) stated in *Public Service Commission for the State of New York* v. *Federal Power Commission*, an experimental regulation cannot be objectionable merely because it introduces a change of policy, instead 'the legal system does not compel rigidity, or bureaucratic inflexibility, least of all in an area like energy policy where flexibility may be essential in the public interest ... [in fact] it [is] the genius of the administrative process to be flexible in response to observed development' so an agency should 'switch rather than fight the lessons of experience'.[88]

The principle of legal certainty does not prevent the introduction of legal change in the legal order, either by enacting sunset clauses or experimental laws or regulations. The principle of legal certainty will only be endangered if the 'rules of the game' are breached, in other words, laws and regulations may be temporary and/or have an experimental character but private actors must be able to predict their rights and duties and be protected against sudden legislative changes. The lack of a clear legal framework for the enactment of sunset clauses and experimental laws and regulations may be the real foe to the principle of legal certainty (see Chapter 3). Their temporary duration is not.

---

[87] Andrew J. Wistrich, 'The Evolving Temporality of Lawmaking' (2012) 44 *Connecticut Law Review* 737, 825.

[88] *Public Services Commission for the State of New York* v. *Federal Power Commission,* 167 U.S. App. D.C. 100, 511 F.2d 338 (1974).

5. The principle of equal treatment

5.1 INTRODUCTION

As described in Chapter 2, any experiment implies distinguishing between two separate groups: the control and the sample groups. Experimental laws and regulations should share this characteristic with natural science experiments, if their results are intended to be valid. While a differentiation may easily threaten the idea that all citizens should be equal before the law, it is a more complex issue to claim that experimental legislation discriminates against a group of citizens. It is thus important to understand whether sunset clauses, and particularly experimental legislation, can imperil the principle of equal treatment. The first step in this analysis requires a study of the meaning(s) of this principle in light of the literature and case law of the jurisdictions under analysis and, where relevant, the influence of the European Court of Justice (CJEU) and European Court of Human Rights.

5.2 MEANING(S) OF THE PRINCIPLE OF EQUAL TREATMENT

The principle of equal treatment (equal protection or equality) has been described as 'the standard' of the Dutch Constitution.[1] Article 1 imposes the equal treatment of all inhabitants and forbids discrimination on any

[1] Grondwet voor het Koninkrijk der Nederlanden, text as of the version of the Statute of 27 June 2008 (Stb. 272) and Statute of 27 June, 2008 (Stb. 273). Dutch Constitution, art. 1 reads: 'Allen die zich in Nederland bevinden, worden in gelijke gevallen gelijk behandeld. Discriminatie wegens godsdienst, levensovertuiging, politieke gezindheid, ras, geslacht of op welke grond dan ook, is niet toegestaan'. ['All persons in the Netherlands shall be treated equally in equal circumstances. Discrimination on the grounds of religion, belief, political opinion, race or sex or on any other grounds whatsoever shall not be permitted.] P.W.C. Akkermans, C.J. Bax and L.F.M. Verhey, *Grondrechten: grondrechten en grondrechtsbescherming in Nederland* (W.E.J. Tjeenk Willink, 1999) 50: the principle of equal treatment is depicted as the 'standard of the new Constitution'.

subjective ground. This is far from being a specificity of the Netherlands: the principle of equal treatment must be of cardinal importance for any state that wishes to qualify itself as a *Rechtsstaat*.[2] In the United States, the equal protection clause constitutionalized in the Fourteenth Amendment of the United States Constitution also safeguards 'equality'.[3] This 'equality' has traditionally been defined in the literature as the 'theory … that every man's civil liberty is the same [as] that of others – that all men are equal before the law in rights, privileges, and legal capacities'.[4] Article 3 of the German Constitution also defines 'equal treatment' as the equality of all persons before the law.[5]

Despite the central place in the constitutions under analysis, the principle of equal treatment is a relatively recent creation of law. In 1789, article 1 of the Declaration of the Rights of the Man and the Citizen granted a central place to the idea of 'equality'.[6] In the United States, the ideas about equality of rights started to be discussed in the mid-nineteenth century, where they '[coexisted] with ideas about rights derived from natural law or from the nature of republican society'.[7]

---

2 A.D. Belinfante and J.L. De Reede, *Beginselen van het Nederlandse Staatsrecht* (Kluwer, 2012) 263.

3 Section 1 of the Fourteenth Amendment of the United States Constitution reads: 'All persons born or naturalized in the United States, and subject to the jurisdiction thereof, are citizens of the United States and of the State wherein they reside. No State shall make or enforce any law which shall abridge the privileges or immunities of citizens of the United States; nor shall any State deprive any person of life, liberty, or property, without due process of law; nor deny to any person within its jurisdiction the equal protection of the laws'.

4 Thomas M. Cooley and Andrew C. McLaughlin, *The General Principles of Constitutional Law in the United States of America* (Little, Brown and Company, 1898) 247.

5 Basic Law of the Federal Republic of Germany, art. 3(1).

6 See Declaration of the Rights of Man and Citizens of 1789, art. 1, which reads: 'Les hommes naissent et demeurent libres et égaux en droits. Les distinctions sociales ne peuvent être fondées que sur l'utilité commune'. ['Men are born and remain free and equal in rights. Social distinctions may be based only on considerations of the common good'.] A few years later, the idea of 'equality' reacquired a central dimension with art. 3 of the Declaration of the Rights of Man and Citizen of 1793, which reads 'Tous les hommes sont égaux par nature et devant la loi'. ['All men are equal by nature and before the law'.]

7 W. Nelson, *The Fourteenth Amendment: From Political Principle to Judicial Doctrine* (Harvard University Press, 1988) 13.

However, it was during the twentieth century that the principle of equal treatment acquired particular importance due to the civil rights movement.[8]

More recently, it has been argued in the Dutch literature that the principle of equal treatment acts at three levels: first, it constitutes an abstract framework which binds the legislator;[9] it is a horizontal principle which constrains public administration;[10] thirdly, it is regarded as a fundamental right of any citizen.[11] Although the Aristotelian formula 'treat equals equally and unequals unequally' is still today widely accepted as a general formulation of the principle of equal treatment,[12] it is too vague to truly reflect the meaning of this principle.[13] Treating citizens 'equally' is a relative concept. First, it depends on the context and point of view from which one is looking, and secondly, it implies a clear definition of what can and should be understood as 'equal'. The legal concept of 'equality' refers to the 'similarity of relevant conditions or circumstances'.[14] Whenever the latter is verified, the principle of equal treatment must be applied.

The German Constitutional Court has explained on several occasions that the principle of equal treatment is applicable both to the imposition

---

8 T. Loenen, *Het gelijkheidsbeginsel* (Aers Aequi Libri, 1998) 9.

9 G.H. Addink, *Algemene beginselen van behoorlijk bestuur* (Kluwer, 1999) 153.

10 J.H. Gerards, 'Het gelijksheidsbeginsel in het bestuursrecht' in R.J.N. Schlössels, A.J. Bok, H.J.A.M. van Geest and S. Hillegers (eds), *In beginsel: over aard, inhoud en samenhang van rechtsbeginselen in het bestuursrecht* (Kluwer, 2004) 45.

11 Akkermans, Bax and Verhey, *Grondrechten: grondrechten en grondrechtsbescherming in Nederland*, n. 1 above, 49.

12 In Germany, see the interpretation of the principle of equal treatment by the German Constitutional Court, for example, 1 BvR 1239/85, 11 October 1988 (BVerfGE 79, 1), para. 17, 2 BvR 1397/09, 19 June 2012, para. 53; 'Der allgemeine Gleichheitssatz des Art. 3 Abs. 1 GG gebietet, alle Menschen vor dem Gesetz gleich zu behandeln sowie wesentlich Gleiches gleich und wesentlich Ungleiches ungleich zu behandeln'. ['The general equal protection clause of article 3, paragraph 1 of the German Constitution states that before the law all men should be equally treated, treating equals equally and unequals unequally'.] In the Netherlands, see Bart van Klink, *De wet als symbool: over de wettelijke communicatie en de Wet gelijke behandeling van mannen en vrouwen bij de arbeid* (W.E.J. Tjeenk Willink, 1998) (dissertation) 184.

13 Loenen, *Het gelijkheidsbeginsel*, n. 8 above, 23.

14 A.D. Belinfante and J.L. De Reede, *Beginselen van het Nederlandse Staatsrecht*, n. 2 above, 263.

of 'unequal burdens and [grant of] unequal privileges'.[15] This principle prohibits 'any exclusion of privileges contrary to equality, which grants a preferential treatment to a group of people, while depriving another one'.[16] Equal protection may imply 'a challenge to laws that allocate benefits or impose burdens on a defined class of individuals'.[17]

The principle of equal treatment cannot be understood as a simplistic imposition of general equality, because not only do most laws or regulations imply the classification of individuals but they also apply a different treatment of different persons or things, and the distinguishing of different circumstances is inherent to lawmaking.[18] Instead, it is important to distinguish between (a) lawful unequal treatment, and (b) discrimination.[19] The latter will generally constitute a violation of the principle of equal treatment, while the first may not only be legal but also necessary to guarantee the compliance with this principle (different treatment for different situations).

Since German legislators are bound by the prohibition of arbitrariness in the context of the principle of equal treatment, any differentiation here must be objective and equitable.[20] The complexity of discovering whether there is a violation of the principle of equal treatment lies in tracing the thin line between permissible differentiation and impermissible differentiation.[21] The grounds for differentiation will be accepted if they are clearly objective and in line with the concrete circumstances. In addition,

---

[15] German Constitutional Court, 2 BvL 5/00, 8 June 2004, para. 56: 'Der allgemeine Gleichheitssatz des Art. 3 Abs. 1 GG … gilt für ungleiche Belastungen wie auch für ungleiche Begünstigungen'. ['The general equal protection clause of article 3, paragraph 1 of the German Constitution is valid for unequal burdens as well as for unequal privileges'.]

[16] German Constitutional Court, 2 BvR 1397/09 19 June 2012, para. 53: 'Verboten is daher auch ein gleichheitswidriger Begünstigungsausschluss, bei dem eine Begünstigung einem Personenkreis gewährt, einem anderen Personenkreis aber vorenthalten'. ['An exclusion of privileges is therefore also contrary to equality and forbidden, whenever a privilege is granted to a group of people, but denied to another one'.]

[17] Geoffrey R. Stone, Louis Michael Seidman, Cass R. Sunstein, Mark V. Tushnet and Pamela S. Karlan, *Constitutional Law* (Aspen Publishers, 2005) 251.

[18] Jerome A. Barron and C. Thomas Dienes, *Constitutional Law in a Nutshell* (Thomson/West, 2005) 274.

[19] Akkermans, Bax and Verhey, *Grondrechten: grondrechten en grondrechtsbescherming in Nederland*, n. 1 above, 50.

[20] H.D. Horn, *Experimentelle Gesetzgebung unter dem Grundgesetz* (Duncker and Humblot, 1989) 317.

[21] Stone *et al.*, *Constitutional Law*, n. 17 above, 501.

a lawful differentiation implies placing oneself in the position of the legislator and consider the *underlying objectives* of this differentiation as well as the *means* used to attain it.

In the United States, legal classifications and differentiations will not violate the equal protection clause if they are 'reasonable in relation to the objectives of the law'.[22] The 'reasonableness' of this differentiation can be explained in light of several factors which appear in the literature and jurisprudence of the three countries under analysis. First, considering the German Constitutional Court case law, the differentiation made by legislators can only be justified and accepted by those who are treated unequally if it is proportional.[23] Secondly, the criteria or terms on which legislators differentiate must have a *strict relationship with the objective* for which it is carried out. Hence, lawful differentiations are also dependent on the relevance of the differentiation criteria and must observe the principle of proportionality. In general, this assertion is dependent on a casuistic analysis.

Temporary differentiations, in the sense of affirmative action (or positive discrimination), have been widely accepted and put into practice in several countries as a means to promote opportunities for participation in society of under-represented groups.[24] Temporary differentiations are tools to achieve full equality in the long run. This is not, however, the challenge posed to equal treatment by sunset clauses and particularly experimental legislation. The primary goals of this legislative instrument do not necessarily include achieving a common level playing-field, but rather observe the effects of the implementation of different rules for two groups of citizens. At first sight, experimental legislation goes against the

---

[22] Barron and Dienes, *Constitutional Law in a Nutshell*, n. 18 above, 274–5.

[23] Horn, *Experimentelle Gesetzgebung unter dem Grundgesetz*, n. 20 above, 318. See also the Decision of the German Constitutional Court of 20 December 1961 BVR 320/57, BVerfGE 21, 12, 27 (Allphasenumsatzsteuer): 'Die … Vorteile der Typisierung müssen im rechten Verhältnis zu der mit der Typisierung notwendig verbundenen Ungleichheit der … Belastung stehen. Nur dann ist diese Ungleichheit von den Betroffenen hinzunehmen'. ['The advantages of the typification must have a direct relationship with the inequality of burden in question. Only then will this inequality be accepted by all those affected'.]

[24] See Treaty on the Functioning of the European Union, Art. 157(4) where it is explicitly stated that 'with a view to ensuring full equality in practice between men and women in working life, the principle of equal treatment shall not prevent any Member State from maintaining or adopting measures providing for specific advantages in order to make it easier for the underrepresented sex to pursue a vocational activity or to prevent or compensate for disadvantages in professional careers'.

perception of equal treatment as equality before the law. It does so in principle for a good reason (see Chapter 2), but the difficulty lies in examining whether the experimental differentiation is always 'good enough' to be qualified as a lawful differentiation. Since the implementation of sunset clauses does not imply a different treatment of citizens, the relationship between this legislative instrument and the principle of equal treatment will be very briefly analyzed in the following paragraphs. Greater attention will be paid to experimental legislation.

5.3 PRINCIPLE OF EQUAL TREATMENT AND SUNSET CLAUSES

In Germany, in the 1980s, it was questioned whether temporary legislation (sunset clauses included) could be responsible for possible violations of the principle of equal treatment.[25] Legislators should consider whether the expiration of a temporary law could create a situation of considerable unequal treatment or disadvantage for legal cases occurring later.[26] This argument is rejected here. The later occurrence of a situation may mean that past, present and future situations are not 'equal' and consequently, deserve a differentiated treatment. Sunset clauses do not endanger the principle of equal treatment as they merely confer a temporary character to legislation. According to the German Constitutional Court, unlawful differentiation would only occur if the legislator could at that time already foresee a future change in circumstances, which would place citizens after the sunset in a position of inequality. Otherwise, the legislator is free to revise laws or terminate them as long as citizens are not discriminated against on the basis of existing or foreseeable subjective criteria.[27]

In 2004, the Dutch Supreme Court was asked to assess whether a temporary regulation, derogating from general penitentiary rules, infringed the principle of equal treatment. As elaborated in example 5.1, the Court rejected these arguments.

---

[25] Carl Böhret and Werner Hugger, *Test und Prüfung von Gesetzentwürfen: Anleitungen zur Vorabkontrolle und Verbesserung von Rechtsvorschriften* (Carl Heymanns Verlag KG, 1980) 52.

[26] *Ibid.* 52.

[27] 1 BvL 33/51 of 21 July 1955, BVerfGE 4, 219.

EXAMPLE 5.1 TEMPORARY REGULATION ON DRUG SMUGGLING

In the Netherlands, violation of the principle of equal treatment by a regulation containing a sunset clause was claimed in 2004 before the Dutch Supreme Court (Hoge Raad der Nederlanden). This case involved an appeal from a case regarding the application of a temporary regulation on drug smuggling through Schiphol airport.[28] The appellant argued that the application of this temporary act, instead of the general criminal rules, resulted in a violation of the principle of equal treatment as required, amongst others, by Article 14 of the European Convention of Human Rights (ECHR). The defendant appealed for sentence reduction on the grounds that he had received unequal treatment due to the application of a temporary act which imposed a special regime for drug smuggling suspects arrested at Schiphol airport. The Hoge Raad considered that, in this case, the violation of the principle of equal treatment was not at stake since no subjective discrimination had taken place: the defendant was judged solely on the grounds of the committed crime. The regulatory regime in the temporary legislative act had no effect at this level. Furthermore, a distinction was made between 'unequal treatment', which did not always mean that the principle of equal treatment had been infringed, and 'prohibition of discrimination'. In this case, the Supreme Court considered that equal situations were being treated equally and unequal situations, unequally. In addition, as to the application of a temporary act, it was affirmed that the fairness of this regulation was justified by the emergency circumstances which motivated its enactment and which had not disappeared at that time.[29] The

[28] Judgment of the Hoge Raad of 23 November 2004 (cassatie), LJN: AR2435 no. 00582/04.

[29] It is interesting to see that in the Parliament the same issue was discussed. The then Minister of Justice answered to the objections of possible violation of the principle of equal treatment by arguing that 'the situation of necessity had been caused by the group of criminals at stake' and 'in any case, there is always penitentiary differentiation of convicted criminals according to their sentences'. See Brief van de Minister van Justitie, Drugssmokkel Schiphol, Kamerstukken II, 28 192, no. 36.

temporary character of the legislative act was consequently considered to be irrelevant for the analysis of the case and the appeal was rejected.

In brief, sunset clauses do not introduce an unlawful differentiation between citizens placed in equal situations, endangering the principle of equal treatment. Moreover, the application of different rules to present and future circumstances should be qualified as lawful, unless a specific change in circumstances is foreseeable and legislators intentionally use sunset clauses as a mechanism to discriminate against a group of citizens in the future.

5.4 EXPERIMENTAL LEGISLATION AND THE PRINCIPLE OF EQUAL TREATMENT

The definition and the nature of experimental legislation, as described in Chapter 2, imply that experimental regulations will only be applied to a part of the population (sample group) for the sake of the validity of the experiment. While the experiment lasts, not all citizens will be equal before the law and this implies differentiating between citizens who would otherwise be 'equals' in the sense underlying the principle of equal treatment.[30] Some citizens may be benefited, while others will be disadvantaged. This potential and abstract conflict between the implementation of experimental laws and the principle of equal treatment almost goes without saying, according to the Dutch Council of State.[31]

Equal treatment is a dynamic principle, in other words, what is considered unequal will vary from time to time and from place to place. The measure of equality should be based on the consideration of the concrete individual needs and the circumstances faced by citizens.[32] Legitimate and objectively justified unequal treatment may thus be lawful

---

[30] David Keyaerts, 'De wetgever en experimentalisme: de juridische grenzen van een wetgevingsmodel' (2013) 1 *Tijdschrift voor Wetgeving* 30.

[31] Opinion of the Dutch Council of State of 23 August 2004, No. W05.04.0365/III, Experimentenwet vooropleidingeisen, selectie en collegegeld-heffing; see also the Opinion of the Dutch Council of State in the context of the Report of the Interdepartementale werkgroep experimenteerbepalingen, *Het proberen waard* (23 May 2000), Bijvoegsel Staatscourant, 10 October 2000, no. 196.

[32] Loenen, *Het gelijkheidsbeginsel*, n. 8 above, 10–11.

in many cases. This perception can equally be detected in the United States, where it has been underlined that a differentiation in the grant of privileges can be authorized in the name of the general welfare, 'if [it results] from the nature of the case that there cannot be a general participation'.[33] This is exactly the case of experimental legislation: a differentiation between the 'legislative treatment' given to the sample and control groups is essential to guarantee the validity of the experiment. However, this does not mean that any differentiation grounded on an experimental law or regulation should be allowed: only an 'objective' differentiation will be lawful.

5.4.1 Experimental Legislation and Objective Differentiation

The Dutch experiment aiming to assist single parents and promote their integration in the labour market (WWB Alleenstaande ouders) is an illustration of the difficulty in justifying a lawful experimental differentiation between citizens (see example 5.2).[34]

EXAMPLE 5.2 EXPERIMENTAL REGULATION ON SINGLE-PARENT FAMILIES

This experiment involved granting subsidies, bonuses or education possibilities to single parents who lived in one of the 30 municipalities which joined the experiment. In this case, there was a double differentiation: first, a territorial one, since the experiment was only applicable to a number of municipalities; and secondly, between single- and two-parent families. The first differentiation was necessary for the experiment, since the group volunteering for the experiment would be treated as the sample group. The second differentiation needs to be analyzed in the light of its underlying context and motive: most single parents (usually, women) struggle with combining a job and bringing up

[33] Cooley and McLaughlin, *The General Principles of Constitutional Law in the United States of America*, n. 4 above, 248.

[34] Besluit van 25 augustus 2008 tot vaststelling van een algemene maatregel van bestuur als bedoeld in artikel 83 van de Wet werk en bijstand inzake een experiment met betrekking tot de bevordering van de arbeidsinschakeling van alleenstaande ouders met een bijstandsuitkering (Tijdelijk besluit bevordering arbeidsinschakeling alleenstaande ouders WWB), Stb. 2008, 351. [Temporary regulation on the integration of single parents into the labour market.]

their children. Unable to work full time, the annual income of these families tends to be lower than most couples, placing this group in a vulnerable situation. Single parents often become dependent on social security benefits and subsidies in order to survive. The experiment entailed a differentiated treatment between single parents with children aged under 12 and couples with children, and single parents living in the participating municipalities and the ones residing elsewhere.

The experiment in question had a double motive or objective: on the one hand, to assist single parents at work, notably by ensuring some stability at their workplace; and, on the other hand, to improve the economic situation of this group, empowering them through additional education and assistance. In light of the meaning and dimensions of the principle of equal treatment, it is difficult to see here room for possible discrimination. 'Being a single parent residing in one of the 30 eligible municipalities' qualifies as an 'objective' ground for differentiation. Furthermore, the objective of this socially innovative experiment was to assess to what point providing the mentioned economic and additional benefits could assist single parents to enhance their labour position and, in the long run, become independent of social benefits. It appears, therefore, that no discrimination was involved: the unequal treatment was connected with the objective of the experiment and the differentiation was objectively justified.

In Germany, the argument that the different treatment underlying experiments can breach the principle of equal treatment has been rejected. An important judicial decision in this context was delivered by the Bavarian Constitutional Court in 2006: at stake was the challenge of the constitutionality of an experimental disposition which temporarily abolished a form of opposition proceedings in Mittelfranken.[35] The objective of this experiment was to examine in which areas and to what extent the opposition procedure (*Wiederspruchsverfahren*) was unnecessary from a practical legal and administrative perspective. This

[35] Decision of the Bavarian Constitutional Court of 15 November 2006, Vf. 6-VII-05 Vf., Vf.12-VII-05, BeckRS 2009, 31698: at stake was the constitutionality of art. 15(21) of the Gesetzes zur Ausführung der Verwaltungsgerichtordnung in der Fassung der Bekanntmachung vom 20 Juni 1992 (GVBI S.162, BayRS 34-1-I), zuletzt geändert durch Gesetz vom 23 Juni 2006 (GVBI S.330). See J.F. Lindner, Experimentelle Rechtssetzung durch Rechtsverordnung – Am Beispiel des Hochschulrechts (2007) 23 *Die Öffentliche Verwaltung* 1004.

court considered that this experimental law did not breach the principle of equal treatment since, first, 'the introduction of an experimental disposition with a testing character does not exceed the leeway of the Bavarian legislator'.[36] Secondly, the Bavarian Constitutional Court considered that the selection of Mittelfranken as the sample group was objectively justified, considering its dimension and structure, which meant that it could be qualified as the 'average administrative region'. According to this court, this differentiation should be regarded as a guarantee that the experiment could later be extended to the whole Bavarian territory, should its results be positive.[37] Thirdly, the temporary duration of the test for a clear period was also found to be necessary in order to gather enough information. In addition, the differentiation at stake was fully justifiable taking into consideration the objective of the experiment. The court rejected the demand of the applicant of the pressure group (Popularklage) of extending the experiment to the whole Bavarian territory.[38] This would have deprived the temporary law under analysis of its experimental character.

The definition of objective criteria appears to be the key to respond to the theoretical tension between experimental legislation and the principle of equal treatment. This can also been seen in EU case law. In *Société Arcelor Atlantique and others* (C-127/07), the compatibility of the scheme for greenhouse gas emission allowance trading introduced by the European Parliament and Council Directive 2003/87, as amended by Directive 2004/101, with the principle of equal treatment was analyzed.[39] This Directive introduced a phased and experimental implementation of the greenhouse gas emission allowance trading scheme. The 'step-by-step' approach of this Directive enabled EU Member States to progressively extend the scope of this trading scheme to different industries. Advocate General Maduro expressed in this case no concern regarding any potential discrimination between the applications representing the steel sector.[40] Maduro argued that this was a case of 'legislative experimentation' that required 'that the new policy [is] applied to only a limited

[36] Decision of the Bavarian Constitutional Court of 15 November 2006, Vf. 6-VII-05 Vf., Vf.12-VII-05, BeckRS 2009, 31698, III.

[37] *Ibid.* V, 2, b) bb).

[38] *Ibid.* III.

[39] *Société Arcelor Atlantique et Lorraine and others* v. *Premier ministre and others* (C-127/07), Judgment of the European Court of Justice (Grand Chamber) of 16 December 2008 [2008] ECR I-09895.

[40] *Ibid.* Opinion of Advocate General Poiares Maduro of 21 May 2008, paras 47 and 48.

number of its potential subjects. ... As a result, the policy is artificially circumscribed so that its consequences can be tested before its rules are extended, if appropriate, to all operators who might, in the light of its objectives, be subject to it'. The Advocate General argued in this case that the 'discrimination which experimental legislation inevitably entails is compatible with the principle of equal treatment only if certain conditions are satisfied'. He points out two criteria: the transitory character of experimental laws and the definition of 'the trial measure in accordance with certain objective criteria'.[41]

Besides the definition of objective criteria, another legitimate ground for unequal treatment in the case of experimental legislation has been argued in the Netherlands: 'temporary inequality' might be a stepping stone to achieve greater justice.[42] The unequal treatment underlying experimental legislation is only temporary and it enables the legislator to gather more information about new rules, their effectiveness and justice. The Council of State has affirmed that in fact legal experiments require 'a [justification of] special fairness' due to the violation of the principle of equal treatment and the deviation from a standard or rule. This was argued in the context of the above-mentioned experiment regarding the integration of single parents in the labour market.[43] The Council of State refused to accept in this case that the alleged fairness of a certain measure could be used as a 'justification' for its inequality. In fact, the mentioned 'special (degree) of fairness' does not mean that any violation of the principle of inequality will be justified by the former. In addition, the principle of equal treatment already appeals to 'sentiments of justice and fairness'.[44]

---

[41] *Ibid.* paras 47 and 48.

[42] Opinion of the Dutch Council of State of 23 August 2004, No. W05.04.0365/III, Voorstel van wet houdende tijdelijke regels betreffende experimenten in het hoger onderwijs op het gebied van vooropleidingseisen aan en selectie van aanstaande studenten en op het gebied van heffing van collegegeld (see the justification of the experiment at stake and the Ministerial reply to the Opinion).

[43] Opinion of the Dutch Council of State of 31 August 2007, No. W12.07.0229/III, Ontwerpbesluit tot vaststelling van een algemene maatregel van bestuur als bedoeld in artikel 83 van de Wet werk en bijstand inzake een experiment met betrekking tot de arbeidsinschakeling van alleenstaande ouders met kinderen tot 16 jaar (Tijdelijk besluit experiment WWB alleenstaande ouders), Kamerstukken II, 2006/2007, 30 545, no. 33.

[44] Akkermans, Bax and Verhey, *Grondrechten: grondrechten en grondrechtsbescherming in Nederland*, n. 1 above, 49.

The interaction of principles of law – in this case, justice and equal treatment – implies finding an adequate balance between them,[45] rather than claiming that an experiment disregards the principle of equal treatment but promotes justice. It is due to a 'checks and balances' analysis that priority is given to one principle under some circumstances, and to another principle under other circumstances.

Unequal treatment could potentially arise in the case of experimental legislation due to the differentiated implementation of experiments by different agents and when the legal framework is too broadly defined. This concern was expressed by the German literature in the case of the 'freedom to promote employment' (section 10 'freie Förderung' SGB) granted to German agencies for employment. This leeway included the possibility to enact experimental clauses as a means of furthering innovation in this field.[46] This is, however, far from being a problem specific to experimental clauses. Administrative institutions are necessarily bound by the principle of equal treatment which, allied to other principles of good administration, shape their discretion and prevent arbitrariness. Potential violations of the principle of equal treatment can be prevented by defining clear limits to the enactment and implementation of experimental regulations.

In brief, it is intrinsic to the nature of experimental laws and regulations to differentiate; and this differentiation is lawful as long as it is (i) temporary, and (ii) justified on objective criteria. Two additional criteria must be added to this list: (iii) voluntary participation when possible, and (iv) the proportionality of the differentiation. The proportionality criterion is analyzed in a separate chapter (see Chapter 6).

5.4.2 Voluntary Participation in the Experiment

In *New Ice Co.* v. *Liebman*, Justice Brandeis stated that 'it [was] one of the happy incidents of the federal system that a single courageous State

---

[45] Arend Soeteman, 'Rechtsbeginselen en positivisme?' (2009) 38(1) *Rechtsfilosofie and Rechtstheorie* 5.

[46] See A. Gagel, *Grundsicherung und Arbeitsförderung: Loseblatt-Kommentar* (C.H. Beck, 2009) (online at beck-online.de), s. 10 Freie Förderung Rn, 1–19: the discretion of the employment agencies should inevitably be limited by the principle of equal treatment 'on the one hand, in the processing of essentially equal situations by the same institution, on the other, in the unequal treatment of different institutions on the grounds of a different administrative practice' ['einerseits bei der Bearbeitung wesensgleicher Sachverhalte durch ein dieselbe Agentur, anderseits bei Ungleichbehandlungen durch verschiedene Agenturen aufgrund einer jeweils unterschiedlichen Verwaltungspraxis'].

may, *if its citizens choose*, serve as a laboratory: and try novel social and economic experiments without the risk to the rest of the country'.[47] Brandeis' words can be interpreted in the sense that citizens should not be obliged to participate in an experiment; rather consent should be given. Voluntary participation can change a participant's appreciation of the (un)lawfulness of the differentiated treatment. However, citizens are not or cannot always be directly requested to provide their consent as far as the implementation of laws is concerned.

Municipalities in the Netherlands and Germany may sometimes choose to register or not for an experiment, but citizens are neither directly consulted nor is their consent asked for these purposes. If it would be possible to imagine an experiment which was voluntary instead of being compulsory, or that a fair compensation would be given to those harmed by the experimental regime, then discussions regarding the principle of equal treatment would be complex. The first option was suggested by the Dutch Council of State in 2003 in an opinion regarding an experiment in the health care sector.[48] This institution expressed its concern regarding the nature of the experiment and questioned whether companies could be requested to adhere to the experiment or whether they would be compelled to do so and, in this case, what the financial consequences for these actors would be. This question was raised but there appears to be no simple answer to this dilemma: on the one hand, the idea of experiment as conceived in natural sciences requires randomized but informed and voluntary participants. On the other, it might not always be feasible to request the direct consent of all inhabitants of a certain region as to the implementation of a law. In addition, it may be argued that citizens have already indirectly given their consent to participate in the enactment of experimental regulations since the adoption of these legislative instruments is already comprised in the general legislative power.

As long as the differentiated treatment imposed by the experiment is reasonable, citizens in the control or sample groups to which less beneficial or 'burdensome' rules are applied should not be entitled to invoke the violation of the principle of equal treatment. In general, consent will not be asked or given, but (formal) legislators could equate this possibility whenever experimental laws may directly interfere with certain fundamental rights of citizens. An illustration can be found in the

---

[47] *New State Ice Co. v. Liebmann*, 285 U.S. 262 (1932), dissenting opinion Justice Brandeis (emphasis added).

[48] Opinion of the Dutch Council of State, Wijziging van de Wet tarieven gezondheidszorg in verband met experimenteren, prestatiebekostiging en enige maatregelen – WTG ExPres*)*, Kamerstukken II, 2003–2004 29 379, 4.

case of 'voting experiments' which allows citizens to vote electronically. In the United States, Germany, and in the Netherlands, there have been several attempts to experimentally introduce and expand the use of Internet voting.[49] However, due to the lack of reliability, functionality and security of electronic voting systems, these systems have not been widely used.

It is worth noting that in 2009, the German Constitutional Court held the electronic voting systems (employed notably in the context of the 2005 elections for the Bundestag) to be unconstitutional.[50] Taking into account the shortcomings of the electronic voting system, the Court affirmed that the Federal Voting Machines Ordinance (Bundeswahlgeräteverordnung) was unconstitutional because the voting machines used did not meet the constitutional requirements of the principle of the public nature of elections. The public nature of elections implied that 'every citizen must be able to fully understand the key steps in the elections without any special technical knowledge'. However, this declaration of unconstitutionality should not be interpreted as a prohibition of electronic voting or of the enactment of experiments with this system. Instead 'the legislature is not precluded from using electronic voting machines in the elections if the (constitutionally required) possibility of reliable accuracy control is guaranteed'.

As long as there are risks associated with Internet voting, citizens should not be compelled to use electronic instruments to exercise their

---

[49] In the Netherlands, the following experimental law on electronic voting has been adopted: Wet van 11 December 2003, houdende tijdelijke regels ter zake van experimenten in het kader van het project 'Kiezen op Afstand' (Experimentenwet Kiezen op Afstand), Stb. 2003, 569 (expired 1 January 2010). In 2007, a Dutch evaluation report on electronic voting emphasised that no instrument of electronic voting was entirely secure. Adviescommissie inrichting verkiezingsproces, *Stemmen met Vertrouwen* (Ministerie van Binnenlandse Zaken en Koninkrijksrelaties, 2007), available at www.kiesraad.nl/sites/default/files/Stemmen_met_vertrouwen_1.pdf. In 2013, a new committee was formed to reassess if it would be possible to reintroduce secure electronic voting in the Netherlands. In the United States, the Help America Vote Act of 2002, Pub. L. 107-252, aimed to improve the efficiency of the voting process, implying the introduction of voting machines. States and localities may legislate further on the implementation of this act, which has been criticized over the years due to several failures in the security of the voting process and the lack of reliability of the voting machines.

[50] German Constitutional Court, 2 BvC 2, 4/07, 3 March 2009, BVerfGE 123, 39, see paras 120–63.

right to vote. Instead, informed consent to participate in such experiments should at all times be required.

5.5 EXPERIMENTAL LEGISLATION AND THE PRINCIPLE OF EQUAL TREATMENT: CONCLUDING REMARKS

At first sight, objective, temporary and proportionate differentiations required by the implementation of experimental legislation do not infringe the principle of equal treatment. However, additional attention should be paid whenever the division between the sample and control group may lead to (or conceal) an indirect discrimination on the grounds of gender, race, ethnic background, sexual orientation or any other ground mentioned in the constitutional dispositions of the countries under analysis. The German Constitutional Court has pointed out that the authorization of differentiations between groups of citizens should be stricter whenever the unequal treatment can lead to discrimination against a minority.[51] This occurs in the case of regulations on part-time employment which often affect more women than men, and can thus uncover indirect discrimination against that group.

Moreover, the argument that an experimental differentiation should be allowed because it aims in abstract to enhance fairness or justice does not substantiate a solid ground of justification. The objectivity and proportionality of the differentiation do. The German Constitutional Court has established that one of the most important boundaries of differentiation is the prohibition of arbitrariness. Any differentiation must be objectively justified and should only be allowed if it results from a casuistic (and not abstract) analysis that this differentiation is proportionate.[52] Legislators should objectively justify any experimental differentiation by the learning

---

[51] Judgment of the German Constitutional Court, 2 BvR 1397/09, 19 June 2012, para. 57.

[52] German Constitutional Court, 2 BvR 1397/09, 19 June 2012, paras 54 and 55; German Constitutional Court, 2 BvL 5/00, 8 June 2004, para. 58: 'Nähere Maβstäbe und Kriterien dafür, unter welchen Voraussetzungen im Einzelfall der allgemeine Gleichheitssatz durch den Gesetzgeber verletzt ist, lassen sich nicht abstract und allgemein, sondern nur bezogen auf die jeweils betroffenen unterschiedlichen Sach- und Regelungsbereiche präzisieren'. ['Other measures and criteria for this, under which the principle of equality is violated by the legislature in a specific case, cannot be abstract and general, but rather relative and specific to each affected case and areas of regulation'.]

objectives of the experimental regulation and by its nature. Still, a relevant and intricate question arises in respect of the issue of 'proportionality', which may imply examining the concrete unequal treatment at stake and the potential detriment for those citizens submitted to the experimental regulation or those omitted from it. The following chapter is devoted to the principle of proportionality.

6. The principle of proportionality

> What is law? Is it what is on the books, or what is actually enacted and obeyed in a society? Or is law what must be enacted and obeyed, whether or not it is on the books, if things are to go right?
>
> Bernard Schlink, *The Reader* (1995)

6.1 THE PROPORTIONALITY INQUIRY

Both sunset clauses and experimental legislation break with the traditional paradigm of permanent legislation. Breaking with tradition does not need to be regarded as a 'bad thing'. As Justice Holmes stated: 'the past gives our vocabulary and fixes the limits of our imagination … continuity with the past is not a duty. It is only a necessity'.[1] This 'vocabulary' may be used to assist judges in assessing whether legislative choices have been reasonable, but it should be complemented by an active search of facts.[2] Instead, in light of the lack of information and rapid technological and social developments, it might not even be reasonable to regulate a situation 'forever'. Instead, sunset clauses and experimental legislation may be a proportionate choice, particularly as far as the limitation of freedom and property of citizens is concerned. Sunset clauses and experimental regulations will not always limit fundamental rights, but the choice to do so on a temporary and/or an experimental basis should pass a proportionality inquiry.

The importance of performing a proportionality assessment responds to the Dutch Council of State's argument that experimental legislation

---

[1] Max Lerner, *The Mind and Faith of Justice Holmes: His Speeches, Essays, Letters, and Judicial Opinions* (Transaction Publishers, 1989) 35.

[2] David M. Speak, *Living Law: The Transformation of American Jurisprudence in the Early 20th Century* (Garland Publishing, 1987) 47: referring to Justice Brandeis' demonstration of reasonableness in his brief filed in the context of *Muller v. Oregon*, 208 U.S. 412 (1908). Brandeis built on the existing case law, but actively searched for empirical data and information from other jurisdictions to demonstrate that the Oregon law in question was not unreasonable.

should be regarded as a 'last resort mechanism'.[3] Legislators should demonstrate that experimental regulations as well as sunset clauses are suitable, necessary and proportionate *stricto sensu* to attain a determined objective. This is far from being a specificity of these temporary legislative instruments: 'proportionality of laws and judicial decisions belongs to the very core of justice and equity'; therefore, a 'disproportionate legal rule is no law'.[4]

The idea of justice and proportionality are inseparable.[5] A proportionality test is particularly important when inequality concerns, such as the ones posed by experimental regulations, are at stake. As explained above, it is intrinsic to the nature of any experimental regulation to differentiate, but only proportionate differentiations can be considered lawful.

Since the principle of proportionality implies a highly casuistic assessment of circumstances, the analysis of this principle will remain limited. Once again, the focus of this analysis will be on experimental legislation due to legislative differentiation introduced by the latter.

6.2 GENERAL CONSIDERATIONS ON THE PRINCIPLE OF PROPORTIONALITY

The principle of proportionality, originally inspired in German law,[6] is laid down in Article 5(4) of the Treaty on the European Union and further developed in Protocol II on the application of the principles of subsidiarity and proportionality annexed to the Treaties. This principle has played a central role both in the case law of the European Court of Justice (CJEU)[7] and of the European Court of Human Rights (ECtHR).[8]

---

[3] See the Opinion of the Dutch Council of State in the context of the Report of the Interdepartementale werkgroep experimenteerbepalingen, *Het proberen waard* (23 May 2000), Bijvoegsel Staatscourant, 10 October 2000, no. 196.

[4] Aurelien Portuese, 'Principle of Proportionality as Principle of Economic Efficiency' (2013) 19(5) *European Law Journal* 612.

[5] Adrienne de Moor-van Vugt, *Maten en gewichten: het evenredigheidsbeginsel en Europees perspectief* (Schoordijk Instituut, 1995) (dissertation) 6.

[6] In the EU context, see Tor-Inge Harbo, 'The Function of the Proportionality Principle in EU Law' (2010) 16(2) *European Law Journal* 158. See also Takis Tridimas, 'Proportionality in Community: Searching for the Appropriate Standard of Scrutiny' in Evelyn Ellis (ed.), *The Principle of Proportionality in the Laws of Europe* (Hart Publishing, 1999) 65.

[7] See for example, *Internationale Handelsgesellschaft mbH* v. *Einfuhr- und Vorratsstelle für Getreide und Futtermittel* (11-70), Judgment of the CJEU of 17 December 1970 [1970] ECR 1125.

The proportionality balancing is, however, a criterion in expansion mode throughout the world, particularly in Commonwealth systems.[9] The principle of proportionality has been increasingly used by the US Supreme Court, notably through the timid equivalent of a 'means-ends analysis', but cannot be qualified as a fundamental principle of this legal order.[10]

Considering, for example, the proportionality review performed by the CJEU and following the traditional German formulation,[11] it is possible to distinguish three stages[12] in this phased test:[13] (i) effectiveness or suitability; (ii) necessity; and (iii) proportionality *stricto sensu* of a means to attain a certain end, in other words, the means should not be overly onerous. As Bernhard Schlink explains, 'proportionality' means that:

> if you pursue an end, you must use a means that is helpful, necessary, and appropriate. A means that doesn't help to reach the end isn't a real means – to use it would be out of proportion. It is also out of proportion to use a means that does more than necessary, for example, a means which is more harmful or more expensive than necessary. It is equally out of proportion to use a means that is inappropriate because, even though it is necessary, by using it you do more harm than the end is worth or you spend more than you gain.[14]

---

[8] Jeremy McBride, 'Proportionality and the European Convention on Human Rights' in Evelyn Ellis (ed.), *The Principle of Proportionality in the Laws of Europe* (Hart Publishing, 1999) 23.

[9] For a 'global' approach to the expansion of the principle of proportionality, see Alec Stone Sweet and Jud Mathews, 'Proportionality Balancing and Global Constitutionalism' (2008) 47 *Columbia Journal of Transnational Law* 72.

[10] E. Thomas Sullivan and Richard S. Frase, *Proportionality Principles in American Law: Controlling Excessive Government Actions* (Oxford University Press, 2009); Bernhard Schlink, 'Proportionality in Constitutional Law: Why Everywhere but Here?' (2012) 22 *Duke Journal of Comparative and International Law* 291.

[11] Paul Craig, *EU Administrative Law* (Oxford University Press, 2012) 591.

[12] According to Paul Craig, it is uncertain whether EU courts use a two- or a three-step proportionality test, but this scholar argues that there is evidence that the 'proportionality *stricto sensu*' criterion has been used when 'the court has found that the measure was both suited and necessary to achieve the desired end, but the applicant argues that the burden placed on it by the measure should nonetheless be regarded as disproportionate to the benefits secured', see Paul Craig, *EU Administrative Law* (Oxford University Press, 2012) 602.

[13] Aharon Barak distinguishes four elements in this context: (i) identification of proper purpose; (ii) rational connection; (iii) necessity; (iv) proportionality *stricto sensu*. See Aharon Barak, *Proportionality: Constitutional Rights and Their Limitations* (Cambridge University Press, 2012).

[14] Schlink, 'Proportionality in Constitutional Law', n. 10 above, 291.

The mentioned proportionality assessment departs from the goal formulated by the legislator and then seeks to determine, first, the causality: would the enactment of a sunset clause or an experimental regulation be conducive to that end? Christoph Engel calls the second test 'comparing institutions': does the legislator have other instruments to achieve the mentioned goals? Considering all relevant circumstances, is it necessary to adopt a sunset clause or an experimental law? And are these instruments the least intrusive choices?[15] This last consideration brings us to the final dimension of the test: proportionality *stricto sensu*: legislative or regulatory instruments should not be manifestly disproportionate, in other words, onerous in relation to the aim to be attained. In the following paragraphs, the proportionality test is applied to the context of sunset clauses and experimental legislation.

6.3 PROPORTIONALITY TEST, SUNSET CLAUSES AND EXPERIMENTAL LEGISLATION

The multistaged proportionality review should be performed by the legislator as an '*ex ante* reflection' on the chosen legislative instruments. In the specific case of experimental legislation, the 'proportionality test' refers not only to the differentiation to be executed in order to distinguish between the sample and control groups, but also to the necessity of a temporary disposition and its duration. This is a common aspect to be considered in the case of sunset clauses: it might not be suitable, necessary or strictly proportionate to terminate laws referring to realities that do not change rapidly or fulfil any of the functions stated in Chapter 2. The periodic termination of laws should, for example, not impose disproportional compliance burdens on private actors. In addition, the duration of a sunset clause or of an experimental regulation should be reasonable, consider all relevant circumstances and the legislative aim pursued.

The proportionality of the duration of a sunset or experimental provision can only be assessed on a casuistic basis. To illustrate, the Bavarian Constitutional Court in the decision explained above, considered that the temporal extension of a two-year test run was an adequate

[15] Christoph Engel, 'The Constitutional Court: Applying the Proportionality Principle as a Subsidiary Authority for the Assessment of Political Outcomes' in Christoph Engel and Adrienne Héritier (eds), *Linking Politics and Law* (Nomos, 2003) 285, 287.

period.[16] Although the definition of the duration of a provision falls within the discretion of the legislator, this court argued that an (experimental) act should last for the period required to obtain the necessary information.[17] Hence, an experimental regulation should live long enough to allow legislators to gather meaningful information and perform a significant evaluation of this act.[18] Excessively short or long experimental periods will fail the proportionality test. The same applies to disproportionate extensions of the experimental period.

In the United States, in *T. Atchison and S.F. Ry. Co.* v. *Summerfield*, the District Court acknowledged that although it was allowed to experiment in that case, the 'experiment [would be] unlawful if unduly prolonged'.[19] Although sunset clauses have deserved less attention in the context of a proportionality review, the above considerations are equally valid for sunset clauses.

Proportionality concerns arise not only during the lawmaking process but also when courts are asked to appreciate the proportionality of regulations: should the temporary and/or experimental character of an act be taken into consideration to circumvent the stringency of the proportionality test? After all, one could argue that 'it is just an innocent experiment'. This position is conceivable, but this is not the position adopted here. A proportionality test is required but all relevant circumstances should be considered. To wit, the urgency of a legislative act, the rapid developments of the sector or insufficient information as to a novel social problem must be contemplated. Judges may conclude that a temporary measure was in that case proportionate, but a permanent law would not have been. In practice, it is difficult to draw the line between the consideration of relevant circumstances leading judges to conclude that flexible and temporary legislative acts should be adopted; and 'flexibilizing' the proportionality test.

A source of inspiration for this difficulty comes from the ECtHR in *Pasko* v. *Russia* which involved the discussion of the violation of a

---

[16] Decision of the Bavarian Constitutional Court of 15 November 2006, Vf. 6-VII-05 Vf., Vf.12-VII-05, BeckRS 2009, 31698, V, 2-b) aa).

[17] *Ibid.*: 'Die Erstreckung des Probelaufs auf einen Zeitraum von-zunächst-zwei Jahren ist nicht sachwidrig. Es ist nicht zu beanstanden, dass dieser überschaubare Zeitraum für erforderlich gehalten wurde, um sachlich fundierte Daten zu erhalten'.

[18] J.F. Lindner, 'Experimentelle Rechtssetzung durch Rechtsverordnung – Am Beispiel des Hochschulrechts' (2004) *Die öffentliche Verwaltung* 1004, 1008.

[19] *T. Atchison and S.F. Ry. Co.* v. *Summerfield*, 128 F.Supp. 266, 274 (D.D.C.) (1955).

legality requirement by a presidential decree on a list of information classified as state secrets.[20] According to Patricia Popelier, the flexible interpretation of the legality requirements carried out by the ECtHR in this case can be explained by the acknowledgement that in cases where it is necessary to provide a swift response to imperative circumstances, Acts of Parliament or a parliamentary authorization might take too long, which can justify the use of another legislative instrument, such as, in the *Pasko* case, a presidential decree.[21] Besides, the fact that the decree had a temporary character could have also played a role in the acknowledgement of the ECtHR. A higher level of flexibility of courts can thus be expected when legislation has to respond to emergency situations or when the legislative procedure for the adoption of formal laws is too slow and puts at risk the effectiveness of the legislative act. This flexibility only means that courts are considering all relevant circumstances.

In general, US courts review agencies' rulemaking by taking 'a hard look' in order to guarantee agency rationality. However, Daniel Farber argues that the level of stringency of this review should depend on 'whether the agency is taking a dynamic or a static approach to regulation'.[22] As the scholar explains, the scrutiny should be lowered 'when an agency plans to monitor a rule's implementation and make appropriate modifications'.[23] This is the case of experimentation. Nonetheless, the agency should demonstrate the rationality – and proportionality – of its choice, notably by evidencing that 'its action will not cause irreparable injury'. A regulatory experiment is designed to gather relevant information and experience regarding the implementation of new regulations; and 'it has a process in place that will in fact result in a reappraisal of current policy as the new information is developed', including evaluations.[24] This academic position, which indirectly includes a judgment of reasonableness, has been supported by the case law in the United States.

The US Court of Appeals (District of Columbia) in the *United Telegraph* case ruled that 'the court's inquiry into the factual underpinnings of agency action authorizing a temporary program or giving it

[20] *Pasko* v. *Russia*, Application no. 6951/01, ECtHR.

[21] P. Popelier, 'La loi aujourd' hui (le principe de légalité)' in I. Hachez *et al.* (eds), *Les sources du* droit *revisitées*, vol. 2, *Normes internes infraconstitutionnelles* (Anthemis, 2013) 17.

[22] Daniel A. Farber, 'Environmental Protection as a Learning Experience' (1993) 27 *Loyola of Los Angeles Law Review* 791, 806.

[23] *Ibid.* 806.

[24] *Ibid.*

interim approval will *appropriately be less searching* than if [the court was] faced with the institution of a permanent program'.[25] This perspective had already been evidenced in 1961 in *Connecticut Committee Against Pay TV* v. *FCC*, where the same court explained that 'the very purpose of the projected experiment is to explore these unknown and unpredictable factors'.[26] In 1985 in *Maryland People's Counsel* v. *Federal Energy Regulatory Commission* (FERC), this Commission also pleaded for 'an indulgent review' of experimental regulations based on the 'experimental character' of the legislative instruments at stake. In this case, the US Appeal Courts (District of Columbia Circuit) demonstrated more resistance to this argument when not grounded in solid arguments, but acknowledged that since the experiment would be shortly coming to an end, it did not give rise to 'heavy reliance interests'.[27]

In conclusion, sunset clauses and experimental legislation will be considered lawful, and, in the case of the latter, may introduce lawful differentiations, if these legislative instruments are the most reasonable responses to a social or technological problem. Courts may be less demanding in the review performed of these legislative acts, considering their temporary and provisional characters and rapid changes of the sector. However, the duration of these legislative instruments and the differentiation introduced by experimental legislation must be legitimate to achieve the pursued goal, suitable, necessary and strictly proportional to the legislative aims pursued.

---

25 *United Telegraph Workers* v. *Federal Communications Commission*, 141 U.S. App. D.C. 190, 436 F.2d 920 (1970) (emphasis added): at stake was the enactment of the Mailgram experiment which involved a change in the system of handling telegrams. Under the experimental programme, postal employees, rather than those of Western Union, would scan and insert the messages into envelopes for mailing.

26 *Connecticut Committee Against Pay TV* v. *Federal Communications Commission*, 112 U.S. App. D.C. 248, 44 P.U.R.3d 50, 301 F.2d 835 (1961).

27 *Maryland and People's Counsel* v. *Federal Energy Regulatory Commission*, 245 U.S. App. D.C. 377, 66 P.U.R. 4th 542, 761 F.2d 780 (1985).

PART III

Beyond the law

Chapter 2 depicted sunset clauses and experimental legislation as multifunctional legislative instruments that could be employed in innovative regulatory fields. Notwithstanding these virtues, these types of temporary legislation have not received sufficient attention from legislators or from the literature in general. In the 1980s, Peter DeLeon investigated the reasons behind the resistance to terminate policies, concluding that six plausible explanations could be provided: intellectual reluctance, institutional permanence, dynamic conservatism, anti-termination coalitions, legal obstacles and high start-up costs.[1] In this study, the reasons offered by this scholar are also taken into consideration but are categorized into 'legal' and 'non-legal reasons'. Part II examined the first possible source of reluctance to use sunset clauses and experimental legislation: violation of fundamental principles of law. In principle and as long as these legislative instruments are enacted within a legal framework, no fundamental legal principles will be endangered. Therefore, the opening enigma of this study partially remains: if sunset clauses and experimental regulations can perform multiple functions and do not encounter substantial legal hurdles, why have they not received a more prominent place in lawmaking? In addition, are legislators willing to enact these legislative instruments, and if not, is this motivated by the second category of

---

[1] Peter DeLeon, 'Policy Termination as a Political Phenomena' in Dennis Palumbo (ed.), *The Politics of Program Evaluation* (Sage Publications, 1987); Peter DeLeon, 'Policy Evaluation and Program Termination' (1983) 2 *Policy Studies Review* 631.

reasons – the 'non-legal obstacles'? In the third part of this book, this analysis goes beyond the legal literature in search of these non-legal factors.

7. Sunset clauses and experimental legislation beyond the law

> Es ist nicht genug zu wissen, man muss auch anwenden.
> Es ist nicht genug zu wollen, man muss auch tun.
> [Knowing is not enough, we must apply.
> Willing is not enough, we must apply.]
>
> Johannes W. Goethe, *Wilhelm Meisters Wanderjahre* (1795)

7.1 INTRODUCTION

Legislators are not only influenced by existing law and legal principles, but also – and often primarily – by the 'constraints and resources in [these actors'] milieu, including the behavior of implementing agencies',[1] interest groups and politics. Scholars and practitioners in these areas have analyzed the reasons behind the scarce use of policy phenomena or instruments that often perform comparable functions to sunset clauses and experimental legislation. This is the case of policy termination and policy experimentation. Policy termination has been defined as 'the cessation of a public entity … or a policy cycle'.[2] Legislation cannot be understood detached from policy-making: novel policies often give rise to new laws that are regarded as their implementation vehicles, but policy can also be greatly determined by lawmaking.[3] Due to this connection, the odds are that the factual reasons why legislators do not consistently employ sunset clauses or experimental legislation might be similar to the

---

[1] Robert B. Seidman, 'Justifying Legislation: A Pragmatic, Institutionalist Approach to the Memorandum of Law, Legislative Theory, and Practical Reason' (1992) 29 *Harvard Journal on Legislation* 1, 5.

[2] Michael Howlett and M. Ramesh, *Studying Public Policy: Policy Cycles and Policy Subsystems* (Oxford University Press, 1995) 263.

[3] Ittai Bar Siman Tov, 'Lawmakers as Lawbreakers' (2010) 52 *William and Mary Law Review* 805, 841: Gert-Jan Veerman and Robin Mulder, *Wetgeving met Beleid* (Boom Juridische uitgevers, 2010) 43; see also Ivor Burton and Gavin Drewry, *Legislation and Public Policy: Public Bills in the 1970–74 Parliament* (Macmillan Press, 1981).

ones behind the reluctance to terminate policies or experiment with them, or take their results into consideration when enacting new policies.

In this chapter, diverse non-legal challenges behind the enactment and implementation of sunset clauses and experimental legislation are examined: first, the intellectual and ideological reluctance to use these legislative instruments; secondly, the lack of information regarding sunset clauses and experimental legislation; thirdly, the role played by politics in the adoption of sunset clauses and experimental legislation. Although these issues have a 'factual' nature, they are also legally relevant for a complete understanding of the legislative instruments under analysis.

7.2 INTELLECTUAL AND IDEOLOGICAL RELUCTANCE

Contrary to the judicial decision-making process, which is largely grounded in formal, written opinions, jurisprudence and literature, and expected to be objective, the legislative process is characterized by a number of subjective factors that make it difficult to rationally justify some legislative choices.[4] Intellectual and ideological elements play an important role in this context. In the section on intellectual reluctance, sunset clauses and experimental legislation will be analyzed separately. The scepticism toward these legislative instruments refers to distinct perceptions or misperceptions. Since the role of ideology in the adoption of specific legislative instruments is less clear, sunset clauses and experimental legislation will be jointly analyzed.

7.2.1 Intellectual Reluctance

(a) Sunset clauses and the reluctance towards 'termination'

In Part I, Jefferson's words 'the earth belongs to the living' were quoted not only to explain the relevance of sunset clauses but also to evidence that the need to terminate laws periodically is far from being a recent concern. Nonetheless, it is this exact fear that the earth *only* belongs to the living, and that termination of life is projected onto the extinction of

---

[4] Seidman, 'Justifying Legislation', n. 2 above. It should be emphasised that judicial decision-making is not always totally objective; emotions, for example, play an important role, see for example, Maria Ijzermans, *De overtuigingskracht van emoties bij het rechterlijk oordeel* (Boom Juridische Uitgevers, 2011).

laws, that may explain the legislators' reluctance to enact sunset clauses.[5] By adopting these clauses, lawmakers might have the psychological perception that they are not leaving a legislative 'legacy' in the legal order that goes beyond their terms of office. Jefferson's concern may seem less relevant in a time where legislation is highly policy-driven. Still, the life of most statutes and regulations remains considerable, revealing indirectly the mentioned reluctance towards termination. In the Netherlands, for example, the average duration of a statute is 40 years, while a regulation has a 'life expectancy' of 21 years.[6]

In addition, there is a widespread perception that the durability of laws reflects their social, political and economic importance: the longer laws last, the more influential they are, or seem to be.[7] This disinclination towards the enactment of temporary policy or legislative instruments is shared by both legislators and policy-makers. It is easier to adopt new laws and policies than to extinguish the existing ones. A possible explanation for this concerns the prejudice against policy termination: terminating a policy often implies acknowledging a policy failure.[8] However, this concern is ill-founded since, first, the effectiveness of laws decreases with time, especially when they are not regularly applied.[9] Secondly, obsolete laws do not produce a significant influence in society and are often regarded as a dead letter. Thirdly, a revision or termination of laws to fit the evolution of society and technology is susceptible to increasing the quality and effectiveness of legislation (see Chapter 2).

Termination is necessary to avoid the degradation of laws that no longer serve a useful purpose or lag behind technology and society. 'Termination is the ultimate adjustment of people, policies, programs, systems, and institutions that have ceased to work well. Death, divorce … [and] the repeal of legislation … can be seen as examples of termination [but] the sense of finality that coincides with termination gives way to a

5 Jörg Steinhaus, *Gesetze mit Verfallsdatum* (Books on Demand, 2008) 44.

6 P.O. de Jong and M. Herweijer, *Alle regels tellen – de ontwikkeling van het aantal wetten, AMvB's en ministeriële regelingen in Nederland* (WODC/Boom, 2004) 45–6.

7 Forrest Maltzman and Charles R. Shipan, 'Change, Continuity, and the Evolution of the Law' (2008) 52(2) *American Journal of Political Science* 252.

8 See Peter DeLeon, 'Public Policy Termination: An End and a Beginning' (1978) 4 *Policy Analysis* 369.

9 See Anthony D'Amato, 'Legal Uncertainty' (1983) 71(1) *California Law Review* 1.

spirit of rebirth and creation'.[10] Therefore, termination of laws and policies should not be dominated by the fear of admitting failure or extinction. It is instead an opportunity to incorporate novelties and improve the quality of law and policy-making. As mentioned in Chapter 2, the ability to sunset obsolete laws and policies and ensure that the law does not lag behind can have a positive influence on investment policies.[11] To wit, the relevant circumstances and the political or social context in which the termination occur are more important than the legislative instrument chosen. In brief, the unconscious need to hold on to the duration of laws as a synonym of their importance is therefore unjustified.

Sunset clauses are not the only legislative instruments affected by a 'psychological' or intellectual scepticism, which is often difficult to support by substantial evidence. Experimental legislation is often regarded with comparable scepticism due to its terminological and partial methodological resemblance to scientific experiments.

(b) Experimental legislation and scepticism towards the experimental method

A potential explanation for the unsurmountable suspicion aimed at experimental legislation lies in its apparent resemblance to scientific experiments.[12] This perception creates the idea that legislators could be tempted to experiment with fundamental rights and freedoms of citizens. This argument is examined below.

Experimentation originated, not without a struggle, in the fields of natural and, later, social sciences with Bacon, Bernard or Comte, but it was only afterward that the influence of this method was extended to policy- and lawmaking.[13] The terms 'scientific' or 'experimental' method are still frequently associated with natural sciences.[14] Experiments are employed as a widespread source of information in this field and

---

[10] Mark R. Daniels, *Terminating Public Programs: An American Political Paradox* (M.E. Sharpe, 1997) 31.

[11] *Ibid.* 36.

[12] See also in the context of legislative experiments (and not experimental laws), Christoph Engel, *Legal Experiments: Mission Impossible?* (Eleven International Publishing, 2013) 17–27.

[13] For a historical perspective on the origins of experimental legislation, see James Williams, 'Experiment in Legislation' (1888) 14 *Law Magazine and Review* 299.

[14] See for example, Frederick K. Beutel, *Experimental Jurisprudence and the Science State* (Gieseking Verlag, 1975) 55.

sometimes even regarded as the primary method of research. The 'experimental method' was traditionally considered the scientific method used by natural sciences, whereas social sciences would only use the 'observational method'. The acknowledgement of the insufficiency of the latter in social sciences, particularly in case-based research, underpinned the growing interest in experiments.[15] In the field of political science, for example, the initial disinclination towards the experimental method found its basis in Lawrence Lowell's traditional claim: 'we are limited by the impossibility of experiment. Politics is an observational, not an experimental science'.[16] Nowadays, experiments have earned their place in experimental political science, as well as in other social sciences.[17] However, experiments are still not welcomed by everyone with open arms.

The 'experimental method' acquired a negative connotation after the Second World War. Although the basic principles of this method were defined in the Nuremberg Code,[18] it was also during this war that exceptionally hideous experiments were performed. Some decades later, in the field of social sciences, the notorious Stanford prison experiment (see example 7.1) exposed the dangers of psychological experiments and their inherent ethical problems.[19]

---

[15] John Gerring and Rose McDermott, 'An Experimental Template for Case Study Research' (2007) 51(3) *American Journal of Political Science* 688.

[16] See A. Lawrence Lowell, 'The Physiology of Politics' (1910) 4 *American Political Science Review* 1; James Druckman, Donald P. Green, James H. Kulinski and Arthur Lupia, 'The Growth and Development of Experimental Research in Political Science' (2006) 100(4) *American Political Science Review* 627.

[17] See for example, James Druckman, Donald P. Green and James H. Kulinski, *Cambridge Handbook of Experimental Political Science* (Cambridge University Press, 2011).

[18] The Nuremberg Code was a code of medical ethics which revolutionized the way experiments should be conducted. The Code introduced the ten principles which should guide experimentation.

[19] Philip G. Zimbardo, 'On the Ethics of Intervention in Human Psychological Research' (1973) 2 *Cognition* 243.

EXAMPLE 7.1 STANFORD PRISON EXPERIMENT

In 1971, a homogeneous sample of volunteers (college male students) was selected to participate in a two-week experiment on 'prison life'. The roles of 'guards' and 'prisoners' were randomly assigned and the subjects were placed in a mock prison in the Stanford campus. They were being closely monitored by researchers. Not long after the experiment started, the 'prisoners' rebelled against the 'guards' and thereafter abuses of authority began. The students playing the role of 'guards' started displaying aggressive behaviour towards the 'prisoners'. A number of guards were hostile, arbitrary and humiliated the prisoners. Due to these abuses of authority, the experiment had to be terminated before the end of the period determined beforehand. Considering the background of the subjects, nothing could have predicted that this experiment would have produced such dramatic results. Philip G. Zimbardo, the researcher behind the 'Stanford Prison Experiment', later explained 'the Lucifer effect', which turns ordinary people into 'bad creatures' capable of committing horrendous acts as follows: a particular dangerous combination of conditions, the fact that people are used to obeying authority, and the habit of playing social roles making people unable to reflect beyond these roles.[20]

It is not surprising that the images of these abusive experiments are evoked when the term 'experiment' is mentioned. The risk that experimental laws may also go too far and put fundamental rights at stake might emerge as one of the explanations for the legislator's reluctance to adopt the experimental method.

The implementation of the experimental method in the field of lawmaking can pose more challenges than in any other science because in law 'man is not only the master of the experiment but also its subject

[20] See Philip G. Zimbardo, *The Lucifer Effect: Understanding How Good People Turn into Evil* (Random House Trade Paperbacks, 2008). See also Craig Haney and Philip G. Zimbardo, 'The Past and the Future of U.S. Prison Policy: Twenty-Five Years after the Stanford Prison Experiment' (1998) 53(7) *American Psychologist* 709.

and object': laws are tested in the real world, having in most cases an irreversible impact in the life and business of citizens.[21]

In brief, experimental legislation is not an implementation *tout court* of the scientific method. Therefore, the term 'experimental legislation' should not evoke the past abuses committed in medical experiments. Experimental laws involving, for example, experimental legislative prescriptions on dynamic speed limits on Dutch highways[22] cannot be compared to eugenic medical experiments. The object of scientific experiments and that of experimental legislation is substantially different: experimental laws or regulations are designed to test the effectiveness of new rules, and not those of new products or services. These should have already been sufficiently tested under laboratory conditions. Experimental legislation is a 'search for facts' which seeks to test the effectiveness of law and its adaptability to a socio-economic context, but which, from a methodological point of view, does not comprise a scientific verification of a legal prescription.[23]

7.2.2 Role of Ideology

Peter DeLeon argued in the 1980s that ideology (understood as 'a set of beliefs about the role and scope of government') can influence the support or resistance of policy termination.[24] He argued that Republicans were more interested in limiting the role and scope of government than Democrats, which meant that they would also be more inclined to

---

21 See J. Boulouis, 'Note sur l'utilisation de la méthode expérimentale en matière de réformes' in *Mélanges Trotabas* (LGDJ, 1970) 29.

22 See the report, *Evaluatie praktijkvoeren Dynamische Maximumsnelheden* (evaluatie rapport van Rijkswaterstaat, Ministerie van Verkeer en Waterstaat, Dynamische Maximumsnelheden, 15 July 2010), Bijvoegsel Kamerstukken II, 2010–2011, 32 646, no. 1, 9. The legislative act in question was the Experimenteerverkeer besluit ten behoeve van een experiment met een dynamisch maximum snelheid van 130km/h op enkele wegvakken onder beheer van het Rijk, Stc. 2011, 2549. The experiment consisted in the application of a dynamic speed limit in selected highways or part of them in order to verify the effects of this measure on the traffic flow, environment and road safety.

23 Sandrine Chassagnard-Pinet, 'Argumentation and Judicial Decisions' in Dov. M. Gabbay, Patrice Canivez, Shahid Rahman and Alexandre Thiercelin (eds), *Approaches to Legal Rationality* (Springer, 2010) 160.

24 DeLeon, 'Policy Evaluation and Program Termination', n. 1 above; Susan E. Kirkpatrick, James P. Lester and Mark R. Peterson, 'The Policy Termination Process: A Conceptual Framework and Application to Revenue Sharing' (1999) 16(1) *Policy Studies Review* 210, 227.

terminate certain policies.[25] This was not only true in the 1980s but also in the 1990s Republican-controlled Congress, where sunset clauses were suggested as 'a means of ending [the] cycle of statutory debasement'.[26] This conclusion has not been supported by recent research. Instead, there is mixed evidence as to the role played by ideology in policy choice and policy termination.

In the Netherlands, a number of initiatives to enact experimental laws and sunset clauses have been put forward by the government or have been suggested by Members of Parliament from more right-wing or centre parties. One of the first references to sunset clauses in the Dutch political debate, for example, was made in the 1986 election programme of the Volkspartij voor Vrijheid en Democratie (VVD) party that suggested the adoption of sunset clauses.[27] Sunset clauses were considered to be useful instruments for the control of public expenditure, execution of generally required government cuts and, consequently, improvement of the efficiency of public policies. At first glance, it would appear that Dutch centre and right-wing parties are more receptive to temporary legislation than other parties which often raise queries as to the possible legal problems of the implementation of these instruments. An illustration would be the interventions of the Christen-Democraten Appèl (CDA) party on the temporary regulation of drug smuggling into Schiphol airport (see Chapter 5). However, during the Lubbers II government, some sunset clauses were suggested and, in many cases, included in reform or crisis package measures,[28] regional legislation[29] and tax legislation.[30] There is insufficient evidence to connect the enactment of sunset clauses with the ideology of the political parties with majority in this period (CDA and VVD). Instead, economic concerns and the need to introduce 'better regulation' strategies have certainly played a more significant role.[31]

---

[25] *Ibid.* 227.

[26] *Ibid.*

[27] VVD electoral programme for the 1986 elections for the Parliament (Tweede Kamer) 14, available at http://dnpp.eldoc.ub.rug.nl/FILES/root/programmas/Verkiezingsprogramma/1986/vvd86.pdf.

[28] Sanering procedures, Vergaderjaar 1985–1986, 19 579, nos. 1–2.

[29] Wijzing van de wet houdende nieuwe bepalingen met betrekking tot provinces (Provinciewet) of 19 March 1988, art. 113a (3, 4).

[30] Invorderingswet van rijksbelastingen. Andere dan invorrechten en accijnzen was later renamed Invorderingswet 1990, Stb. 1990, 221. The original version of art. 71 contained a sunset clause, the current version does not.

[31] OECD, *Better Regulation in Europe: The Netherlands* (OECD, 2010) 15; OECD, *Regulatory Reform in the Netherlands* (OECD, 1999).

A similar conclusion can be drawn from a number of German examples. The Christian-Democrat '*keine Experimente*' slogan used in 1957 by Konrad Adenauer gave the sign of stability at the different policy levels that many Germans were longing for during that turbulent period: no medical, social or political experiments, just stability and continuation of good policies. This aversion towards 'experiments' and changes does not mean that this political party would nowadays be averse to the enactment of experimental laws.[32] The concrete topic and circumstances should determine the legislative instrument chosen. This appears to be equally applicable to sunset clauses in Germany, since in the last decade, a number of sunset clauses have been suggested by political parties with distinct ideologies.

In Germany, members of the Sozialdemokratische Partei Deutschlands (SPD) party have defended the inclusion of sunset clauses to combat excessive bureaucracy and regulatory pressure in different political programmes.[33] Sunset clauses were presented as an important instrument to eliminate excessive burdens imposed on private actors. Moreover, this was not the only party aware of the virtues of this instrument. During the 2005–2009 CDU/CSU (Christlich-Soziale Union in Bayern)/SPD, government sunset clauses were also proposed or even included in statutes of significant importance. This is the case of the Gemeinsame-Dateien-Gesetz which is due to sunset in 2017.[34] This statute regulates the collection of police data connected with terrorism.

In conclusion, there is not sufficient evidence that ideology plays a clear role in the decision to enact sunset clauses or experimental legislation. Instead, the nature of the subject to be regulated, and the social, economic and political circumstances, appear to determine the decision to adopt a sunset clause or an experimental law.

---

32 This was notably the conclusion withdrawn from a meeting with a member of the CDU.

33 See for example, the following policy promoted, amongst others, by the SPD in Bremen: Senatskanzlei Bremen, Handelskammer, Industrie- und Handelskammer Bremerhaven and Arbeitsnehmerkammer Bremen, *Bürokratieabbau in Bremen: Das Land Bremen geht neue Wege* (2008), available at www.rathaus.bremen.de/sixcms/media.php/13/Broschuere_Buerokratieabbau_im_Land_Bremen.pdf.

34 Gesetz zur Errichtung gemeinsamer Dateien von Polizeibehörden und Nachrichtendiensten des Bundes (Gemeinsame-Dateien-Gesetz), *Bundesgesetzblatt* Jahrgang 2006 Teil I No. 66 3409. Article 5 contains a ten-year sunset clause.

7.3 LACK OF INFORMATION OR EXPERTISE

The common disinclination toward sunset clauses and experimental legislation can often be elucidated in light of the lack of information regarding these instruments or the expertise to implement them. The absence of unbiased information might underlie the above-mentioned intellectual reluctance to adopt these legislative instruments. There is, however, limited information and empirical evidence on this topic.

According to Gerber and Patashnik, policy-makers do not experiment more often with policies not because they are truly sceptical about these legislative instruments, but because they are unaware of their multiple functionalities.[35] What is more, policy- and lawmakers do not always have sufficient information, resources or know-how to enact and implement them.[36] Furthermore, even when this information is available, politicians and policy-makers might not be interested in taking full advantage of it.[37] Policy-makers often have excessively optimistic beliefs about the effects and side-effects of policies, dismissing the importance of experiments without considering that novel and untested policies are susceptible to having unexpected consequences when implemented. Besides, these unrealistic expectations are also due to the extensive delegation chains and the reliance on expert knowledge that might give a misrepresentation of the real meaning of the information provided since 'each official tries somewhat to make his part of government look like what the officials above him want it to look like'.[38]

In the United States, sunset clauses are far from being an unknown instrument and, although no comparative empirical data is available, this instrument seems to be considered more often by lawmakers and regulators than in the Netherlands or Germany. In a Dutch report on sunset clauses presented in 2010, it was concluded on the grounds of a

---

[35] Alan S. Gerber and Eric M. Patashnik, 'Missing Opportunities to Solve Problems' in Alan S. Gerber and Eric M. Patashnik (eds), *Promoting the General Welfare: New Perspectives on Government Performance* (Brookings Institution Press, 2006) 10.

[36] *Ibid.* 10.

[37] Robin Hanson, 'Decision Markets for Policy Advice' in Alan S. Gerber and Eric M. Patashnik (eds), *Promoting the General Welfare: New Perspectives on Government Performance* (Brookings Institution Press, 2006) 151.

[38] *Ibid.* 151.

number of interviews with multiple lawmakers that a number of them were not acquainted with this legislative instrument.[39]

In Germany, Renate Mayntz argued that the most significant problem in political decision-making was not the lack of expertise to use new legislative instruments, notably instruments based on evidence, but the lack of willingness to do so.[40] Political reasons often underlie this unwillingness to seek the 'truth of the facts'. Facts can be uncomfortable to deal with, leading to disregard for such facts, for the 'truth of empirics' has been part of the so-called fact-free politics and populism which easily spreads in times of crisis.[41] These political reasons will be further explained in the following section.

7.4 POLITICAL RATIONALITY

As explained in Chapter 2, sunset clauses and particularly experimental legislation emerged as instruments employed to rationalize the legislative process, namely, by observing and learning from the results of the experiments and evaluation reports. By submitting new laws to 'a reality test' and taking into account facts or evidence in their decisions, legislators should be able to take rational decisions. Since consulting the Oracle of Delphi is no longer an option for decision- and lawmakers, drafters must instead turn to 'reason informed by experience' and 'must possess the potential for self-correction'.[42] This implies, according to Robert Seidman, adopting devices for testing and improving legislation in the light of the gathered experience, including the adoption of sunset clauses (see also Chapter 1).[43] These arguments appear to be fairly logical, but lawmaking is far from being a rational process. Politics and interest groups play a decisive role at this level, pushing policy and

---

39 ZENC, *Horizonwetgeving Dichterbij: onderzoek naar horizonwetgeving en regeldrukvermindering voor bedrijven* (ZENC, 2010).

40 Renate Mayntz, 'Speaking Truth to Power: Leitlinien für die Regelungen wissenschaftlicher Politikberatung' (2009) 1 *DMS-Der modern Staat, Zeitschrift für Public Policy, Recht und Management* 5.

41 See Ruud Kole, 'Fact Free Politics' (2011) 38(2) *Beleid en Maatschappij* 251; Jan Walburg, 'Fact-free and Evidence-free Politics' (2011) 9(6) *Maandblad Geestelijke Volksgezondheid* 597.

42 Seidman, 'Justifying Legislation', n. 2 above, 18.

43 *Ibid.* 75.

legislative decisions in the direction of politically desirable solutions, which are not necessarily those that promote the public interest.[44]

Policy persistence or legislative inaction towards repeal of ineffective legislation in cases where there are no rational reasons to maintain ineffective legislation exemplify the mentioned problem. In the fields of political economy[45] and political science,[46] scholars have argued that there is a tendency for policies to persist 'even when [their] original rationale is no longer applicable or has been proved invalid'.[47] Excessive policy and legislative persistence can be adverse to both sunset clauses and experimental legislation since both legislative instruments have a temporary character. The pursuit of political persistence is thus the first side of political rationality to be analyzed.

7.4.1 Political Persistence

In the 1980s, Arno Korsten pointed out that the number of ineffective policies was growing at an alarming rate in the Netherlands.[48] Comparable observations have been made elsewhere, notably in the United States. As Philip Horward explains, such tendency is not surprising since 'it is much more difficult to repeal a law than it is to pass it in the first place, because, once enacted, an army of special interests surrounds each law'.[49] The preservation of a law in the legal order may favour diverse private actors who might be interested in maintaining the status quo, diverting the attention of legislators from the truly important matters, notably the effectiveness and efficiency of laws. This phenomenon might

---

44 Mary Wiktorowicz and Raisa Deber, 'Regulating Biotechnology: A Rational-Political Model of Development' (1997) 40 *Health Policy* 115.

45 Stephen Coate and Stephen Morris, 'Policy Persistence' (1999) 89(5) *American Economic Review* 1327.

46 Iris Geva-May, 'When the Motto is "Till Death Do Us Part": The Conceptualization and the Craft of Termination in the Public Policy Cycle' (2001) 24(6) *International Journal of Public Administration* 263.

47 Coate and Morris, 'Policy Persistence', n. 46 above.

48 Korsten, *Dynamisch bestuur: beleidsdynamiek als beleidsbeëindiging en opvolging, bijdrage aan het Liber Amicorum voor Prof. Dr. R. in 't Veld: Trajectmanagement* (Boom Lemma uitgever, 2010), also available at www.arnokorsten.nl.

49 Philip K. Howard, 'Showcase Panel IV: A Federal Sunset Law, The Federalist Society 2011 National Lawyers Conventions' (2012) 16 *Texas Review of Law and Politics* 339, 348.

explain why policy termination and the enactment of sunset clauses have remained 'underattended subject[s]' in the countries under analysis.[50]

In Germany, Michael Bauer has argued that this lack of interest in policy termination is surprising for two reasons: from a practical point of view, the limited policy-making capacity of most countries would require governments to terminate ineffective policies instead of incurring maintenance costs; and, from a theoretical point of view, the conception of policy analysis as the main instrument for a comprehensive and systematic understanding of the policy process should mean that policy cycles, including termination, should be thoroughly examined.[51]

Political opposition is one of the main explanations for the reduced enactment or incorrect implementation of sunset clauses.[52] A number of additional explanations can be added to this tendency to oppose policy termination. First, maintaining policies – regardless of their reduced effectiveness – can be pointed out as a way of ensuring the survival of organizations such as regulatory agencies.[53] According to the literature, there seems to be 'an institutional bias in favor of the status quo: agreement is required to change a policy, but no agreement is required to sustain it'.[54] The maintenance of these organizations has equally been justified on the grounds of the investment made in human capital, which would be wasted if agencies would be extinguished.[55] Significant sunk costs in the training of employees are often behind the decision not to terminate policies.[56] Traditionally, this sunk cost argument was rejected by the rational choice theory of micro-economics and qualified as the 'sunk cost fallacy'.

---

[50] Peter DeLeon, 'Afterward: the Once and Future State of Policy Termination' (1997) *International Journal of Public Administration* 2197; Jacob Gersen, 'Temporary Legislation' (2007) 74 *University of Chicago Law Review* 247. See also the literature review performed by Michael W. Bauer, *The Policy Termination Approach: Critique and Conceptual Perspectives*, Working Paper Series, WP #1/2009 (2009), available at www.sowi.hu-berlin.de/lehrbereiche/politikundverwaltung/wps/working-paper-1.

[51] Bauer, *The Policy Termination Approach: Critique and Conceptual Perspectives*, n. 51 above, 2.

[52] Jan Funke, *Bürokratieabbau mit Hilfe zeitlich befristeter Gesetze: zu den Erfolgsbedingungen der Sunset-Gesetzgebung* (AVM, 2011) 90.

[53] Stella Z. Theodoulou and Chris Kofinis, *The Art of the Game: Understanding American Public Policy Making* (Thomson Wadsworth, 2004) 206.

[54] Coate and Morris, 'Policy Persistence', n. 46 above.

[55] Geva-May, 'When the Motto is "Till Death Do Us Part"', n. 47 above.

[56] Eugene Bardach, 'Policy Termination as Political Process' (1976) 7 *Policy Sciences* 126.

More recently, it has been counter-argued that, under certain circumstances, it might be rational to allow sunk costs to influence decision-making on the grounds of informational content, reputational concerns or financial and time constraints.[57] In the United States, sunset commissions employed a considerable number of people to whom training had to be provided. These sunk costs do not appear to be a sufficiently convincing argument to maintain obsolete or ineffective laws. Since sunset commissions are a typical US institution, this first argument does not appear to be applicable to Germany and the Netherlands. In addition, administrative agencies do not exert the same influence on the legislator in Europe as they appear to do in the New World. As earlier mentioned, sunset clauses have not been used in Germany to increase legislative oversight and limit the growing power of agencies, but rather to abolish outdated and obsolete regulations on a systematic basis and thus improve the quality of regulation.[58]

Secondly, in the United States, politicians fear that policy termination can trigger political reprisals from special interest groups.[59] The influence of these interest groups frequently means that policies can continue to exist even when their public interest justification has disappeared.[60] Interest groups play an important role in the political decision-making process and may lobby, for example, to ensure the maintenance of the status quo, notably when subsidies are at stake, even when these no longer serve a substantial goal. This is not an issue limited to the American context. In Germany and the Netherlands, the relevance of interest groups and lobbyists in legislative decision-making has also been discussed.[61] Lobbyism is a well-known form of influencing political decision-making and ultimately lawmaking. Although lobbyism is not illegal, the lack of transparency in the process of influencing lawmaking

---

57 R. Preston McAfee, Hugo M. Mialon and Sue H. Mialon, 'Do Sunk Costs Matter?' (2010) 48(2) *Economic Inquiry* 323.

58 Bertelsmann Stiftung, *Sunset Legislation and Better Regulation: Empirical Evidence from Four Countries* (Bertelsmann Stiftung, 2010) 17, available at www.bertelsmann-stiftung.de/cps/rde/xbcr/SID-E8B3D0D1-5443791C/bst_engl/xcms_bst_dms_35739__2.pdf.

59 See Geva-May, 'When the Motto is "Till Death Do Us Part"', n. 47 above.

60 Coate and Morris, 'Policy Persistence', n. 46 above.

61 For an overview on lobbyism in Germany, see Thomas Leif and Rudolf Speth (eds), *Die stille Macht. Lobbyismus in Deutschland* (Wiesbaden Westdt, 2003). For the Netherlands, see for example, M.P.C.M. van Schendelen, *Lobbyen in Nederland* (Sdu Uitgevers, 1998).

and the involvement of donations to political parties contribute to its bad reputation.[62] Private funding may not 'buy' political decisions but it often helps.

In October 2013, the substantial donations made by the family owning BMW to the German Christian-Democratic (CDU) party hit the headlines, as it was rumoured that this was a response to the successful lobbying of the German government at the EU level to abandon an agreement to cap EU car emissions.[63]

Interest groups in Germany also try to maintain the status quo and block propose policy changes that might be disadvantageous to them. This has been verified, for example, in the energy sector, where during many years the main energy suppliers exerted substantial pressure on political decision-makers.[64] The influence of lobbyists in the lawmaking process may delay policy and legislative changes which would be advantageous for the public in general. Nonetheless, 'in our modern society lobbyism appears to be an indispensable and increasingly more accepted activity'.[65] According to a study elaborated in 2007 by Popelier and Van Gestel (and others), consultations could be employed to limit the negative aspects of lobbyism.[66]

Thirdly, to the 'outside world', the maintenance of ineffective policies is regularly justified on the grounds of conservatism, political inertia, and economic or legal arguments. This aspect is inevitably connected to the argument presented above. Whenever a sunset is suggested, the threat of termination can trigger 'a plethora of political games', in no way related to the essence of the agency's politics or procedures, but solely focused

---

[62] Maciej Drozd, 'Lobbying-Regulierung in europäische Vergleich. Eine kurze Evaluation rechtlicher Rahmenbedingungen' (2006) *Zeitschrift des DIPA* 78.

[63] Dietmar Hawnarek, Christoph Pauly and Gerald Traufetter, 'Merkel's patrons: donation from BMW owners raises eyebrows', *Der Spiegel*, 15 October 2013, available at www.spiegel.de/international/europe/cdu-gets-donation-from-bmw-owners-during-co2-talks-a-927954.html.

[64] Wolfgang Gründinger, *The Energy Transformation in Germany: Why Interest Groups Win – and Why They Lose*, Working Paper (2012), available at www.wolfgang-gruendinger.de/wp-content/uploads/2011/10/phd-prospectus-short.pdf.

[65] J.A.G. van Mierlo, 'Lobbyen' in N.A.A. Baakman and J.A.G. van Mierlo (eds), *Overheid en onderneming. Een inleiding* (Maastricht University, 2001) 315–16.

[66] Patricia Popelier, Rob van Gestel, Koen van Aeken, Victoria Verlinden and Peter van Humbeeck, *Consulteren over ontwerp-regelgeving* (Sigma, 2012).

on avoiding abolition and ensuring that their interests are furthered.[67] These interest groups will lobby to impede the adoption of sunset clauses, and if they are employed, they will unite efforts to guarantee their reauthorization.

Three Dutch scholars, Camps, Kickert and Korsten, suggested in the 1980s that stronger incentives for policy termination were required and sunsetting could be a viable way of achieving it.[68] Since the influence of interest groups is an inevitable part of the political game, these political obstacles standing in the way of policy and legislative termination might in reality be extremely difficult to overcome, following the notion of 'he who pays the piper, calls the tune'. Yet large companies 'paying the piper' are nevertheless not the only ones 'bearing the cost'. Enhanced transparency (see also Chapter 3) may, however, empower citizens to participate in this process and assist them in questioning who should be allowed to call the tune.

7.4.2 Reputational and Electoral Concerns

Reputational concerns and electoral incentives are also critical elements influencing the decision to enact experimental regulations or to sunset legislation. Both legislative instruments are based on evaluations and have a temporary character, which means that if their implementation is transparent, the effects of these laws will be earlier or periodically exposed. Politicians may often feel uncomfortable with the exposure of the outcomes of their laws and policies. According to the literature, not all politicians will be equally influenced by these reputational concerns and allow them to interfere with the chosen instruments.[69]

Better informed politicians will be less interested in the reputational costs of reversing a policy experiment even if the performance of the policy is disappointing at first.[70] These politicians know that, in most cases, more time is required in order for meaningful results to be produced. Politicians who are exclusively interested in maintaining a

---

[67] Landon Curry and Patricia Shields, *Attitudes Toward Sunset Review in Texas*, study prepared for the 1990 Annual Meeting of the Southwestern Political Science Association, Fort Worth, 29 March 1990, at 5, available at https://digital.library.txstate.edu/bitstream/handle/10877/3966/fulltext.pdf.

[68] Th.W. Camps, W.J.M. Kickert and A.F.A. Korsten, 'Horizonwetgeving, een nieuwe coloradokever' (1982) 2(4) *Bestuur* 10, 12.

[69] Andreas Bernecker and Christina Gathman, *Trial and Error? Policy Experimentation during the US Welfare Reform*, Working Paper (March 2013).

[70] *Ibid.*

good reputation will *a contrario* terminate an experiment, as soon as it starts to produce negative effects susceptible to being contested. These reputational concerns are connected with the desire to be re-elected that is presumed to influence the legislators' choice regarding both the public policy goals to be achieved and the type of legislation to be employed.[71]

According to the political economy literature, legislators driven by a short-run electoral horizon have the propensity to opt for policy programmes and laws that produce rapid results. This choice may not, however, be one that maximizes the public interest.[72] This reasoning can be applied to experimental legislation which, regardless of the duration of the underlying programme, always requires a reasonable duration, which depending on the field may be shorter or longer, but it must last long enough to produce significant results. However, this also means that politicians might be able to 'play' with this instrument: in fields requiring experiments that exceed the term of the legislative assembly but that have a high risk of negative results, politicians might be less reluctant to enact them. In this case, politicians could leave potential problems to the following government. However, when there is a high probability that experimental laws will produce positive results in the long run, not contributing to re-election, politicians might be indifferent to enacting these experiments. In brief, if lawmakers would like to see fast and positive results, they might be reluctant to take the risk of adopting experimental laws that only produce long-term results. Such long-term effects characterize education and other social fields.

Electoral concerns are visible in the case of both sunset clauses and experimental legislation. Politicians may tend, for example, to avoid these legislative instruments because, should the parliamentary majority change, the new government will have to evaluate a sunset clause or an experiment that might be contrary to a new political programme or budget.[73] A new government with a different perspective on policy priorities could be tempted to execute a pro forma evaluation, terminate the law, or devote less time and resources to the evaluation. As mentioned in Chapter 4, according to the German literature, these clauses cannot be capriciously terminated before they attain their natural 'sunset'. These legislative instruments can thus be inconvenient since implementing sunset clauses enacted by a previous government can interfere with the

---

[71] Linda Cohen and Matthew Spitzer, 'Term Limits' (1992) 80 *Georgetown Law Journal* 477, 486.

[72] *Ibid.* 490.

[73] Funke, *Bürokratieabbau mit Hilfe zeitlich befristeter Gesetze*, n. 53 above, 57–8.

new government's policy programme.[74] Example 7.2 on the German Anti-Child Pornography Law demonstrates how a change in the government coalition can drastically alter the legislator's position towards a law and its sunset clause.

EXAMPLE 7.2 ANTI-CHILD PORNOGRAPHY LAW

In the summer of 2009, the introduction of a sunset clause into the highly controversial German Anti-Child Pornography Law (Gesetz zur Bekämpfung der Kinderponographie in Kommunikationsnetzen) was proposed by the coalition government (CDU/CSU/SPD) and later adopted in the Bundestag. This Act was designed to block access to child pornography websites.[75] Curiously, in 2010, when this controversial law was finally signed by the President and published, the government decided that this law did not match the new government policy. After the elections in October 2009, the Free Democratic Party (FDP) replaced the SPD in the coalition government. This political party soon expressed its disinclination towards the Anti-Child Pornography Law. In 2010, a non-application directive was issued and after the 2011 review this law was repealed.

7.4.3 Capture by Special Interest Groups and Politicians

Since legislation is traditionally designed to solve societal or economic problems, citizens expect legislators to take relevant information into account and choose the most efficient instrument to achieve this goal. Nonetheless, as previously demonstrated, this is not what happens in the 'real world': legislators' decisions are repeatedly influenced by other

[74] *Ibid.* 57–8.

[75] Gesetz zur Bekämpfung der Kinderpornographie in Kommunikationsnetzen, Bundesgesetzblatt 2010 Teil I, No. 6, 22 February 2010. See Marcel Rosenbach and Christian Stöcker, 'The Law that nobody wanted: now Internet legislation embarrasses new German government', *Der Spiegel*, 18 February 2010, available at www.spiegel.de/international/germany/the-law-that-nobody-wanted-new-internet-legislation-embarrasses-german-government-a-678782.html.

factors, in particular constituency casework[76] and special interest groups.[77] Private interest theories of regulation have been based on the assumption that regulation is a result of the actions of individuals or groups driven to maximize their self-interest.[78] The public choice literature has devoted great attention to the influence exerted by special interest groups in regulation and explained how regulators were 'captured' by them.[79]

Special interest groups are a significant problem since they might influence politicians to give preference to the solutions that further their interests instead of those that would advance the public interest.[80] The influence of special interest groups deserves particular attention in this chapter since the literature has attempted to establish a connection between the enactment of sunset clauses and experimental legislation and special interest groups. There are, however, divergent perceptions of this 'connection'.

Richard Myers and Rebecca Kysar argue that sunset clauses can increase the opportunities for these groups to exert their influence on the regulator.[81] Zachary Gubler, on the contrary, claims that the lack of popularity of experimental legislation among US federal agencies can be explained in light of the disinclination of special interest groups towards experimental regulations.[82] The implications of these arguments are

---

76 'Constituency casework' is the assistance provided by Congressmen to constituents in order to solve their problems with government agencies.

77 Mordecai Lee, 'Political-Administrative Relations in State Government: A Legislative Perspective' (2006) 29 *International Journal of Public Administration* 1021, 1029.

78 Bronwen Morgan and Karen Yeung, *An Introduction to Law and Regulation: Text and Materials* (Cambridge University Press, 2007) 43.

79 As an illustration, see Sam Peltzman, 'Toward a More General Theory of Regulation' (1976) 19 *Journal of Law and Economics* 211; George J. Stigler, 'The Theory of Economic Regulation' (1971) 2 *Bell Journal of Economics and Management Science* 3; Richard Posner, 'Theories of Economic Regulation' (1971) 5 *Bell Journal of Law and Economics and Management Science* 335.

80 Lee, 'Political-Administrative Relations in State Government', n. 78 above, 1030.

81 Richard E. Myers, 'Responding to the Time-Based Failures of the Criminal Law Through a Criminal Sunset Amendment' (2008) 49 *Boston College Law Review* 1327, 1373; Rebecca M. Kysar, 'Lasting Legislation' (2011) 159 *University of Pennsylvania Law Review* 1007; Rebecca M. Kysar, 'The Sun Also Rises: The Political Economy of Sunset Provisions in the Tax Code' (2006) 40(2) *Georgia Law Review* 335.

82 Zachary J. Gubler, 'Experimental Rules' (2014) 55 *Boston College Law Review* 129.

different: the first position tries to demonstrate that sunset clauses open the door to new rent-seeking opportunities for special interest groups, in particular in tax legislation, and argues that preference should be given to permanent legislation. The second position appears to contradict the first by suggesting that, in a political economy rationale, these groups would be willing to 'pay less' for temporary laws. The contents and field of law in question determine the attitude of special interest groups which will be willing 'to pay more' for an experimental law, if this provides them with larger benefits in the long run. There is thus no contradiction between the two positions; rather the difference of perspectives relates to the divergent fields of application. Kysar has tax law in mind; while Gubler refers to experiments with regulations to be enacted by federal agencies.

In Chapter 2, sunset clauses and experimental legislation were described as instruments suitable to advance the quality of legislation and public administration. However, according to the literature, these functions have been 'captured' by politicians and special interest groups.[83] Rebecca Kysar argues that, in the field of tax law, sunset clauses have been recently employed 'as apparatuses that underestimate the revenue costs of legislation or fit the legislation within predetermined budget constraints … and function as rent-extracting mechanisms'.[84] By enacting sunset clauses that involve tax cuts instead of permanent laws, lawmakers could reduce the estimation of the revenue costs of these laws, since the calculation would only take the sunset period into account. However, in practice, the original plan was to renew these tax cuts later. Moreover, sunset clauses have been used to circumvent budgetary constraints and enact laws meant to last under the 'cover' of a temporary provision.[85]

In the United States, it has been argued that the above-mentioned rent-extracting mechanisms will be at stake when legislative modifications imply modifying the benefits granted to a group. The uncertainty underlying sunset clauses (for example, whether or not the law will be terminated upon the sunset date or renewed for an additional period) may produce a negative influence in the democratic process since it can encourage interest groups to lobby for the option that benefits them the

[83] The term 'capture' should be partially understood in the sense developed by the Public Choice theorists (see for example, Stigler, 'The Theory of Economic Regulation', n. 80 above.

[84] Kysar, 'The Sun Also Rises', n. 82 above, 339.

[85] Manoj Viswanathan, 'Sunset Provisions in the Tax Code: A Critical Evaluation and Prescriptions for the Future' (2011) 82 *New York University Law Review* 656.

most.[86] This is a perfect scenario for legislators to 'extract rents from sunset date to sunset date, without regard to what is actually the optimal policy choice'.[87] The successive sunsets create opportunities for well-organized interest groups to lobby for the renewal of these sunset clauses. According to Kysar, this phenomenon shifts the potential original benefits of these sunset clauses from the 'poorly organized majority with diffuse interest to a highly organized minority by creating occasions for rent-extraction'.[88] The described rent-extraction mechanism (or at least its awareness) appears, however, to be a typically US reality, since the Netherlands and Germany have never known a period of abundant regulatory sunsets as the United States has. In addition, as it results *a contrario* from Chapter 2, sunset clauses are not connected with tax legislation in these European countries.

7.5 ENACTMENT OR IMPLEMENTATION PATHOLOGIES

As previously stated, sunset clauses and experimental laws and regulations have not been adopted on a systematic basis. However, when these instruments are enacted and prove to be less effective than originally expected, the focus is precisely on this failure and not on the underlying reasons for the ineffectiveness. The 'sunset fad' in the 1980s in the United States was replaced in the 1990s by a strong disappointment with this instrument, which was partially explained by the excessive number of poorly considered sunset clauses.[89] According to a report of the Bertelsmann Stiftung, the failure of sunset clauses can often be explained by the 'limited time and resources available for sunset review, lack of acceptance, and unrealistic expectations with regard to the effects of sunsetting'.[90] The elements highlighted by that report were the results of a comparative study including the United States and Germany. In the first country, particularly serious implementation deficiencies have been identified in recent years contributing to a general disenchantment with this legislative instrument. As Gary Marchant and Lyn Gaudet explain,

---

86 *Ibid.* 678.

87 *Ibid.* 678, 680.

88 Kysar, 'The Sun Also Rises', n. 82 above, 340.

89 See Richard C. Kearney, 'Sunset: A Survey and Analysis of the State Experience' (1999) 50 *Public Administration Review* 49.

90 Bertelsmann Stiftung, *Sunset Legislation and Better Regulation*, n. 59 above.

even when 'Congress complied with the technical requirements of temporary legislation', it did not comply 'with its spirit'.[91] Many laws were reauthorized but their effects were not truly re-examined. Congress regularly overlooked the fact that the central goal of sunset clauses was not termination, but guaranteeing legislative oversight.

During the Reagan administration, 175 organizations were analyzed for potential termination, however, only a small minority of them was extinguished. According to a study by Herbert Kaufman, the termination of these agencies was determined 'by luck' and not by clear patterns.[92] The 1980s 'sunset fad', which spread at state level throughout the United States, came to an end in the 1990s. By then, 12 states had already suspended or repealed sunsetting.[93]

Since 1990, the interest in sunset clauses has progressively diminished at the state level and nowadays the enactment of these dispositions in the context of agency review has become sporadic.[94] Numerous reasons have been suggested for the decreasing interest in sunset clauses in the United States: lobbies against sunset clauses; ineffective sunset reviews; lack of adequate evaluation criteria to apply to agencies under review; and excessive burdens.[95] John Finn suggests that if the 'measure of success' of sunset clauses would be the frequency with which they lead to expiration or non-renewal of the statutory provisions to which they are connected, then it would be clear that the great majority of sunset clauses are not effective.[96] Finn explains that most sunset clauses were not adequately reviewed and terminated, but rather automatically renewed.

---

[91] Lyn M. Gaudet and Gary Marchant, 'Administrative Tools for More Adaptive and Responsive Regulation' in Gary Marchant, Braden R. Allenby and Joseph R. Herket (eds), *The Growing Gap Between Emerging Technologies and Legal Ethical Oversight: The Pacing Problem* (Springer, 2011) 167, 178.

[92] Herbert Kauffman, *Are Government Organizations Immortal?* (Brookings Institution, 1976); Kirkpatrick, Lester and Peterson, 'The Policy Termination Process', n. 25 above, 211.

[93] Bertelsmann Stiftung, *Sunset Legislation and Better Regulation*, n. 59 above, 10.

[94] Thomas W. Merrill (as one of the panelists), 'Showcase Panel IV: A Federal Sunset Law, The Federalist Society 2011 National Lawyers Convention' (2012) 16(2) *Texas Review of Law and Politics* 339, 342.

[95] Bastian Jantz and Sylvia Veit in Bertelsmann Stiftung, *Sunset Legislation and Better Regulation*, n. 59 above, 10.

[96] John E. Finn, 'Sunset Clauses and Democratic Deliberation: Assessing the Significance of Sunset Provisions in Antiterrorism Legislation' (2009) 48 *Columbia Journal of Transnational Law* 442, 495.

To wit, during the 1970s and 1980s, in Alabama, Arkansas and Louisiana, the legislators compromised the goals of sunset review by enacting too many sunset clauses that were required to be evaluated at the same time. The pressure to evaluate or to renew sunset provisions was often solved by automatic renewals or superficial evaluations.[97] In the mentioned context, there are several examples that illustrate the failed implementation of this instrument, such as in the case of the Commodity Futures Trading Commission, an example of 'a non-serious attempt to diminish the power of the agency', which, despite the chorus of criticism, was renewed on several occasions.[98]

Sunset clauses were not the only temporary instrument 'suffering from a deficient implementation syndrome'. There are also examples of experimental laws whose ineffectiveness can be attributed to poor execution. An example of a failed experiment in education is the Georgia Private School Tax Credit Law designed to integrate minorities and low-income children by giving them the possibility to attend a private school (see example 7.3).[99] This state law was considered to be socially innovative since it would give 'the opportunity for children to have choices in education' despite their families' low incomes.[100] The lack of an *ex ante* defined framework influenced the result of the first phase of the experiment: many students who were granted a scholarship did not transfer to a private school; some of the eligible students did not even come from disadvantaged families; other low income students wishing to change to another school were not contemplated for a subsidy; and the absence of accountability facilitated multiple abuses.[101] Not only did the experiment fail to attain the objective of promoting the transfer of children to private schools, but it also turned out to be an expensive mistake.

---

[97] See Anthony R. Licata, 'Zero-base Sunset Review' (1977) 14 *Harvard Journal on Legislation* 505.

[98] The Commodity Futures Trading Commission still exists, for more information, see www.cftc.gov/index.htm.

[99] See the report of the Southern Education Foundation, *A Failed Experiment: Georgia's Tax Credit Scholarships for Private Schools* (2011), available at www.southerneducation.org/pdf/Failed%20Experiment-SEF%20full%20report.pdf.

[100] *Ibid.* 8.

[101] *Ibid.*

EXAMPLE 7.3 GEORGIA TAX CREDIT SCHOLARSHIP FOR PRIVATE SCHOOLS

As stated on the website of Georgia's Department of Education, the Georgia Private School Tax Credit Law was designed to allow 'eligible private citizens and corporations to receive tax credits for donations to Student Scholarship Organizations (SSOs). SSOs will provide student scholarships to parents of eligible children who plan to attend private schools'. Nonetheless, no clear income limits regarding the eligibility of students were established in advance; some of the affiliated schools were not eligible for the subsidy; no accountability systems were established; and little attention was paid to the execution of the experiment. New income caps have been defined so as to overcome the above-mentioned original deficiencies of this law.[102]

Alongside the political elements explained above, the hasty and inconsiderate enactment of these dispositions[103] and the lack of a clear framework for the implementation of these instruments have been pointed out as some of the underlying problems. Contrary to what the two examples might suggest, the United States is not the only jurisdiction struggling with these difficulties. The Netherlands and Germany face similar problems. Two categories of problems susceptible of contributing to the 'failure' of sunset clauses and experimental legislation will be put forward: deficiencies at the design level, and implementation problems.

7.5.1 Problems at the Design or Enactment Level

(a) Deficient goals and evaluation criteria

In many of the early cases of sunset laws, no objectives were defined and, when there were review criteria, these were often methodologically

---

102 For more information, see the official website of the Georgia Department of Education, www.gadoe.org/.

103 See Anthony R. Licata, 'Zero-base Sunset Review', n. 98 above.

deficient.[104] Instead of solving these problems, these deficiencies contaminated sunset reviews in other US states since most sunset laws were inspired by the first of their kind enacted in Colorado and Florida.[105]

The failure of sunset review of agencies in the 1980s in the United States can be partially explained by the fact that most sunset reviews were not conducted while taking into account whether the agency's programme had been fulfilled and to what extent.[106] The first sunset clauses employed in the late 1970s in the United States did not require the programmes to be evaluated or merely defined very broad public policy evaluation criteria (for example, 'whether or not there is a reasonable relationship between the exercise of a state's police power and the protection of the public health').[107] These pathologies undermined the original purposes of sunset clauses of offering legislative oversight and promoting programme effectiveness. In these cases, evaluators could not conclude whether a programme had been effective at the time of the sunset because they were not provided with the 'measure of effectiveness', in other words, the clear objectives to be attained.

(b) Duration of sunset clauses and experimental legislation

Jacob Gersen and Eric Posner have argued that 'the timing of a law can be just as important as its content'.[108] This statement referred to the 'timing' of laws, rather than to the temporary limitation of legislation. The first issue refers to the timing of effects, the second to the implementation of a law as a whole (effects included). Nevertheless, this is equally applicable to sunset clauses and experimental laws and regulations, where the duration of these legislative instruments determines their effectiveness. As mentioned in Chapter 3, the definition of the duration of these instruments, particularly under uncertain conditions, can constitute one of the most troublesome aspects of their enactment.

---

[104] Lewis Anthony Davis, 'Review Procedures and Public Accountability in Sunset Legislation: An Analysis and Proposal for Reform' (1981) 33 *Administrative Law Review* 393, 398.

[105] *Ibid.* 397.

[106] *Ibid.* 395.

[107] *Ibid.* 396. The example given as to a vague evaluation criteria were inserted in the Colorado Review Stature s. 24-34-104(8)(b)(III).

[108] Jacob E. Gersen and Eric A. Posner, 'Timing Rules and Legal Institutions' (2007) 121 *Harvard Law Review* 543.

According to a study performed in 1990 by Kearney, most sunset clauses were characterized by incorrect sunset review periods.[109] Excessively short periods burdened sunset commissions with constant reviews and did not provide for meaningful results. This was the case of the production tax credits (see Chapter 4) that were designed to stimulate investment in renewable energy and hence advance clean energy innovation.[110] These tax credits were subject to a sunset, which could be renewed for the period of one to three years. However, it takes three to seven years to develop a wind farm, which meant that, due to this disparity in duration, entrepreneurs would be uncertain as to the renewal of the tax credit. This could consequently slow down long-term investment.[111]

The definition of a duration period has also been regarded as the Achilles heel of experimental legislation. The credibility of experimental legislation as an effective learning instrument depends on compliance with the 'rules of the game', namely, a meaningful duration. At the time of the drafting of an experimental law, legislators do not know enough about the complexities of the subject-matter to be regulated but they must ensure that the experiment lasts long enough to produce significant results. This includes the guarantee that experiments will not be terminated before their objectives are achieved. Experiments should only be terminated early if there are solid grounds to believe that the underlying goals cannot be attained, or their continuation produces more damages or costs than benefits. In some cases, it can be unclear whether the termination of an experiment is based on the already observed results or on the influence of special interests and public opinion. An illustration of this complexity was visible in the Dutch 'dentist experiment' (see example 7.4) which was designed to stimulate the deregulation of dentistry tariffs. This experiment was terminated before the results were conclusive.

---

[109] Kearney, 'Sunset: A Survey and Analysis of the State Experience', n. 90 above, 51.

[110] Erin Dewey, 'Sundown and You Better Take Care: Why Sunset Provisions Harm the Renewable Energy Industry and Violate Tax Principles' (2011) 52 *Boston College Law Review* 1105.

[111] *Ibid.*

EXAMPLE 7.4 DUTCH DENTIST EXPERIMENT

In the Netherlands, dental professions and their tariffs have been regulated by the Dutch Healthcare Authority since 2006. An attempt to deregulate this market was made in 2012: as of 1 January, dentists were allowed to determine their own tariffs on an experimental basis (*experiment met de vrije prijsvorming in de mondzorg*). This possibility was already foreseen in the Healthcare Market Organization Statute,[112] which allows the Dutch Healthcare authority to enact an experiment through a policy rule and temporarily deviate from existing tariffs.[113] Contrary to the original predictions of the regulator, the deregulation of dentists' rates resulted in higher prices. The patients soon complained and this strong public opinion against the deregulation of tariffs was confirmed by a monitoring report of prices published by the Dutch Healthcare Authority with reference to the first trimester of 2012.[114] In this period, a 6 per cent increase in the prices had been observed, but the Dutch Healthcare Authority predicted that more time was required in order to allow patients and healthcare providers to adapt to the new market conditions.[115] The regulator suggested in this context a partial return to a regulated system, namely, by introducing a regulated 'dentist season ticket' for youth dental care. However, a further step was taken. In June, the Dutch Parliament voted and

[112] Wet marktordening gezondheidszorg Wet van 7 juli 2006, houdende regels inzake marktordening, doelmatigheid en beheerste kostenontwikkeling op het gebied van de gezondheidszorg (Wet marktordening gezondheidszorg), Stb. 2006, 415; this statute has been revised multiple times since 2006 and a number of revisions are still pending; for the most recent version, see www.wetten.overheid.nl.

[113] See for example, Besluit inzake aanvulling procedure en uitbreiding van kortdurende kleinschalige experimenten met AWBZ-zorg, Aanwijzing van de Staatssecretaris van Volksgezondheid, Welzijn en Sport van 8 mei 2008, MC-U-2847325 op grond van artikel 7 van de Wet marktordening gezondheidszorg inzake aanvulling procedure en uitbreiding van kortdurende kleinschalige experimenten met AWBZ-zorg, Stcrt. 2008, 92.

[114] Letter to Minister Schippers (VWS) and to Parliament about the progress of the experiment with the free determination of prices in dental care, 25 June 2012, available at www.rijksoverheid.nl/documenten-en-publicaties/kamerstukken/2012/06/25/kamerbrief-over-experiment-vrije-prijzen-mondzorg.html.

[115] *Ibid.*

approved a motion in favour of the termination of this experiment, despite the concerns of the Minister that it was too soon to terminate the experiment.

In the context described in example 7.4 and less than one year after the enactment of the experiment, the responsible Minister announced the termination of the 'dentist experiment'.[116] Several associations of Dutch dental care professionals initiated judicial proceedings at the court of The Hague, requesting the invalidation of the (ministerial) instruction that determined the termination of the experiment or the prohibition on the state to implement this order.[117] The petitioners grounded their request on the conflict between this instruction and the principles of good administration, namely, the obligation to state reasons in writing for all decisions, the principle of legal certainty and the prohibition of arbitrariness.[118] The petitioners argued that the interruption of the experiment was based on insufficient and premature information. Although the Dutch court acknowledged that the sudden termination of the experiment was questionable from a policy consistency point of view, it underlined as well that the Minister of Public Health was allowed to exercise discretion and modify implemented policy, even if this implied damaging previous expectations.[119] According to the court, the termination of the experiment would only be unacceptable if the Minister, after considering the available information, should necessarily have reached another decision. However, this was not the case since there were elements pointing in the direction chosen by the Minister.

The example of the Dutch 'dentist experiment' demonstrates the difficulty in ensuring that an experimental law or regulation endures for a meaningful period of time, despite public opinion. The above-mentioned example of the German Anti-Child Pornography Law is a similar example of a temporary act which due to a change in politics and the lack of social consensus was terminated just one year after its enactment.

---

116 Regeling aanwijzing ex artikel 7 Wet marktordening gezondheidszorg (stopzetten experiment vrije tarieven mondzorg), Aanwijzing van de Minister van Volksgezondheid, Welzijn en Sport van 12 juli 2012, no. MC-U-3122855, op grond van artikel 7 van de Wet marktordening gezondheidszorg, inzake stopzetten experiment vrije tarieven mondzorg, Stcrt. 2012, 14943.

117 *Rechtbank 's-Gravenhage,* 12 September 2012, LJN: BX7092.

118 *Ibid.*

119 *Ibid.*

Abrupt termination is, in most cases, a negative product of political pressure, since a few months are not sufficient to observe meaningful results.

7.5.2 Intricacies at the Implementation Level

(a) Disregard for participation of stakeholders

The lack of meaningful citizen participation or disregard for the input of stakeholders in the review process have also been regarded as noteworthy deficiencies of sunset clauses.[120] The latter was visible in the sunset review process of the Civil Aeronautics Board, where the criticism pointed out by citizens was not taken into account.[121] More recently, Michael Crain argued that sunset clauses have not achieved a significant level of public participation due to the lobbying activity of special interest groups.[122]

In the Netherlands, in the context of the Wientjes Commission,[123] representatives of different sectors were allowed to express their concerns as to the regulatory burdens imposed on companies and offer possible solutions. In Germany, it is unclear whether and how the participation of stakeholders is considered.[124] It is not clear from the literature on sunset clauses or on experimental legislation how the stakeholder's input is taken into consideration and whether the objection based on the lack of meaningful participation is still valid.

In the above-described context, it is possible to refer to the intricacies of general consultations in the context of lawmaking. Consultations were originally conceived to allow minorities and groups with reduced democratic participation to have a say in the lawmaking process. However, the participation of stakeholders is not always meaningful: consultations are often captured by special interest groups which tend to be active participants in these processes; the influence of the stakeholders concerns

---

[120] Kearney, Sunset: A Survey and Analysis of the State Experience, n. 90 above, 50, 55.

[121] *Ibid.* 50.

[122] Michael D. Crain, 'Time for the Sun to Rise on Federal Sunset Legislation' (2000) 8 *Public Law* 10, 13.

[123] See for example, Letter from the Commissie Regeldruk to the Minister of Justice, Dr. E.M.H. Hirsch Ballin, 2 December 2008, available at www.rijksoverheid.nl/documenten-en-publicaties/rapporten/2010/08/27/advies-commissie-wientjes-over-horizonbepalingen-in-wetgeving.html.

[124] Bertelsmann Stiftung, *Sunset Legislation and Better Regulation*, n. 59 above, 21.

mostly cosmetic revisions of the law or regulation and rarely affects the policy choices made.[125]

(b) Evaluation and validity of experiment

The design of experimental laws and regulations determines to a great extent the reliability and validity of the results obtained.[126] This can be a problem caused by deficiencies both at the enactment and implementation levels. In addition, the fact that experimental laws and policy experiments 'occur in the real world' and not under laboratory controlled conditions already puts at stake the possibility to generalize from the results obtained and apply them later elsewhere.[127] This means, for example, that the effectiveness of experiments in the context of the so-called 'laboratories of democracy' (see Chapter 2) may vary across place, time and policy or legal field.

The lack of a solid experimental design has been pointed out in the United States as one of the main deficiencies of experimental regulations.[128] Many experiments performed by the Federal Energy Commission were undertaken on an 'ad hoc' basis and with reduced review of existing case law connected with the enactment of experimental regulations without an adequate experimental design. Experimental legislation faces an obvious objection: the lack of random assignment, which characterizes experiments that aim at being valid and to produce results that can be generalized to a wider public. While a casuistic approach must always be taken, the existence of methodological guidelines could confer objectivity on experimental legislation. None of the countries under analysis possesses a clear legal or methodological framework (see Chapter 3 for a proposed framework). In Germany and in the Netherlands, the literature has attempted to provide legal guidelines, but no references to the methodology of experimental legislation have been made.[129]

---

125 Patricia Popelier, Rob van Gestel, Koen van Aeken, Vicky Verlinden and Peter van Humbeeck, *Consultaties in de Wetgevingspraktijk: Een zoektocht naar internationale best practices* (Politeia, 2008) 132–5.

126 Paul B. Mohler, 'Experiments at the FERC: In Search of a Hypothesis' (1998) 19 *Energy Law Journal* 281, 302.

127 See Mark Carl Rom, 'Taking the Brandeis Metaphor Seriously: Policy Experimentation within a Federal System' in Alan S. Gerber and Eric M. Patashnik (eds), *Promoting the General Welfare: New Perspectives on Government Performance* (Brookings Institution Press, 2006) 256–82.

128 Mohler, 'Experiments at the FERC', n. 127 above, 304.

129 The most complete works on experimental legislation in Germany only focus on the relationship between this legislative instrument and fundamental principles of law, see Hans-Detlef Horn, *Experimentelle Gesetzgebung unter dem*

(c) Inadequate evaluation or disregard for the results of evaluation reports

Sceptics of the virtues of a broader enactment of sunset clauses and experimental legislation have argued that the information gathered is often disregarded by legislators. The mentioned legislative instruments are often not adequately evaluated or their results are not taken into account.

Sometimes the results of an experiment are experienced as being negative because they are 'ahead of their time'. This was the case of the German experiment with the qualification of lawyers in the 1970s (see example 2.1). More competences were given to federal states to decide on this qualification, on what should be included in the Bachelor of Law programmes and how it should be tested. This experiment was established with the participation of different states, including Hamburg, Bremen, Baden-Württemberg, Nordrhein-Westfalen and Rheinland-Pfalz. The 'new' model of legal education (*einstufige Juristenausbildung*) was regarded as an alternative to the two-step qualification, implying sitting for state exams. This experiment aimed to enhance the interaction between theory and practice and ensure that students could perform different traineeships during their education. This experiment was introduced in 1971 for the period of ten years and abolished in 1981.[130] Due to its controversial character, this type of legal education was abolished in the 1980s without an adequate evaluation, and without considering indication of change.

The Dutch law on the risk reference index for youth[131] (*verwijsindex risico's jeudigen*') suggests that the above-mentioned sceptics might have a point: in 2008, a new law was proposed completely ignoring the then ongoing experiment (*proeftuin*) and its results. The Council of State

---

Grundgesetz (Duncker and Humblot, 1989); Volker Maaβ, *Experimentierklauseln für die Verwaltung und ihre verfassungrechtlichen Grenzen* (Duncker and Humblot, 2001). For the Netherlands, Simon Bulut and Gert-Jan Veerman, *Over horizon- en experimenteerbepalingen* (Ministerie van Justitie, 2010).

[130] Ernst E. Hirsch, 'Experimentierklausel' (1971) 26 *Juristenzeitung* 286.

[131] Wet van 4 februari 2010 tot wijziging van de Wet op de jeugdzorg in verband met de introductie van een verwijsindex om vroegtijdige en onderling afgestemde verlening van hulp, zorg of bijsturing ten behoeve van risico jongere die bepaalde risico's lopen te bevorderen (verwijsindex risicojongeren), Stb. 2010, 89.

criticized this and advised reference to the experiment and consideration of the evaluation report of the experiment.[132]

Legislators do not always feel constrained by evaluation reports. An example is the experiment with reduced VAT rates on labour intensive services. In this case, the European Commission decided to ignore the negative results verified in the different Member States, and convert the experimental Directive into a permanent one (see example 7.5).

EXAMPLE 7.5 RESULTS OF THE EXPERIMENTAL DIRECTIVE ON REDUCED VAT RATES

At the end of the four-year experimental period, the participating Member States provided the European Commission with information regarding the evaluation of the experiment.[133] The reports were far from enthusiastic. Based on this evidence, the Commission concluded that there was no direct causal link between reduced rates of VAT and job creation.[134] Furthermore, the evidence in some Member States demonstrated that lower rates of VAT were not fully reflected in prices.[135] In conclusion, the reduced VAT rates on labour intensive services did not achieve the original objectives for which they were introduced. Despite the mixed evidence, in 2006, the Council adopted Directive 2006/18/EC which allowed Member States either to

[132] Opinion of the Council of State of 17 October 2008, Kamerstukken II, 2008/2009, 31 855, no. 4 on voorstel van wet houdende wijziging van de Wet op de jeugdzorg in verband met de introductie van een verwijsindex waarin jeugdigen kunnen worden gemeld die bepaalde risico's lopen (verwijsindex risico's index jeugdigen), 14. Following the ministerial reply to this Opinion (included in the same document), the advice of the Council of State was that the evaluation report of the experiment should be taken into consideration.

[133] See Report from the Commission to the Council and the European Parliament, *Experimental Application of a Reduced Rate of VAT to Certain Labor-intensive Services*, SEC(2003)622/ COM/2003/0309 final. For more detailed information on the Member States, see *Evaluation Report on the Experimental Application of a Reduced Rate of VAT to Certain Labor-intensive Services*, Commission Staff Working Paper, COM(2003)309 final/SEC/2003/0622 final.

[134] *Ibid.*

[135] See Report from the Commission to the Council and the European Parliament, n. 134 above.

continue applying this reduced VAT rate until 31 December 2010 or to start applying it, if they had not already participated in the experiment. In 2009, regardless of the existing evidence, the Council adopted Directive 2009/47/EC which allowed the optional use of reduced rates for certain labour-intensive local services on a permanent basis.

The reduced VAT rates example demonstrates that the legislator may turn a blind eye to all existing evidence when the political statement behind the experiment is more important than the results observed.

7.6 COSTS AND BURDENS

The burdens of the implementation of sunset clauses and experimental legislation designed to produce information and test the effectiveness of new laws and regulations can be compared, to a certain extent, to those of conducting empirical studies: both are costly and time-consuming, remaining fairly unused by lawyers.[136] The enactment of sunset clauses and experimental legislation is burdensome in multiple ways.

Guido Calabresi, in his book *A Common Law for the Age of Statutes*, evidenced his scepticism towards sunset clauses, arguing that the implementation of this instrument would require significant resources.[137] In fact, the literature has been highly critical as to the employment of sunsets in determined fields, such as tax law, since these legislative instruments would misrepresent the true costs of legislation.[138] It has been argued that sunset clauses employed in the context of production tax credits designed to stimulate investment in renewable energy can 'frustrate the simplicity goal of the tax system by increasing the costs of compliance'.[139] If the sunset is frequent (as in the mentioned case), taxpayers must spend additional resources in order to ensure that their projects are completed before the sunset date in order to obtain the

---

[136] Laurens Walker, 'Perfecting Federal Civil Rules: A Proposal for Restricted Field Experiments' (1988) 51 *Law and Contemporary Problems* 67, 70.

[137] Guido Calabresi, *A Common Law for the Age of Statutes* (Cambridge University Press, 1992) 61.

[138] William G. Gale and Peter R. Orzag, 'Sunsets in the Tax Code' (2003) 99 *Tax Notes* 1153, 1157.

[139] Dewey, 'Sundown and You Better Take Care', n. 111 above, 1122.

production tax credit and avoid being submitted to new rules which differ from the previous ones.

According to the study performed by Kearney in 1990, most states in the United States did not have any real perception of the actual costs of sunset clauses. Whereas sunset clauses should theoretically lead to savings since they imply the termination of agencies; in practice, Kearney concluded that it was difficult to calculate if there were effective savings and if they compensated for the costs implied by sunset clauses.[140] The excessive costs of sunset review, often outweighing the benefits, have been difficult to calculate since the enactment of the first sunset clauses. No substantial improvements at this level have been described more recently.[141] However, this 'story' can have a different ending, provided that we analyze the costs of the lawmaking process as a whole and enact sunset clauses within a clear framework. Temporary legislation does not necessarily imply higher costs: such instruments simply 'allocate the costs between the current-period and future-period legislature'. Jacob Gersen affirms that 'the higher transaction costs of temporary legislation during the sunset year may be partially, if not entirely, offset by lower relative transaction costs in the time periods prior to the sunset'. According to Gersen, the intuition that temporary legislation is 'more costly' is not supported by either theoretical or empirical claims.[142]

In Germany, it was also claimed that sunset clauses also appeared to be a costly instrument since they lead to savings in the first years of implementation, due to the reduction in the number of regulations; but later, as more legislative oversight was required, the costs would increase.[143] It is worth remembering that a number of German states have adopted general sunset clauses, meaning that a significant number of regulations must be extinguished. In order to avoid the unwise extinction of regulations, states will have to incur 'legislative oversight' costs.

There is scarce literature on implementation costs of experimental legislation; however, this does not mean that these legislative instruments have not received the same objections as sunset clauses. The implementation of experimental laws implies transaction costs of informing judges and lawyers about the temporary experimental rules and training them in

---

[140] Kearney, 'Sunset: A Survey and Analysis of the State Experience', n. 90 above, 54.

[141] Davis, 'Review Procedures and Public Accountability in Sunset Legislation', n. 105 above, 396.

[142] Gersen, 'Temporary Legislation', n. 51 above, 263.

[143] Bertelsmann Stiftung, *Sunset Legislation and Better Regulation*, n. 59 above, 19.

the introduced specificities; (delay) costs of the application of beneficial rules to those that are not included in the sample group; the implicit costs of potential errors of implementing ineffective rules; and monitoring and evaluation costs.[144]

Although temporary laws require 'multiple rounds of enactment costs' and permanent laws do not, this does not mean that the former will be more costly than the latter, since all laws must fulfil the same constitutional, legal and procedural enactment requirements and respective costs.[145] It is difficult to conclude whether sunset clauses and experimental laws are more costly than permanent laws and particularly inefficient ones: the maintenance costs of temporary laws may be lower because they last, in principle, fewer years and no repealing costs will be incurred when the sunset is approaching.[146] However, the efficient monitoring of sunset clauses and experiments can undoubtedly counterbalance the mentioned lower costs, being determinant in a cost-benefit analysis of these instruments.

In conclusion, sunset clauses and experimental legislation require a clear enactment and implementation framework. Notwithstanding the discussed objections, legislators should not be discouraged by the examples of ineffective laws that were passed and implemented without explicit goals, for an insignificant duration or without an adequate evaluation methodology. Sunset clauses and experimental laws can perform differently and better.

7.7 PRELIMINARY CONCLUSION

Returning to the opening quotation of this chapter, it can now be argued that lawmakers are often aware of the existence of sunset clauses and experimental legislation, but are unwilling or unable to implement them. The examples of ineffective sunset clauses and experimental legislation may too easily influence the decision not to adopt these types of laws, whereas one should first question why these laws have failed and what could have been done to prevent it.

At the end of Part II, it was clear that most legal hesitations could be resolved by taking a good look at the current interpretation of the fundamental principles under analysis and designing a clear legal framework for the enactment and implementation of sunset clauses and

---

144 Walker, 'Perfecting Federal Civil Rules', n. 137 above.

145 Gersen, 'Temporary Legislation', n. 51 above, 263.

146 *Ibid.* 247.

experimental legislation. While acknowledging the difficulty to control political forces, a similar conclusion is reached here. As described in this chapter, most cases of failed sunset clauses or experimental laws were not exclusively explained by political elements but also by the non-existence of a clear and accurate framework. It is this framework that will guarantee the reliability and validity of sunset clauses and experimental laws. If the goals and results of the evaluation performed with regard to these legislative instruments are clear, transparent and accurate, there will be less room for political misappropriation of sunset clauses and experimental laws and regulations. In Chapter 8, final guidelines are provided for the enactment of sunset clauses and experimental legislation.

PART IV

Conclusion

8. Conclusion

> *Ex facto jus oritur* … no law, written or unwritten, can be understood without a full knowledge of the facts out of which it arises and to which it is to be applied. But the struggle for the living law has not been fully won.
>
> Louis Brandeis[1]

8.1 THOUGHTS ON A LEGISLATIVE MIDWAY BETWEEN PAST AND FUTURE

New and old dilemmas characterize modern day lawmaking: we are inevitably bound by a nostalgia for the past but we long for the promising future. Tomorrow's laws will always seem more attractive than today's laws are. Still, we hold on to yesterday's rules because they are 'safe', predictable and long-standing. But are they better? Is the 'rule of law' always 'a law of [lasting] rules'? Or is it a law of rules that draws its inspiration from society, savours it and improves the 'recipe' from time to time to guarantee a law does not turn 'sour' as time goes by? In this book, two tools for this iterative and learning approach to law have been explored: sunset clauses and experimental legislation. They have been presented as a midway between eternity and innovation; an appearance of lasting certainty and the certainty of a temporary rule; equality in poverty and temporary inequality in the pursuit of wealth; laws that remain and laws that move forward. They are instruments at the crossroads between the information society and the ignorance society that promise more flexibility and learning opportunities than permanent legislation. They are not a panacea, but they are useful and deserve more attention from lawmakers.

This study navigated through different theoretical approaches to lawmaking as an experimental, learning and evidence-based process which

---

[1] Louis Brandeis, 'The Living Law', an address delivered before the Chicago Bar Association, 3 January 1916, available at www.law.louisville.edu/library/collections/brandeis/node/223.

should be characterized by periodic monitoring and, in some cases, periodic termination. This book adopts the perspective that laws should be adapted to the evolution of the times. Briefly, sunset clauses and experimental legislation respond to the need to confer more flexibility on lawmaking so as to adapt it to changing times and allow legislators to legislate as they learn from the gathered information.

8.1.1 Flexibility in Lawmaking

Both sunset clauses and experimental legislation offer flexibility to legislators and regulators, notably thanks to the possibility to define adaptable goals and enable the adjustment of laws and regulations according to the evolution of circumstances. These instruments offer a complementary perspective that grants 'time flexibility'. To wit, sunset clauses and experimental regulations allow the legislators and regulators to rethink the necessity of particular rules and their contents in light of their effects, changes in circumstances or the evolution of state-of-art technology or of society. In the meantime, legislators can test the new rules in the 'real world' and gather information. This flexible approach to lawmaking designed to test the effects of a novel legal solution and draw lessons from it brings us to the second pillar: the importance of developing an iterative 'learning by doing' process to meet the challenges of legislating in a changing society. This is a valuable approach that is not specific to the regulation of highly innovative or technical fields but that characterizes a number of policy and legal reforms.[2]

8.1.2 Learning by Doing

Similarly to natural sciences, experimentation in law is said to be motivated by the lack of information: the effects and side-effects of a new policy are unknown, the response of citizens and private actors to policies aimed at stimulating innovation are equally uncertain and the potential risks may demand caution. As underlined by Jacob Gersen, it is precisely this 'cognitive bias' which constitutes a valid justification for enacting temporary legislation.[3] Experimenting with a law can be

---

[2] Andreas Bernecker and Christina Gathmann, *Trial and Error? Policy Experimentation during the US Welfare Reform*, University of Manheim Working Paper (2013), available at http://adam.vwl.uni-mannheim.de/fileadmin/user_upload/MACRO/Bernecker___Gathmann_13-05.pdf.

[3] Jacob E. Gersen, 'Temporary Legislation' (2007) 74 *University of Chicago Law Review* 247, 268.

regarded as a means of gathering more information and overcoming this bias.[4] The 'learning by doing' approach takes into account the complexities of complex and innovative fields, while simultaneously assessing the response of individual behaviour to new legal rules and enabling flexible adaptations of legislation to the lessons learned.[5] This learning approach is also said to be particularly suitable for federal states, where policy innovation can flourish through experimentation at state level: states can learn from each other and, theoretically, the federal legislator could also draw lessons from states.[6] Although experimental legislation was traditionally regarded as a typical instrument and a privilege of federal systems, there are recent claims in the literature that experimentation is equally (or even more) suited for uni-jurisdictional systems.[7] The Netherlands is an example of a unitary state where experimental legislation is currently being enacted.

Experimental regulations are a tool for the rationalization of the legislative process since they expand the experience of legislators with the implementation of a new law, by testing it in a part of the territory and gathering more information on the effects and effectiveness of a regulation. 'In today's fast changing regulatory world, information is critical to informed and just decisions. [Experimental regulations] of good design provide information that can be found no other way. The

---

4 This was claimed in the Netherlands in a pilot project implemented in the field of labour law: Tijdelijke regels voor een pilot ter bevordering van de participatie van personen met een arbeidsbeperking met behulp van loondispensatie (Tijdelijke wet pilot loondispensatie), advies van Raad van State en nader rapport (see reaction of the State Secretary of Social and Labour Affairs to the Opinion of the Council of State of 2 October 2009, No. W12.09.0349/III, Kamerstukken II, 2009–2010, 32165, no. 4, 2. The Council of State considered, on this and other occasions, that the general objective of an experiment could not be to gather information since legislation does not have an inquiring function.

5 Hasan Bakshi, Alan Freedman and Jason Potts, *State of Uncertainty: Innovation Policy through Experimentation* (NESTA, 2011) 4, 16, available at www.nesta.org.uk/library/documents/Provocation_14_State_of_Uncertainty_v7.pdf.

6 Christos Kotsogiannis and Robert Schwager, 'On the Incentives to Experiment in Federations' (2006) 60 *Journal of Urban Economics* 484.

7 Susan Rose-Ackerman, 'Risk Taking and Reelection: Does Federalism Promote Innovation?' (1980) 9 *Journal of Legal Studies* 593.

real world is a laboratory that is nonpareil in quickly providing information which permits policymakers to reject hypotheses that do not work and embrace those that do'.[8]

However, sunset clauses and experimental legislation remain underexamined and underestimated. In this book, different legal and non-legal objections which might be raised to these instruments have been examined. In the following section, a number of conclusions and 'instructions for the use of sunset clauses and experimental legislation' are presented.

8.2 CONCLUSIONS AND INSTRUCTIONS FOR USE

This research was motivated by a perplexity encountered in the literature: sunset clauses and experimental legislation appear to be able to perform multiple functions in different policy fields, including innovative and fast-changing fields; and yet they are not integrated into the 'regulators' daily toolbox'. The mentioned legislative instruments could assist legislators and regulators in regulating innovative products, services and policy programmes under uncertain circumstances and limited information. Sunset clauses and experimental legislation may avoid regulatory delays and inconsistencies. However, these legislative instruments are seldom employed and no straightforward answer for this fact has been provided. Legal and non-legal objections have been raised in the three countries under analysis. Temporary legal dispositions are not well received by traditional scholars, who support the long-lasting character of legislation. While the Netherlands appears to be the most 'inexperienced' and sceptical country with regard to a broader enactment of sunset clauses, and, particularly, experimental legislation, less reservations have been expressed in Germany and in the United States. Continuity is still nowadays an important characteristic of legislation. However, this legal stability should not open the doors to a rigid legal paradigm impervious to changing social norms and practices.[9]

[8] Paul B. Mohler, 'Experiments at the FERC' (1998) 19 *Energy Law Journal* 281, 304.

[9] Stefanie A. Lindquist and Frank C. Cross, *Stability, Predictability and the Rule of Law: Stare Decisis as Reciprocity Norm*, Working Paper (2012), available at www.utexas.edu/law/conferences/measuring/The%20Papers/Rule%20of%20Law%20Conference.crosslindquist.pdf.

Other fundamental principles of law do not seem to be endangered by sunset clauses and experimental legislation either. The German Constitutional Court has been favourable to the enactment of temporary legislation, particularly experimental legislation, rejecting objections regarding the violation of principles of law. As explained in Chapter 5, an objective differentiation between rules will not put at stake the principle of equal treatment. As far as the principle of proportionality is concerned, it was concluded in Chapter 6 that sunset clauses and experimental legislation may, under certain circumstances, be a more appropriate and effective choice than permanent rules. It can thus be concluded that sunset clauses and experimental legislation as such do not violate any fundamental principle of law. However, just like any other form of legislation, they may do so, if no adequate legal framework is observed.

A number of non-legal elements appear to play a role in explaining why sunset clauses and experimental legislation have not been used on a systematic basis (see Chapter 7). These reasons include the lack of information and experience; intellectual misperceptions regarding sunset clauses and experimental legislation; the influence of special interest groups; and the appropriation of results by political actors. These factors have been responsible for the 'bad reputation' of these legislative instruments and appear to be difficult and undesirable to overcome. Paradoxically, political pressure has been a reason to enact, and not to enact, temporary rules. As argued in Chapter 2, it is sometimes important to think strategically in order to gather sufficient political consensus regarding a new law. This strategy can consist in the enactment of experimental laws or regulations that aim to gather more information and, above all, show the opponents and the public in general that these innovations are harmless. Experimental legislation may achieve through the power of the facts what argumentation and rhetoric could not. Although politics is not regarded as an obstacle in this context but rather an inevitable part of lawmaking, more transparency and accountability should be guaranteed in order to ensure that 'truth' is spoken to power, that the latter listens to it and does not try to misuse sunset clauses and experimental legislation.

To sum up, sunset clauses and experimental legislation are valuable legislative instruments, but clear 'instructions for use' are required.

8.3 INSTRUCTIONS FOR USE OF SUNSET CLAUSES AND EXPERIMENTAL LEGISLATION

8.3.1 Permanent Legislation: General Guidelines

As the term conveys, permanent rules should be designed to regulate lasting phenomena. Change is inevitable; however, while in a number of cases legislation only needs to be updated after several decades, in others five years may result in an outdated status for some rules in relation to new technological developments. In the first scenario, legislators can rightly prefer permanent to temporary rules. Permanent legislation is in principle the most appropriate legislative approach to the regulation of social problems or situations that are not characterized by rapid changes and about which sufficient information has been gathered. The legislator does not foresee in this case rapid changes that can justify the use of temporary instruments. Unexpected social changes must be safeguarded against, but based on centuries of legal experience, legislators can already anticipate that some social phenomena are characterized by a slow evolution.

Permanent legislation can equally be preferred when the legislator is required to establish core legal institutions, principles and material concepts. These must have a lasting nature in order to guarantee the stability of the legal order. Nonetheless, an important line should be drawn between the material content of these principles and concepts and their practical implementation: while the first can resist the change of times and is sufficiently open to respond to them, the second should benefit from new technological and social developments. To wit, it is inconceivable that the legislator would set a date on the due process clause. However, bearing in mind the increasing workload faced by judges, the legislator may experiment with new forms of proceedings which ensure that trials take place within a reasonable period of time (European Convention on Human Rights (ECHR), Article 6). Therefore, institutions and concepts that resist the ravages of time should be granted a quasi-permanent character; however, this does not preclude the legislator from combining this permanence with a temporary or experimental search for better means of implementation.

In brief, permanent legislation should be employed to regulate: (a) core legal institutions, concretization of legal principles and fundamental concepts of a legal order; (b) realities that do not tend to evolve rapidly; and (c) phenomena that are not new and about which sufficient information and experience has been gathered.

8.3.2 Temporary Rules

Sunset clauses and experimental laws and regulations are not necessarily 'last resort' instruments. Moreover, they can in principle be enacted in most fields of law as long as the underlying problem or situation to be regulated is characterized by uncertainty, potential risks, lack of information, rapid mutations and/or requires a rapid and flexible legislative response. Typical examples include the regulation of telecommunications, complex societal phenomena and emerging technologies. As explained in Chapter 2, sunset clauses and experimental legislation may serve different functions. Therefore, on the grounds of the qualification of the problem to be regulated, the legislator must decide on whether (a) sunset clauses or (b) experimental legislation should be chosen. Since emergency legislation is excluded from the scope of this study (see Chapter 1), no reference will be made to this type of situations.

(a) Sunset clauses

Sunset clauses are particularly suitable as a response to rapidly changing fields or circumstances which justify the extinction of the legal regime to be enacted or its significant review. In the case of sunset clauses, the legislator regards the dispositions to be enacted as merely temporary. In some cases, sunset clauses can also be put at the service of 'learning' or 'consensus-finding' functions (see Chapter 2), and be used as alternatives to lasting legislation. This occurs when the legislator is afraid that the situation to be regulated is temporary; or that the current lack of consensus might be resolved in light of new evidence. In any of these conceivable scenarios, the concepts of *termination* and *legislative oversight* should underlie sunset clauses. When sunset clauses are chosen for these two mentioned purposes, the line between this instrument and experimental legislation can be extremely difficult to draw. As explained in Chapter 2, sunset clauses can be put at the service of a number of objectives. The termination of agencies that are no longer required; the extinction of obsolete regulations; responding to temporary problems; or gathering political or social consensus are some of the functions which may be fulfilled by sunset clauses (see Chapter 2). All of them have a common ground: sunset clauses respond to the need to 'unburden' the legal order of rules that no longer fulfil their original goals in an effective or efficient way. In conclusion, sunset clauses should be used when the legislator can foresee the need to terminate a rule or a number of rules in a short period of time. The legislator's prediction should be based, for example, on consultations and/or *ex ante* evaluations.

The enactment of sunset clauses implies a clear framework characterized by transparency and accountability. Legislators should be explicit as to (a) the goals of the sunset clause (in other words, why the disposition should be terminated); (b) the duration of the sunset clause; (c) grounds of reauthorization; (d) evaluation criteria and, if applicable, the composition of an evaluation or sunset commission. Watching the sun set at a distance should not be the legislator's goal: contributing to a more colourful sunrise of tomorrow's laws should be.

(b) Experimental legislation

Contrary to sunset clauses, experimental regulations aim at continuity and are part of an iterative 'learning' or 'persuasion' process that allows the legislator to gather more information regarding either the nature of a new problem, product or service or new legal dispositions translating a new approach to an existing situation. The gathered informational elements can be valuable not only to obtain more information about the effects and side-effects of new rules but also to convince political opponents about the advantages of the introduction of an innovation in the legal order. Experimental regulations are a first step in the enactment of laws that aim at being permanent but which require at first cautious steps to avoid the whole jurisdiction being exposed to the risk of failure of the new law.

In brief, experimental regulations should be the legislator's first choice in the following scenarios: (a) where the legislator is required to regulate new social or technological problems, products or services; (b) where little is known about such problems, products or services, either regarding their nature or their regulation; (c) where incremental changes in the regulated field may be expected, justifying an experimental adaptation of regulation to new realities; (d) where the legislator aims to confer flexibility on the regulation of a rapidly changing field, by experimenting with rules that can ensure the adaptability of regulation to new social and technological phenomena.

Experimental legislation must be 'handled with care' so as not to be misused by politicians who seek the appearance of evidence to disguise their political statements, instead of using facts to further demonstrate them. When enacting experimental legislation, the Congress and national parliaments should remain, to a great extent, the master of the experiment, formulating (a) the explicit goals of the experiment; (b) the direction, extent and scope of the experiment; (c) its duration; (d) the evaluation criteria; and (e) a reasonable deadline for the institution implementing the experiment to decide on the evaluation report.

8.3.3 Limits to the Enactment of Sunset Clauses and Experimental Legislation

Legislators in EU Member States may, however, be obliged to opt for permanent legislation if the enactment of temporary or experimental rules may endanger the implementation of EU law or the fulfilment of international obligations. This can be the case whenever certain rules concern fundamental precepts of a state that are regarded as the legal pillars of a jurisdiction and/or are indispensable for the operability of a state. These would include basic laws on the organization of the judicial system and public administration, state or regional planning and public financial institutions. On such matters, only strictly ancillary experiments should be authorized.

In brief, sunset clauses and experimental legislation should be the legislator's first choice if the above listed criteria are fulfilled, except when this may lead to violating a higher law, including explicit constitutional provisions, EU and international law. In addition, caution should be exercised in the case of experiments with institutional rules, where the core of material concepts should remain untouched, but where the legislator may still be permitted to experiment with strictly procedural rules. These limits vary according to the jurisdictions under analysis, but one over-arching conclusion can be drawn from this study: experimental legislation and sunset clauses are useful multifunctional instruments to concretize a learning, evidence-based approach to lawmaking. They are stepping stones on the pathway to Brandeis' 'living law': allowing laws to sunset and sunrise, and go through experimental periods (and their ordeals) is to give life to legislation and eternity to its role as 'the mirror of society'.

Bibliography

Alexander, L. and Prakash, S., 'Delegation Really Running Riot' (2007) 93 *Virginia Law Review* 1035

Aman, J.A., 'Administrative Law in a Global Era: Progress, Deregulatory Change, and the Rise of the Administrative Presidency' (1988) 73 *Cornell Law Review* 1101

Amar, A.A. *America's Unwritten Constitution: The Precedents and Principles We Live By* (Basic Books, 2012)

Aranson, P.H., 'A Theory of Legislative Delegation' (1982) 68 *Cornell Law Review* 1

Ashford, N.A., Ayers, C. and Stone, R.F., 'Using Regulation to Change the Market for Innovation' (1985) 9 *Harvard Environmental Law Review* 419

Ashford, N.A. and Hall, R.P., 'The Importance of Regulation-induced Innovation for Sustainable Development' (2011) 3 *Sustainability* 270

Ashford, N.A. and Heaton, J.G., 'Regulation and Technological Innovation in the Chemical Industry' (1983) 46(3) *Law and Contemporary Problems* 110

Audretsch, D.A., Heblich, S. and Lederer, A., *Handbook of Research on Innovation and Entrepreneurship* (Cheltenham: Edward Elgar, 2011)

Bakhshi, H., Freedman, A. and Heblich, P.J., *State of Uncertainty: Innovation Policy through Experimentation* (London: NESTA, 2011)

Baldwin, R., 'Is Better Regulation Smart Regulation?' (2005) *Public Law* 499

Balkin, J., *Constitutional Redemption: Political Faith in an Unjust World* (Cambridge, MA: Harvard University Press, 2011)

Bardach, E., 'Policy Termination as Political Process' (1976) 7 *Political Sciences* 126

Barron, D. and Rakoff, T., 'In Defense of Big Waiver' (2013) 113 *Columbia Law Review* 265

Barron, J.A. and Dienes, C., *Constitutional Law in a Nutshell* (St Paul, MN: Thomson/West, 2005)

Bar-Siman-Tov, I., 'Lawmakers as Lawbreakers' (2010) 52 *William and Mary Law Review* 805

Bayern, S.J., 'Against Certainty' (2012) 41 *Hofstra Law Review* 53

Bayles, M.D., 'On Legal Reform: Legal Stability and Legislative Questions' (1977) 65 *Kentucky Law Journal* 638

Beck, U., *Risk Society: Towards a New Modernity* (London: Sage, 1992)
Becker, P., 'Der Parlamentsvorbehalt im Prüfungsrecht' (1990) *Neue Juristische Wochenschrift* 273
Belinfante, A. and De Reede, J., *Beginselen van het Nederlandse Staatsrecht* (The Hague: Kluwer, 2012)
Benjamin, M. and Rai, A.K., 'Fixing Innovation Policy: A Structural Perspective' (2008) 77 *George Washington Law Review* 1
Bernstein, G., 'In the Shadow of Innovation' (2010) 31 *Cardozo Law Review* 2257
Bertelsmann Stiftung, *Sunset Legislation and Better Regulation: Empirical Evidence from Four Countries* (Bertelsmann Stiftung, 2010)
Beutel, F.K., *Some Potentialities of Experimental Jurisprudence as a New Branch of Social Science* (Lincoln: University of Nebraska Press, 1957)
Bickle, M., 'The National Sunset Movement' (1985) 9 *Seton Hall Legislation Journal* 209
Böhret, C. and Hugger, W., *Test und Prüfung von Gesetzentwürfen: Anleitungen zur Vorabkontrolle und Verbesserung von Rechtsvorschriften* (Carl Heymanns Verlag: Cologne, 1980)
Bora, A., 'Innovationsregulierung als Wissensregulierung' in W. Hoffmann-Riem and M. Eifert (eds), *Innovationsfördernde Regulierung: Innovation und Recht II* (Berlin: Duncker & Humblot, 2009) 24
Bouffier, V., 'Normprüfung: Modifizierung des hessischen Befristungskonzepts' (2012) *Zeitschrift für Rechtspolitik* 55
Boulouis, J., 'Note sur l'utilisation de la méthode expérimentale en matière de réformes' in *Mélanges Trotabas* (Paris: LGDJ, 1970) 29
Braeutigam, R.R., 'The Effect of Uncertainty in the Regulatory Delay on the Rate of Innovation' (1979) 43 *Law and Contemporary Problems* 98
Brinktrine, R., 'Organisationsgewalt der Regierung und der Vorbehalt des Gesetzes – zur Reichweite der "Wesentlichkeitstheorie" am Beispiel der Zusammenlegung von Justiz- und Innenministerium in Nordrhein-Westfalen' (2000) 3 *Jura* 123
Brock, B.J., 'Mr. Justice Antonin Scalia: A Renaissance of Positivism and Predictability in Constitutional Adjudication' (1991) 51(3) *Louisana Law Review* 623
Brownsword, R., *Rights, Regulation, and Technological Revolution* (Oxford: Oxford University Press, 2008)
Bruff, H., 'Separation of Powers under the Texas Constitution' (1990) 68(7) *Texas Law Review* 1337
Brüning, C., 'Die kommunalrechtlichen Experimentierklauseln' (1997) *Die öffentliche Verwaltung* 278
Bryce, J., *The American Commonwealth* (3rd edn, London: Macmillan, 1893)

Burkens, M., Kummeling, H.R., Vermeulen, H.R. and Widdershoven, R., *Beginselen van de democratische rechtsstaat: Inleiding tot de grondslagen van het Nederlandse staats- en bestuursrecht* (The Hague: Kluwer, 2012)

Burton, I. and Drewry, G., *Legislation and Public Policy: Public Bills in the 1970–74 Parliament* (London: Macmillan Press, 1981)

Calabresi, G., *A Common Law for Statutes* (Cambridge, MA: Harvard University Press, 1982)

Campbell, D.T., 'Reforms as Experiments' (1969) 24 *American Psychologist* 409

Campbell, R.W., 'Rethinking Regulation and Innovation in the U.S. Legal Services Market' (2012) 9 *New York University Journal of Law and Business* 1

Camps, T.K. and Korsten, A., 'Horizonwetgeving, een nieuwe coloradokever' (1982) 2(4) *Bestuur* 10

Chanos, A., *Möglichkeiten und Grenzen der Befristung parlamentarischer Gesetzgebung* (Berlin: Duncker & Humblot, 1999)

Chassagnard-Pinet, S., 'Argumentation and Judicial Decisions' in D.M. Gabbay, P. Canivez, S. Rahman and A. Thiercelin (eds), *Approaches to Legal Rationality* (Dordrecht: Springer, 2010) 160

Cherry, B., 'Institutional Governance for Essential Industries under Complexity: Providing Resilience within the Rule of Law' (2008) 17 *Common Law Conspectus* 1

Christensen, C., 'Disruptive Innovation for Social Change' (2006) 84(12) *Harvard Business Review* 96

Coate, S. and Morris, S., 'Policy Persistence' (1999) 89(5) *American Economic Review* 1327

Coglianese, C., Zeckhauser, R. and Parson, E., 'Seeking Truth for Power: Informational Strategy and Regulatory Policymaking' (2004) 89 *Minnesotta Law Review* 277

Cohen, L. and Spitzer, M., 'Term Limits' (1992) 80 *Georgetown Law Journal* 477

Conkle, D.O., 'Free Exercise, Federalism, and the States as Laboratories' (1999) 21 *Cardozo Law Review* 493

Cooley, T.M. and McLaughlin, A.C., *The General Principles of Constitutional Law in the United States of America* (Boston, NJ: Little, Brown and Company, 1898)

Craig, P., *EU Administrative Law* (Oxford: Oxford University Press, 2012)

Crain, M.D., 'Time for the Sun to Rise on Federal Sunset Legislation' (2000) 8 *Public Law* 10

Cunningham, L.A., 'The Common Law as an Iterative Process: A Preliminary Inquiry' (2006) 81 *Notre Dame Law Review* 773

Curry, L., 'Politics of Sunset Review in Texas' (1990) 50 *Public Administration Review* 58

D'Amato, A., 'Legal Uncertainty' (1983) 71 *California Law Review* 1

Daniels, M., *Terminating Public Programs: An American Political Paradox* (New York: M.E. Sharpe, 1997)

Davis, A., 'Review Procedures and Public Accountability in Sunset Legislation: An Analysis and Proposal for Reform' (1981) 33 *Administrative Law Review* 393

DeLeon, P., 'Public Policy Termination: An End and a Beginning' (1978) 4 *Policy Analysis* 369

DeLeon, P., 'Policy Evaluation and Program Termination' (1983) 2 *Policy Studies Review* 631

DeLeon, P., 'Policy Termination as a Political Phenomena' in D. Palumbo (ed.), *The Politics of Program Evaluation* (Newbury Park, CA: Sage, 1987) 173

Dewey, E., 'Sundown and You Better Take Care: Why Sunset Provisions Harm the Renewable Energy Industry and Violate Tax Principles' (2011) 52 *Boston College Law Review* 1105

Dewey, J., *The Public and its Problems: An Essay in Political Inquiry* (New York: Holt Publishers, 1927)

Dewey, J., *The Quest for Certainty: A Study of the Relation of Knowledge and Action* (Gifford Lectures, 1929)

Dick, D.L., 'Legal Ethics, Commercial Practice, and the Certainty Imperative: A Cautionary Note' (2013) 40 *Northern Kentucky Law Review* 279

Dombert, M., 'Gesetzesvorbehalt und Breitbandkabel' (1986) *Neue Zeitschrift für Verwaltungsrecht* 277

Doménech Pascual, G., 'Los experimentos jurídicos' (2004) 164 *Revista de Administración Publica* 149

Drozd, M., 'Lobbying-Regulierung in europäische Vergleich. Eine kurze Evaluation rechtlicher Rahmenbedingungen' (2006) *Zeitschrift des DIPA* 78

Druckman, J., Green, D.P. and Kulinski, J.L., 'The Growth and Development of Experimental Research in Political Science' (2006) 100(4) *American Political Science Review* 627

Easterbrook, F.H., Eskridge, W.N., Howard, P.K., Merrill, T.W. and Sutton, J., 'Showcase Panel IV: A Federal Sunset Law, The Federalist Society 2011 National Lawyers Convention' (2011) 16 *Texas Review of Law and Politics* 339

Eifert, M., 'Innovationsfördernde Regulierung' in W. Hoffmann-Riem and M. Eifert (eds), *Innovationsfördernde Regulierung: Innovation und Recht II* (Berlin: Duncker & Humblot, 2009) 11

Eijlander, P. and Gestel, R.J., *Horizonwetgeving: effectief middel in de strijd tegen toenemende regeldruk?: een onderzoek naar de functie van werkingsbeperkingen in wetgeving ter vermindering van regeldruk* (2006), available at www.portill.nl/

Ellerman, A. and Buchner, B.K., 'The European Union Emission Trading Schemes: Origins, Allocation, and Early Results' (2007) 1 *Review of Environmental Policy* 66

Emge, C., *Sicherheit und Gerechtigkeit. Ihre gemeinsame metajuristische Wurzel* (Berlin: De Gruyte, 1940)

Engel, C., 'The Constitutional Court: Applying the Proportionality Principle as a Subsidiary Authority for the Assessment of Political Outcomes' in C. Engel and A. Héritier (eds), *Linking Politics and Law* (Baden-Baden, Nomos, 2003) 285

Engel, C., *Legislative Experiments: Mission Impossible?* (Utrecht: Eleven International Publishing, 2013)

Epstein, L., 'A Definition of Uncertainty Aversion' (1999) 66 *Review of Economic Studies* 577

Eskridge, J.W., 'Dynamic Statutory Interpretation' (1987) 135 *University of Pennsylvania Law Review* 1479

Eskridge, W.N. and Frickey, P.P., *Hart and Sack's, The Legal Process: Problems in the Making and Application of Law* (New York, Foundation Press, 1994)

Eyer, K.R., 'Administrative Adjudication and the Rule of Law' (2008) 60 *Administrative Law Review* 647

Fagan, F., 'After the Sunset: The Residual Effect of Temporary Legislation' (2011) *European Journal of Law and Economics* 209

Fagan, F., *Law and Limits of Government: Temporary versus Permanent Legislation* (Cheltenham: Edward Elgar Publishing, 2013)

Fagerberg, J., 'Innovation: A Guide to the Literature' in J. Fagerberg, D.C. Mowery and R.R. Nelson (eds), *The Oxford Handbook of Innovation* (Oxford: Oxford University Press, 2007) 1

Farber, D.A., 'Environmental Protection as a Learning Experience' (1994) 27 *Loyola of Los Angeles Law Review* 791

Farnam, H.W. and Day, H., *Chapters in the History of Social Legisation in the U.S. to 1860* (Clark, NJ: Lawbook Exchange Ltd, 2000)

Finn, J.E., 'Sunset Clauses and Democratic Deliberation' (2009) 48 *Columbia Journal of Transnational Journal* 442

Firth, L. and Mellor, D., 'The Impact of Regulation on Innovation' (1999) 8 *European Journal of Law and Economics* 199

Fisher, R., *The Design of Experiments* (Edinburgh: Oliver and Boyd, 1966)

Flückiger, A., 'Voter, élire et signer par Internet: le droit expérimental à l'épreuve de la securité' in M. Müller and A. Thomas (eds), *E-voting: Journées 2002 d'information juridique* (Bern, Stämpfli Verlag, 2003) 107

Ford, C., 'Principles-based Securities Regulation in the Wake of the Global Financial Crisis' (2010) 55 *McGill Law Journal* 1

Freund, T., *Kommunale Standardöffnungs- und Experimentierklauseln im Lichte der Verfassung* (Berlin: WVB, 2003)

Friedman, W.G., *Law in a Changing Society* (Los Angeles, CA: University of California Press, 1959)

Fuller, L., *The Morality of Law* (New Haven, CT: Yale University Press, 1969)

Funke, J., *Bürokratieabbau mit Hilfe zeitlich befristeter Gesetze: zu den Erfolgsbedingungen der Sunset-Gesetzgebung* (Munich: AVM, 2011)

Gagel, A., *Grundsicherung und Arbeitsförderung: Loseblatt-Kommentar* (Munich: C.H. Beck, 200)

Gale, W.G. and Orzag, P.R., 'Sunsets in the Tax Code' (2003) 99 *Tax Notes* 1153

Gardner, J.A., 'The "States-as-Laboratories" Metaphor in State Constitutional Law' (1995) 30 *Valparaiso University Law Review* 475

Garrett, B.L. and Liebman, J., 'Experimentalist Equal Protection' (2004) 22 *Yale Law and Policy Review* 261

Gerber, A.S. and Patashnik, E.M., 'Missing Opportunities to Solve Problems' in A.S. Gerber and E.M. Patashnik, *Promoting the General Welfare: New Perspectives on Government Performance* (Washington, DC: Brookings Institution Press, 2006) 10

Gerring, J. and McDermott, R., 'An Experimental Template for Case Study Research' (2007) 51(3) *American Journal of Political Science* 688

Gersen, J., 'Temporary Legislation' (2007) 74 *University of Chicago Law Review* 247

Gersen, J.E. and Posner, J.E., 'Timing Rules and Legal Institutions' (2007) 121 *Harvard Law Review* 543

Gestel, R. von, 'The Deparliamentarisation of Legislation: Framework Laws and the Primacy of the Legislator' (2013) 9 *Utrecht Law Review* 106

Gestel, R. von and Hertogh, M., *Wat is regeldruk?: een verkennende international literatuurstudie* (Nijmegen: Wolf Legal Publishers, 2006)

Geva-May, I., 'When the Motto is "Till Death Do Us Part": The Conceptualization and the Craft of Termination in the Public Policy Cycle' (2001) 24(6) *International Journal of Public Administration* 263

Giddens, A., *Consequences of Modernity* (Stanford, CA: Stanford University Press, 1990)

Gillon, S. and Matson, C., *The American Experiment: A History of the United States* (Stanford, CA: Wadsworth Cengage Learning, 2013)
Ginsburg, T., Masur, S. and McAdams, R.H., 'Libertarian Paternalism, Path Dependence, and Temporary Law' (2014) 81 *University of Chicago Law Review* 291
Ginsburg, T., Melton, J. and Elkins, Z., *The Endurance of National Constitutions*, Chicago Working Papers Series no. 1 (2010)
Gramm, W.L. and Gay, G.D., 'Leading a Regulatory Agency: Lessons from the CFTC' (1994) 17 *Regulation* 1
Greco, G.J., 'Standards or Safeguards: A Survey of the Delegation Doctrine in the States' (1994) 8 *Administrative Law Journal of the American University* 567
Gross, O., 'Chaos and Rules: Should Responses to Violent Crises Always be Constitutional?' (2003) 112 *Yale Law Journal* 1011
Groth, A., *Kommunalrechtliche Experimentierklauseln* (Kiel: Lorenz-Von-Stein-Institut für Verwaltungswissenschaften an der Christian-Albrechts-Universität zu Kiel, 2005)
Hadfield, G., 'Legal Barriers to Innovation: The Growing Economic Cost of Professional Control over Corporate Legal Markets' (2007) 60 *Stanford Law Review* 1689
Hahn, R.W., 'Regulation: Past, Present and Future' (1990) 13 *Harvard Journal of Law and Public Policy* 167
Haltern, U.R., Mayer, F. and Möllers, C., 'Wesentlichkeitstheorie und Gerichtsbarkeit: Zur institutionellen Kritik des Gesetzesvorbehalts' (1997) 3 *Die Verwaltung* 51
Hart, J.H. and Sacks, A.M., *The Legal Process: Basic Problems in the Making and Application of Law* (New York, Foundation Press, 1994)
Hart, L., *The Concept of Law* (Oxford: Oxford University Press, 1961)
Herschel, W., 'Rechtssicherheit und Rechtsklarheit' (1967) 23/24 *Juristenzeitung* 728
Hirsch, E.E., 'Experimentierklausel' (1971) 26 *Juristenzeitung* 286
Hoffmann-Riem, W. and Schneider, J., *Rechtswissenschaftliche Innovationsforschung* (Baden-Baden: Nomos, 1998)
Holznagel, B., 'Innovationsanreize durch Regulierungsfreistellung vom Umgang mit neuen Diensten und Märkten im Medien und TK-Recht' (2006) *Multimedia und Recht* 661
Hoppe, W., Krawietz, W. and Schulte, M., *Rechtsprechungslehre, Zweites Internationales Symposium Münster 1988* (Cologne: Heymanns, 1992)
Horn, H.-D., *Experimentelle Gesetzgebung unter dem Grundgesetz* (Berlin: Duncker & Humblot, 1989)
Howells, J., 'Innovation and Regional Economic Development: A Matter of Perspective?' (2005) 34 *Research Policy* 1223

Howlett, M. and Ramesh, M., *Studying Public Policy: Policy Cycles and Policy Subsystems* (Oxford: Oxford University Press, 1995)
Huber, P.W. and Litan, R.E., *The Liability Maze: The Impact of Liability Law on Safety and Innovation* (Washington, DC: Brookings Institution, 1991)
Iancu, B., *Legislative Delegation: The Erosion of Normative Limits in Modern Constitutionalism* (Heidelberg: Springer, 2012)
Jahrreiss, H., *Gröβe und Not der Gesetzgebung* (Bonn, Schünemann, 1953)
Jevons, W.S., 'Experimental Legislation and the Drink Traffic' (1880) *XXXVII Contemporary Review* 177
Jolls, C., Sunstein, C.R. and Thaler, R., 'A Behavioral Approach to Law and Economics' (1998) 50 *Stanford Law Review* 1471
Kagel, J. and Roth, A., *Handbook of Experimental Economics* (Princeton, NJ: Princeton University Press, 1997)
Karch, A., *Democratic Laboratories: Policy Diffusion among the American States* (Ann Arbor, MI: University of Michigan Press, 2007)
Karkkainen, B.C., 'Toward a Smarter NEPA: Monitoring and Managing Environmental Performance' (2002) 102 *Columbia Law Review* 903
Karkkainen, B.C., 'Information-forcing Environmental Regulation' (2006) 33 *Florida State University Law Review* 861
Kearney, R.C., 'Sunset: A Survey and Analysis of the State Experience' (1990) *Public Administration Review* 49
Keyaerts, D., 'De wetgever en experimentalisme: de juridische grenzen van een wetgevingsmodel' (2013) 1 *Tijdschrift voor Wetgeving* 30
Kindt, J., 'Horizonwetten' (1979) 64 *Economische-Statistische berichten: algemeen weekblad voor handel, nijverheid, financiën en verkeer* 130
Kreveld, J. von, 'The Main Elements of a General Policy on Legislative Quality: Dutch Experience' in A. Kellermann and G.A.-S. Ciavarini (eds), *Improving the Quality of Legislation in Europe* (The Hague: Kluwer Law International, 1998) 91
Kuhn, T.S., *The Structure of Scientific Revolutions* (Chicago, IL: University of Chicago Press, 1996)
Kysar, R.M., 'The Sun Also Rises: The Political Economy of Sunset Provisions in the Tax Code' (2006) 40 *Georgia Law Review* 335
Kysar, R.M., 'Lasting Legislation' (2011) 159 *University of Pennsylvania Law Review* 101
Landman, L.B., 'Competitiveness, Innovation Policy, and the Innovation Market Myth: A Reply to Tom and Newberg on Innovation Markets as the "Centerpiece" of "New Thinking" on Innovation' (1998) 13 *Saint John's Journal of Legal Commentary* 223
Lauroba Lacasa, M.E., 'The Principle of Juridical Certainty and the Discontinuity of Law' (2003) 63 *Louisiana Law Review* 1243

Lawless, R., Robbennolt, J. and Ulen, T., *Empirical Methods in Law* (New York: Aspen Publishers/Wolter Kluwers Law and Business, 2009)
Laws, S., 'Giving Effect to Policy in Legislation: How to Avoid Missing the Point' (2011) 32(1) *Statute Law Review* 1
Lawson, G., 'Delegation and Original Meaning' (2002) 88 *Virginia Law Review* 327
Lee, M., 'Political-Administrative Relations in State Government: A Legislative Perspective' (2006) 29 *International Journal of Public Administration* 1021
Leif, T. and Speth, R., *Die stille Macht. Lobbyismus in Deutschland* (Wiesbaden: Wiesbaden Westdt, 2003)
Leisner, A., *Kontinuität als Verfassungsprinzip* (Tübingen: Mohr Siebeck, 2002)
Leisner, W., '"Gesetz wird Unsinn …" Grenzen der Sozialgestaltung im Gesetzesstaat' (1981) *Deutsches Verwaltungsblatt* 849
Leisner, W., *Staatsrenaissance. Die Wiederkehr der guten Staatsformen* (Berlin: Duncker & Humblot, 1987)
Lerner, M., *The Mind and Faith of Justice Holmes: His Speeches, Essays, Letters, and Judicial Opinions* (Piscataway, NJ, Transaction Publishers, 1989)
Licata, A.R., 'Zero-base Sunset Review' (1977) 14 *Harvard Journal on Legislation* 505
Lindner, J., 'Experimentelle Rechtssetzung durch Rechtsverordnung – Am Beispiel des Hochschulrechts' (2004) *Die öffentliche Verwaltung* 1004
Listokin, Y., 'Learning Through Policy Variation' (2008) 118 *Yale Law Journal* 480
Lobel, O., 'The Renew Deal: The Fall of Regulation and the Rise of Governance in Contemporary Legal Thought' (2004) 89 *Minnesota Law Review* 342
Loenen, T., *Het gelijkheidsbeginsel* (Nijmegen: Aers Aequi Libri, 1998)
Loving, P.E., 'The Justice of Certainty' (1994) 73 *Oregon Law Review* 746
Lowell, A.L., 'The Physiology of Politics' (1910) 4 *American Political Science Review* 1
Lowi, T.J., *The End of Liberalism: The Second Republic of the United States* (New York: W.W. Norton, 1979)
Luce, R., *Legislative Principles: The History and Theory of Lawmaking* (Clark, NJ: Lawbook Exchange, 1971)
Lücke, J., *Vorläufige Staatsakte, Auslegung, Rechtsfortbildung und Verfassung am Beispiel vorläufiger Gesetze, Urteile, Beschlüsse und Verwaltungsakte* (Tübingen: Mohr Siebeck, 1991)

Magat, W.A., 'The Effects of Environmental Regulation on Innovation' (1979) 43 *Law and Contemporary Problems* 4

Majone, G., 'The Rise of the Regulatory State' (1994) 17 *West European Politics* 77

Majone, G., 'The Regulatory State and its Legitimacy Problems' (1999) 22 *West European Politics* 1

Maltzman, F. and Shipan, C.R., 'Change, Continuity, and the Evolution of the Law' (2008) 52(2) *American Journal of Political Science* 255

Mandel, G.N., 'Regulating Emerging Technologies' (2009) 1 *Law, Innovation and Technology* 75

Marchant, G., Allenby, B. and Herkert, J., *The Growing Gap Between Emerging Technologies and Legal Ethical Oversight: The Pacing Problem* (New York, Springer, 2011)

Maxeiner, J.R., 'Legal Certainty: A European Alternative to American Legal Indeterminacy?' (2006) 15 *Tulane Journal of International and Comparative Law* 541

Mayntz, R., 'Speaking Truth to Power: Leitlinien für die Regelungen wissenschaftlicher Politikberatung' (2009) 1 *DMS-Der modern Staat, Zeitschrift für Public Policy, Recht und Management* 5

McGowan, C., 'Congress, Court, and Control of Delegated Power' (1977) 77 *Columbia Law Review* 1

McGraw, T.K., *Prophets of Regulation: Charles Francis Adams, Louis D. Brandeis, James M. Landis, Alfred E. Kahn* (Cambridge, MA: Belknap Press, 1984)

Merrill, T.W., 'Rethinking Article I, Section I: From Nondelegation to Exclusive Delegation' (2004) 104 *Columbia Law Review* 2097

Miller, A., *Toward Increased Judicial Activism: The Political Role of the Supreme Court* (Westport, CT, Greenwood Press, 1982)

Mitchell, M.J., 'Cleaning Up the Closet: Using Sunset Provisions to Clean up Cluttered Criminal Codes' (2005) 54 *Emory Law Journal* 1671

Mohler, P.B., 'Experiments at the FERC: In Search of a Hypothesis' (1998) 19 *Energy Law Journal* 281

Moor-van Vugt, A.d., *Maten en gewichten: het evenredigheidsbeginsel en Europees perspectief* (Tilburg: Schoordijk Instituut, 1995) (Ph.D dissertation)

Morand, C., *Wolfgang Hoffman-Riem, 'Législation expérimen Évaluation législative et lois expérimentales* (Aix-en-Provence, Presses Universitaires d'Aix-Marseille, 1992)

Morgan, B. and Yeung, K., *An Introduction to Law and Regulation: Text and Materials* (Cambridge: Cambridge University Press, 2007)

Müller, W., Bergman, T. and Strøm, K., *Delegation and Accountability in Parliamentary Democracies* (Oxford: Oxford University Press, 2003)

München, I. von, 'Die Zeit im Recht' (2000) *Neue Juristische Wochenschrift* I

Myers, R.E., 'Responding to the Time-based Failures of the Criminal Law Through a Criminal Sunset Amendment' (2008) 49 *Boston College Law Review* 1327

Noll, P., *Gesetzgebungslehre* (Reinbeck: Rowolt Taschenbuch Verlag, 1973)

Oldenziel, H., *Wetgeving en rechtszekerheid: een onderzoek naar de bijdrage van het legaliteitsvereiste aan de rechtszekerheid van de burger* (The Hague: Kluwer, 1998)

Osborne, D., *Laboratories of Democracy* (Cambridge, MA: Harvard Business School Press, 1988)

Ost, F. and Van Hoecke, M., *Temps et Droit* (Brussels: Bruylant, 1998)

Oster, J.S., 'The Scope of Judicial Review in the German and U.S. Administrative Legal Systems' (2008) 9 *German Law Journal* 1267

Page, S., *The Difference: How the Power of Diversity Creates Better Groups, Firms, Schools, and Societies* (Princeton, NJ: Princeton University Press, 2007)

Patterson, E., 'On Legal Stability and Change' (1963) 17 *Vanderbilt Law Review* 179

Peltzman, S., 'Toward a More General Theory of Regulation' (1976) 19 *Journal of Law and Economics* 211

Pennarts, H.F., *Beginselen van behoorlijk bestuur* (Appeldoorn: Maklu, 2008)

Pestalozza, C., 'Gesetzgebung im Rechtsstaat' (1981) *Neue Juristische Wochenschrift* 2081

Petrozzi, U.A., 'The Forgotten Lesson in Quill v. Vacco: A Perspective on the Modern Judicial Role as the Calabresian Remedy to the Statutory Obsolescence' (1998) 44 *Wayne Law Review* 343

Phills, Jr, J., Deiglmeier, K. and Miller, D.T., 'Rediscovering Social Innovation' (2008) *Fall Stanford Social Innovation Review* 39

Popelier, P., *Rechtszekerheid als beginsel van behoorlijke wetgeving* (Antwerp: Intersentia, 1997)

Popelier, P., 'Five Paradoxes on Legal Certainty and the Lawmaker' (2008) *Legisprudence* 51

Popelier, P., 'La loi aujourd'hui (le principe de légalité)' in I. Hachez (ed.), *Les sources du droit revisitées*, vol. 2, *Normes internes infraconstitutionnelles* (Limal: Anthemis, 2013) 17

Popelier, P. and Nieuwenhove, J., *Regelgeving en Tijd. Het Belang van het Tijdsperspectief in de Levenscyclus van Regelgeving* (Bruges: Die Keure, 2009)

Popkin, W.D., *Materials on Legislation: Political Language and the Political Process* (New York, Foundation Press, 2009)

Porter, M., 'The Competitive Advantage of Nations' (1990) *Harvard Business Law Review* 75
Portuese, A., 'Principle of Proportionality as Principle of Economic Efficiency' (2013) 19(5) *European Law Journal* 612
Posner, R., 'Theories of Economic Regulation' (1971) 5 *Bell Journal of Law and Economics and Management Science* 335
Pound, R., *Interpretations of Legal History* (Cambridge: Cambridge University Press, 1923)
Prieger, J.E., 'Regulatory Delay and the Timing of Product Innovation' (2007) 25 *International Journal of Industrial Organization* 219
Puller, S.L., 'The Strategic Use of Innovation to Influence Regulatory Standards' (2006) *Journal of Environmental Economics and Management* 690
Punder, H., 'Democratic Legitimation of Delegated Legislation: A Comparative View on the American, British and German Law' (2009) 58(2) *International and Comparative Law Quarterly* 353
Raban, O. 'The Fallacy of Legal Certainty: Why Vague Legal Standards may be Better for Capitalism and Liberalism' (2010) 19 *Public Interest Law Journal* 182
Raitio, J., *The Principle of Legal Certainty in EC Law* (The Hague: Kluwer, 2003)
Rakhlin, M., 'Regulating Nanotechnology: A Private-Public Insurance Solution' (2008) 10(2) *Duke Law and Technology Review* 1
Ramsay, I., 'Financial Innovation and Regulation: The Case of Securitization' (1993) *Journal of Banking and Finance Law and Practice* 169
Roording, J.F., 'Versnelling van wetgeving: over uiteenlopende ontwikkelingen en eigenwijze actoren' (2012) 27 *Regelmaat* 126
Rothwell, R., 'Industrial Innovation and Government Environmental Regulation: Some Lessons from the Past' (1992) 12 *Technovation* 447
Ruffert, M., 'The Transformation of Administrative Law as a Transnational Methodological Project' in M. Ruffert, *The Transformation of Administrative Law in Europe* (Munich: Sellier, 2007) 10
Sabel, C.F. and Zeitlin, J., *Experimentalist Governance in the European Union: Towards a New Architecture* (Oxford: Oxford University Press, 2010)
Sarnoff, J.D., 'Government Choices in Innovation Funding (with reference to Climate Change)' (2013) 62 *Emory Law Journal* 1087
Sauer, D. and Lang, C., *Paradoxien der Innovation. Perspektiven sozialwissenschaftlicher Innovationsforschung* (Frankfurt: Campus, 1999)
Schacht, W.H., *Cooperative R & D: Federal Efforts to Promote Industrial Competitiveness*, Report for Congress, RL 33426 (Washington, DC: Congressional Research Service, 2008)

Schendelen, M.M., *Lobbyen in Nederland* (The Hague: Sdu Uitgevers, 1998)

Scheuerman, W.E., *Liberal Democracy and the Social Acceleration of Time* (Baltimore, MD: Johns Hopkins University Press, 2004)

Scheurle, K.-D. and Mayen, T., *Telekommunikationsgesetz: Kommentar* (Munich: C.H. Beck, 2008)

Schlink, B., 'Proportionality in Constitutional Law: Why Everywhere but Here?' (2012) 22 *Duke Journal of Comparative and International Law* 291

Schlössels, R. and Zijlstra, S., *Bestuursrecht in de sociale rechtsstaat* (The Hague: Kluwer, 2010)

Schoenbrod, D., 'The Delegation Doctrine: Could the Court Give It Substance?' (1985) 83 *Michigan Law Review* 1223

Schoenbrod, D., 'Delegation and Democracy: A Reply to My Critics' (1998) 20 *Cardozo Law Review* 732

Schroeder, W. and Kostenzer, E.-M., 'Wissenschaftsbasierte Regulierung im EU-Produktrecht' (2013) 48 *Europarecht* 389

Schulze-Fielitz, H., *Theorie und Praxis parlamentarischer Gesetzgebung – besonders des 9. Deutschen Bundestages (1980–1983)* (Berlin: Duncker & Humblot, 1988)

Schumpeter, J., *Capitalism, Socialism and Democracy* (first published in 1939, New York, Harper, 1942)

Schwarzschild, M., 'Keeping it Private' (2007) 44 *San Diego Law Review* 677

Seidman, R.B., 'Justifying Legislation: A Pragmatic, Institutionalist Approach to the Memorandum of Law, Legislative Theory, and Practical Reason' (1992) 29 *Harvard Journal on Legislation* 1

Singleton, R. and Straits, B., *Approaches to Social Research* (Oxford: Oxford University Press, 2005)

Slating, T.A. and Kesan, J.P., 'Making Regulatory Innovation Keep Pace with Technological Innovation' (2011) *Wisconsin Law Review* 1109

Soetema, A., 'Rechtsbeginselen en positivisme!?' (2009) 38(1) *Rechtsfilosofie and Rechtstheorie* 5

Sokolow, A.D., 'The Limited and Contrary Uses of County Charter Reform: Two California Cases' (2004) 36(1) *State and Local Government Review* 7

Staupe, J., *Parlamentsvorbehalt und Delegationsbefugnis: Zur 'Wesentlichkeitstheorie' und zur Reichweite legislativer Regelungskompetenz, insbesondere im Schulrecht* (Berlin: Duncker & Humblot, 1985)

Steinhaus, J., *Gesetze mit Verfallsdatum* (Books on Demand, 2008)

Stephenson, M., 'Information Acquisition and Institutional Design' (2011) 124 *Harvard Law Review* 1422

Stettner, R., 'Verfassungsbindungen des experimentierenden Gesetzgebers' (1989) *Neue Zeitschrift für Verwaltungsrecht* 806

Stewart, R., 'Regulation, Innovation and Administrative Law: A Conceptual Framework' (1981) 69 *California Law Review* 1256

Stolz, F., *Die Rechtssicherheit* (Berlin: De Gruyter & Co., 1955)

Stone, G.R., Seidman, L.M., Sunstein, C.R., Tushnet, M.V. and Karlan, P.S., *Constitutional Law* (New York: Aspen Publishers, 2005)

Strauss, D.A., 'On the Origin of Rules (with Apologies to Darwin): A Comment on Antonin Scalia's the Rule of Law as a Law of Rules' (2008) 75 *University of Chicago Law Review* 997

Sunstein, C., *Laws of Fear: Beyond the Precautionary Principle* (Cambridge: Cambridge University Press, 2005)

Super, D.A., 'Laboratories of Destitution: Democratic Experimentalism and the Failure of Antipoverty Law' (2008) 157 *University of Pennsylvania Law Review* 541

t'Veld, R., *Verandering en bestuur: een pleidooi voor een bescheiden bestuurskunde* (Nijmegen: Afscheidscollege, 1982)

Tamanaha, B.Z., *A General Jurisprudence of Law and Society* (Oxford: Oxford University Press, 2001)

Tarr, G.A., 'Laboratories of Democracy? Brandeis, Federalism, and Scientific Management' (2001) 31(1) *Journal of Federalism* 37

Tegethoff, T., 'Verwaltungsvorschriften und Gesetzesvorbehalt' (2005) *Juristische Arbeitsblätter* 794

Theodoulou, S.Z. and Kofinis, C., *The Art of the Game: Understanding American Public Policy Making* (Belmont, CA: Thomson Wadsworth, 2004)

Timmer, W., *Het doel wel gesteld: een praktijkonderzoek naar de toepassing van doelregelgeving* (The Hague: Boom Juridische uitgevers, 2011)

Van Gestel, R. and Van Dijck, G., 'Better Regulation through Experimental Legislation' (2011) 17(3) *European Public Law* 539

Veerman, G.-J., *Het meesterschap van de wetgevingsjurist* (The Hague: SdU, 2011)

Veerman, G.-J. and Mulder, R., *Wetgeving met Beleid* (The Hague: Boom Juridische uitgevers, 2010)

Vidas, S., 'The Sun Also Sets: A Model for Sunset Implementation' (1976) 26 *American University Law Review* 1170

Viswanathan, M., 'Sunset Provisions in the Tax Code: A Critical Evaluation and Prescriptions for the Future' (2011) 82(2) *New York University Law Review* 657

Voermans, W., *Toedeling van bevoegdheid* (The Hague: Boom Juridische Uitgevers, 2004)

Voermans, W., 'Legaliteit als middel tot een doel' in H. den Juristen-Vereeniging (ed.), *Controverses rondom legaliteit en legitimatie* (The Hague, Kluwer, 2011) 1

Volkmann, U., 'Sicherheit und Risiko als Probleme des Rechtsstaats' (2004) 14 *Juristenzeitung* 696

Walburg, J., 'Fact-free and Evidence-free Politics' (2011) 9(6) *Maandblad Geestelijke Volksgezondheid* 597

Walker, J.L., 'The Diffusion of Innovations among the American States' (1969) 63(3) *American Political Science Review* 880

Walker, L., 'Perfecting Federal Civil Rules: A Proposal for Restricted Field Experiments' (1988) 51 *Law and Contemporary Problems* 67

Westerman, P.C., 'De onmogelijkheid van deregulering' (2006) 81(3) *Nederlands Juristenblad* 132

Westerman, P.C., 'Een nieuwe stijl van reguleren' (2006) 3 *Recht der Werkelijkheid* 33

Westerman, P.C., 'The Emergence of New Types of Norms' in L. Wintgens (ed.), *Legislation in Context: Essays in Legisprudence* (Farnham: Ashgate, 2007) 117

Whitt, R.S., 'Adaptive Policymaking: Evolving and Applying Emergent Solutions for U.S. Communications Policy' (2009) 61(3) *Federal Communications Law Journal* 483

Wiktorowicz, M. and Deber, R., 'Regulating Biotechnology: A Rational-Political Model of Development' (1997) 40 *Health Policy* 115

Wilkinson, M., 'Between Constitutionalism and Democratic Experimentalism' (2007) 70(4) *Modern Law Review* 680

Williams, J., 'Experiment in Legislation' (1888) 14 *Law Magazine Review* 299

Williamson, K.R., *Revisiting and Evaluating the Congressional Review Act* (New York, Nova Science Publishers, 2009)

Wistrich, A.J., 'The Evolving Temporality of Lawmaking' (2012) 44 *Connecticut Law Review* 737

Wolters, A. and Schutte, H., *Innoveren onder voorwaarden: hoe wetten en regels de innovatiemogelijkheden van de agrarisch ondernemen beïnvloeden* (Leiden, LEI, 2006)

Wood, D.P., 'The Rule of Law in Times of Stress' (2003) 70 *University of Chicago Law Review* 455

Worthington, K.A., 'Kendra's Law and the Rights of the Mentally Ill: An Empirical Peek Behind the Courts' Legal Analysis and a Suggested Template for the New York State Legislator's Reconsiderations for Renewal in 2010' (2009) 19 *Cornell Journal of Law and Policy* 213

Wright, J.D. and Ginsburg, D.H., 'Behavioral Law and Economics: Its Origins, Fatal Flaws, and Implications for Liberty' (2012) 106 *Northwestern University Law Review* 103

Yin, G.K., 'Temporary-Effect Legislation, Political Accountability, and Fiscal Restraint' (2008) 84 *New York University Law Review* 174

Young, M.D., 'A Test of Federal Sunset: Congressional Reauthorization of the Commodity Futures Trading Commission' (1978) 27 *Emory Law Journal* 853

Zeitlin, J. and Trubeck, D., *Governing Work and Welfare in a New Economy: European and American Experiments* (Oxford: Oxford University Press, 2003)

Zijlstra, S.E., *Wetgeven: Handboek voor de centrale en decentrale overheid* (The Hague: Kluwer, 2012)

Zimmermann, P., 'Reform der Staatstätigkeit durch generelle Befristung von Gesetzen – Aspekte einer Problembewältigung mit verfassungswidrigen Mitteln' (2003) 22 *Die öffentliche Verwaltung* 943

Zippelius, S.R., *Die experimentierende Methode im Recht* (Mainz: Akademie Mainz, 1991)

Index